RACE, GENDER, AND RHETORIC

RACE, GENDER, AND RHETORIC

THE TRUE STATE OF RACE AND GENDER RELATIONS IN CORPORATE AMERICA

JOHN P. FERNANDEZ
WITH JULES DAVIS

McGRAW-HILL

New York   San Francisco   Washington, D.C.   Auckland   Bogotá
Caracas   Lisbon   London   Madrid   Mexico City   Milan
Montreal   New Delhi   San Juan   Singapore
Sydney   Tokyo   Toronto

137960

Library of Congress Cataloging-in-Publication Data

Fernandez, John P.
    Race, gender, and rhetoric : the true state of race and gender
relations in corporate America / John Fernandez.
        p.   cm.
    Includes bibliographical references and index.
    ISBN 0-07-022008-5
    1. Diversity in the workplace—United States.
I. Title.
HF5549.5.M5F47   1998
331.13'3'0973—dc21   98-28280
                                                                         CIP

McGraw-Hill

A Division of The McGraw·Hill Companies

1 2 3 4 5 6 7 8 9 0   DOC/DOC   9 0 3 2 1 0 9 8

ISBN 0-07-022008-5

The sponsoring editor for this book was *Jeffrey Krames,* the editing supervisor was
John M. Morriss, and the production supervisor was *Suzanne W. B. Rapcavage.*
It was set by North Market Street Graphics.

Printed and bound by R. R. Donnelley & Sons Company.

McGraw-Hill books are available at special quantity discounts to use as
premiums and sales promotions, or for use in corporate training programs.
For more information, please write to the Director of Special Sales, McGraw-Hill,
11 West 19th Street, New York, NY 10011. Or contact your local bookstore.

This book is printed on recycled, acid-free paper containing
a minimum of 50% recycled de-inked fiber.

This book is dedicated to my 3-year-old daughter, Paige Julia Fernandez, who has become the most precious gift in my life. May her African, Portuguese, and Irish heritage suit her well and be a positive force in the world.

I love you big, big bunches.

Acknowledgments

After writing nine books, I am still amazed how a diverse group of people can help me develop new ideas and approaches to old problems like racism and sexism. To this end, I am deeply grateful and indebted to the following:

David Arrington
Pat Delaney
Michele Fernandez
Kristi Georg
Paulette Griffeth-Gerkovich
Ben Johnson
Carol Nehls
Ronald Vargas
Melanie Littlejohn

I want to thank specifically Caroline O'Connell, who helped me find Jeffrey Krames and John Morriss at McGraw-Hill. They were great to work with.

I want to single out Pat Delaney, Ron Vargas, and Paulette Griffeth-Gerkovich for contributing immensely to several chapters.

Finally, Jules Davis's name is on the title page because of her absolutely tremendous contributions to the entire book.

Contents

III
MANAGING RACE AND GENDER
IN THE NEW MILLENNIUM

IV
MANAGING YOUR CAREER

I

RACE AND GENDER RELATIONS IN CORPORATE AMERICA: A 25-YEAR PERSPECTIVE

1

Introduction: Progress, Promises, and Proposals

Most corporate employees, especially corporate leaders, believe that they have a good understanding of the concept of diversity, and of the need to rid their organizations of racism, sexism, and all other "isms." Most, in fact, insist that they and their organizations have largely taken care of the problems of racism and sexism; they have "done" affirmative action and awareness training, so now it's time to stop harping on the issue and get down to the "real work" of the organization. Sometimes they admit that racism and sexism still exist . . . but in the other person's company, never in their own.

This position is sheer wishful thinking. For despite all the time, energy, and money that have been expended over the past three decades, the reality is still this: that corporate America as a whole has failed to effectively address the challenges posed by diversity, particularly with regard to racism and sexism. The major reason for this failure is that companies have not taken a *holistic approach* to eliminating that race and gender discrimination which adversely affects both employees and customers. Rather, they have tried to isolate the race and gender problems and to fix them separately, rather than see them as being part and parcel of a broader range of employee and customer issues that need to be addressed.

Let us remember that the single term "diversity" actually encompasses a wide range of issues. Under its umbrella fall not only race and gender but sexual orientation, age, disability status, and the like. This book will focus upon race and gender, as these are the two demographic characteristics which *everyone* brings to the workforce and generally cannot change or hide. Its thesis, once again, is that corporate America can redress continuing injustices vis-à-vis race and gender in one way and one way only:

by adopting systematic, holistic strategies that simultaneously address broader human resource, customer, and stakeholder issues.

After 34 Years of Equal Employment, How Much Progress Has Been Made?

Thirty-four years have gone by since the passage of the 1964 Civil Rights Act. People of color, and women, have by and large done what they were told to do: Get yourself an education, some credentials, and some experience. Work hard. Don't whine or complain. And yet the same old barriers to full participation in corporate America largely remain in place. While white women have fought their way into the middle ranks of management in some industries, people of color in almost every industry have made only minimal progress beyond the lower levels of management. As for senior management, the faces of a few white women can now be seen around the executive suites. But one will look long and hard, and probably in vain, for any black, Hispanic, Native American, or Asian faces at that level.

So, you still think discrimination is a thing of the past? Well, have a look at this list of just some of the organizations, representing various industry sectors, that have had discrimination suits filed against them in recent years:

Texaco
R. L. Donnelley
United Postal Service
CNA
United Dairy Farmers
Home Depot
Shoney's
Spin magazine
Schering Plough
Nations Bank
The Federal Park Service
Smith-Barney
Lew Lieberbaum & Company
The U.S. military

Nor are today's victims of discrimination exclusively employees. The following are some recent cases of consumer discrimination brought by women and people of color:

Denny's
Avis
Microsoft
American Airlines
Too many financial institutions to list separately

In November of 1996, many Americans turned on their news shows only to be shocked by audiotapes of top corporate executives at Texaco making racist comments about blacks, and by allegations of sexual harassment against several senior executives at CNA. In recent days they also have heard that Avis executives chose to ignore the openly racist treatment of black customers at one of their major franchises, and that many financial institutions and car dealerships were discriminating against women and people of color. They learned that American Airlines had published a guide for its employees that contained offensive stereotypes of Latin American customers, and that even the progressive Microsoft had released software containing racist and stereotyped definitions of Hispanics and Asians.

Many Americans were shocked by all of this, but we at ARMC (Advanced Research Management Consultants) were not. Our work experience as corporate executives and consultants over the past 25 years has convinced us that we will be seeing more and more of such cases, well into the 21st century.

How can this be? Well, let's just say that many people have mistakenly assumed that racism and sexism have all but disappeared from the U.S. corporate landscape. And then too, alas, many whites still firmly believe that the problem lies with people of color; that they would have no difficulty making it in corporate America if they would just get an education and work hard! Even more sadly, some people of color agree with this misguided notion, particularly when it comes to color groups other than their own. Similarly, many men believe that talented women will make it to the top if they get the proper business-related degree, dedicate themselves to work even more than to their family, and "bide their time." Even more so when it comes to customers rather than employees, many people blame women and people of color for the discrimination they face. If they would just supply themselves with money, the right "culture," and the right "attitude," discrimination would disappear tomorrow. For after all, the business world could care less who has the money, so long as they *have* the money. Right?

But the reality is that American corporations are a rather accurate reflection of American society—the good, the bad, and the ugly. And it also is true that those corporations need to recognize that while the Civil Rights Act of 1964 has done good work in dispelling the more overt forms of racial discrimination—the same being true of later legislation focusing on other forms of discrimination—today's discrimination has readily taken on new and more insidious forms. Separate drinking fountains and so on have been replaced by rules, regulations, and procedures that unintentionally discriminate on a basis of race and gender and that deny equitable employment opportunities and fairly priced products and services to women and to people of color. Our point here is that if one needed any proof that American society has by no means succeeded in rising wholly above racism and sexism, one could do no better than look to corporate America. And yet we firmly believe that corporate America could do a *better* job of redressing these evils than has American society as a whole, if it were simply to address the subtler forms of racism and sexism head-on and in a systematic manner, while taking into account the vital roles played by the increasingly powerful and changing customer and other stakeholder groups. But one thing is certain: "Awareness training," in and of itself, isn't going to do the job.

What we also want to make clear in this book is that U.S. organizations face *many* barriers when they attempt to deal effectively with race and gender issues as these pertain to employees, customers, and stakeholders. These barriers have nothing to do with race and gender per se, and everything to do with organizational structure and policy and managerial philosophy and capability. It is when companies ignore these broader concerns that they fail to take a holistic approach to race and gender. And ironically, one result of that failure is that they see many issues as being race- and gender-related, when in fact they are not!

Is It Racism, Sexism, or . . . ?

If it is going to solve the problem of the unfair, inequitable treatment of people of color and of women, both as employees and customers, corporate America must recognize that such treatment is bound up with five other issues:

1. The bureaucratic structure of organizations
2. The subjectivity and irrationality of human beings
3. Inappropriate policies and practices, particularly in the areas of human resources and customer relationships
4. Ineffective implementation of human resources and customer relationship policies and practices, by managers and employees
5. Ineffective managers

What makes racial and gender discrimination such a thorny problem is that often we can't know which of these factors—or which combination thereof—is at work. The following examples should help to illustrate the complexity here.

1. Although she has excellent credentials and an outstanding track record, a female African American midlevel manager remains frustrated by her lack of upward mobility. While it is true she has made it to middle management, she feels she has hit a *cement* ceiling; that she has not been given the power and authority that her white colleagues have; that she is challenged more often than her white colleagues are about her proposals; and that some of her colleagues try to sabotage her at critical moments.

What is the reality here? Is it that her company's bureaucracy is structured in such a way as to lack the resources to reward its top people? That she works for an ineffective manager? That the old bureaucratic way is to move people up *slowly?* That this woman believes she deserves more than she really does? That the company's human resources policies are faulty? Or that she is in fact being discriminated against because of her race and/or gender?

2. A U.S. company, based in Malaysia, has a number of Malaysian employees who feel they are not being treated fairly. These employees believe that more Malaysians should be in senior positions, since after 10 years they have acquired more than enough experience to run the operation smoothly and productively themselves. Further, they believe that American expatriates are being paid too highly and receive benefits and perks denied to the Malaysians. So, what's going on here? Are the Malaysians in fact being discriminated against because of their race, or are they truly not ready to take over the operation? Are the company's policies and practices fair, and if so, are they being implemented effectively? Are the U.S. executives skilled and effective in the United States, but not in Malaysia? Or is some combination of these factors involved?

3. White men can become mired in the problems of discrimination as well. Consider this case of a white, middle-aged manager who feels that he has been stuck for way too long in his present position. He believes that his 20 years of loyal service and positive performance evaluations have merited him a promotion to the next higher level. He has not received any formal career planning or career counseling, but he is bitter because he feels that older white males are being discriminated against— not only because of race and gender, but also because of age. Is he right, or have his managers failed to provide him with honest, candid feedback about his performance, as well as with career planning and counseling?

Does the company perhaps just not have enough higher-level slots open, for deserving employees? Is this middle-aged white male's perception of his strengths and weaknesses inaccurate, or is he being discriminated against owing to some combination of race, gender, and age?

Discrimination issues affect the treatment of customers as well as of employees. Consider the following examples.

1. When a Puerto Rican executive, with tens of thousands of frequent-flyer miles, is mysteriously bumped from a standby list at the gate of a major airline, he is given a vague excuse about computer error. Was he bumped because of the inefficiency of employees, a faulty computer system, or because he is Puerto Rican?

2. A high-salaried woman who makes the financial decisions in her household feels that she does not get the same treatment from financial consultants as men do. Callers ask to speak to her husband; consultants address themselves not to her but to her husband, and they avoid talking with her about complex financial instruments. Are the financial consultants just plain sexist, or is this woman seeing sexism where none exists? Do company policies perhaps dictate that consultants must focus on "the man of the house," because he is thought to be the decision maker?

3. A highly paid black craftsman believes that when he goes to upscale restaurants he is treated with a lack of respect and given poor service because of his race. Is he right, or just being paranoid? Could it be that the restaurant's employees simply don't value quality customer service, regardless of the customer's race? Might they be angry at their managers, and merely taking out that anger on their customers?

We aren't saying that corporations will ever be able to fully eliminate problems such as these. What they can do, however, is to minimize them by recognizing that corporate structures, the shortcomings of employees, ineffective managers, and poor or improperly implemented policies and practices can bring them on. More specifically, they can take the following six steps:

1. Develop new organizational structures so as to become "postbureaucratic organizations."

2. Assist employees with, and hold them accountable for, their technical, professional, and personal development, as that notably includes their compassionate understanding of the problems of racism and sexism.

3. Train managers in managing people, and hold them accountable not only for the management of their employees but for their relationships with customers and stakeholders as well.
4. Educate employees as to how to assess and understand diverse markets and customers.
5. Develop and implement systematic and effective work design, performance appraisals, career planning and development, and reward/recognition systems.
6. Create an environment that is based upon trust and respect, not only for employees but for customers and other stakeholders as well.

Yet again: A day spent in "Diversity and Sensitivity Training" isn't going to cut it. Only a more holistic strategy will work.

The Scope of This Book

In this book we will be closely examining data about human behavior, our minds, and our ways of thinking. Many a competent corporate manager or some employee might ask just how "soft" information of this kind, about race and gender issues, is going to have any impact upon the bottom line in today's climate of downsizing, rightsizing, leveling the organization, and reengineering. Our answer is simple: It is only by means of a broad knowledge of human nature that organizations will ever overcome such persistent ills as racism, sexism, declining morale, lack of team effectiveness, poor stakeholder relations, poor customer service, and loss of market share. For after all, the common denominator of business is people. Businesses are run by people, and people make the products and provide the services that people buy. If businesses fail to understand their people, and fail to make them more effective and compassionate in their interpersonal interactions, then all the reengineering and rightsizing in the world won't help the bottom line one whit. *Our first goal, then, is to present you with very specific strategies to help your employees understand their strengths and weaknesses, as well as to help your organization implement those strategies that will help employees to work more effectively in teams, to surpass customer expectations, and to develop excellent stakeholder relations.*

There's more to it than that, however. If they are going to be competitive in a racially and sexually diverse, technological and global marketplace, organizations are going to have to possess a more detailed, in-depth knowledge of both American and other cultures; of the key cultural traits of specific groups; and of the conflicts that those traits can create. In other words, more and better knowledge will help corporations to understand, value, and appreciate cultural differences. This, in turn, will enable them to segment their markets and to develop goods and services which meet the diverse needs of a diverse marketplace.

It is to further those goals that we here will be presenting a critical analysis of those current and past conflicts among employees, regardless of race or gender, that have hindered and will continue to hinder corporate effectiveness in both the marketplace and the workplace. We have been busy collecting this data over the past 25 years from over 100,000 employees in over 30 different organizations and industries. The key insight to emerge from this data is that employees have certain basic concerns which have little to do with race or gender, and lots to do with their organizations' structure and leadership. That said, let us make clear that our data also shows that significantly large majorities of women and of people of color do believe that gender and/or race discrimination is still widely prevalent. *Our second goal, then, is to present strategies that will help employees and their organizations to determine just how prevalent racism and sexism are within their organizations, and to make measurable progress in dealing with them.*

Our third goal is derived from our intimate understanding of the nature, mindset, and behavior of the old hierarchical bureaucracy, and our recognition that it simply can no longer cut it in today's service-oriented, technological, global marketplace. It can't create high-performance teams of racially and sexually diverse people, and it can't respond to the demands of an increasingly sophisticated and diverse body of customers. *Thus, our third goal is to provide you with an organizational structure that can succeed at doing those things.*

While a great deal has been written about the need for companies to put together diverse teams of people, little has been said about the very real difficulty of forming them, domestically and globally, in the current highly competitive environment. We believe that if a diverse group of employees is to work together effectively, a corporate culture must have a team-oriented bias. For the simple fact is that the services and products which customers require cannot be effectively created, produced, or marketed without strong teams composed of very different people. *Therefore, our fourth goal is to show organizations how to bring very diverse people together and meld them into high-functioning teams.*

We have been saying that customers have diverse needs and desires, and that organizations must learn how to target these varied markets. And that to do that they must have in place high-performance teams of diverse employees who intimately understand and can relate to their customers. Later chapters will detail both the best practices and the *faux pas* of organizations, and all of this in support of *our fifth goal: to explore the fundamental principles accounting for the success—or failure—of market-targeted business strategies.*

We will conclude by presenting a holistic, strategic, human resources initiative which corporations can build into their business plans as a vital component of their global success story. Components of this initiative include leadership, communication, and conflict-resolution skills; recruitment and retention strategies; work design; performance evaluation; rewards and recognition; and career development.

Let us make it clear, however, that we do not pretend in this book to present any easy, comfortable analyses and solutions to problems that will disappear upon their application. Nor will we flatteringly validate what our society, schools, and companies themselves insist that corporate America is really like. Rather, our first and foremost purpose is to set forth what we believe to be the realities presently at work in corporate America. But instead of just grousing about them, we will then be suggesting some approaches to race and gender problems that we truly believe will do much to make corporations competitive in the 21st century.

2

The Search for Solutions

Introduction

This chapter will first look in more detail at the current situation in corporate America—in particular, at some of the major changes that are presently complicating the search for solutions to race- and gender-related problems and the development of global business and marketing strategies. Then we will present an overview of that holistic approach which will have to be taken if we are ever to get beyond the rhetoric of race and gender in corporate America.

The New Workforce

The U.S. labor force has always been diverse, but few would disagree that it has never been more diverse than it is today. In more than half of all married households, both husband and wife hold jobs outside of the home. Indeed, women today make up almost half of the labor force, while less than a tenth of the new entrants to the labor force are white males. At the same time we're definitely seeing a "browning" of the United States. By the turn of the century the majority of California's population will be people of color—this in a state that produces 24 percent of our gross national product and can be reckoned the eighth largest economic power in the world. New York and Texas are seeing a similar trend. Overall, people of color now make up fully one-fourth of the labor force.

Meanwhile, corporate America has been discovering that in order to survive and prosper, it has to continually seek out new opportunities globally. And as a result of mergers and acquisitions, and the siting of plants in foreign countries, many companies' customers and workforces are daily growing more diverse. It is only to be expected that foreign employees will bring to the workplace cultures radically different from those that U.S. corporations have become accustomed to dealing with in the past.

A second factor affecting U.S. corporations—and indeed corporations the world over—is the rising educational level of the workforce, brought on in large part by the demand for smarter, more highly skilled workers. And let's face it, these workers are more demanding. They rightly aspire to move up the corporate ladder, to land the choice job assignments, and in general to be rewarded for their skills and their contributions to the organization. Women are leading this trend, for the simple reason that over the past 10 years and indeed longer than that, they have been receiving more associate's, bachelor's, and master's degrees than men. And more and more of those degrees are in business. In 1971, women accounted for only 9 percent of the nation's business administration degrees; by 1997, the figure had risen to 48 percent. Such highly trained and motivated women are entering the workforce on a full-time, permanent basis, vastly expanding the pool of available talent. That pool looks even vaster, when one recalls that it is also people of color who are finishing college and, in many cases, going on to acquire advanced degrees.

A third factor having a powerful impact upon U.S. corporations is the very different attitude about work and career that prevails today, as opposed to a generation ago. In our training sessions, which include employees of all ages, both 30-year veterans and 30-month rookies, we see a clear generational difference in attitudes toward the work ethic, loyalty to the company, and career expectations. Today, young workers want to feel more flexibility on the part of their employers. Also, they want to be recognized for the value they add, rather than pay their dues and wait their turn. They've seen plenty of downsizing and "restructuring" of workforces, and that has made them far less likely to put their jobs before their other interests; quite simply, they give their first loyalty not to their corporations, but to themselves. Then, too, more and more workers are having multiple careers over the course of their lifetimes, and social mores with regard to achievement, success, and consumption are changing as a consequence. The bottom line: People are saying through their behavior that there is more to life than just their jobs and consumption. A 1996 Bozell Worldwide study supports this observation, finding that the three factors which people all around the world most frequently cite as their top priorities are family life, spiritual life, and good health—not material possessions.

A Frustrated Workforce

As corporations try to adjust to global competition by means of acquisitions, mergers, restructuring, reengineering, and the like, the level of frustration among workers worldwide is increasing, and for good reason. Ewart Wooldridge puts it this way:

> As we put our organizations through processes of downsizing, delayering and derecognition, the simultaneous exhortations for teamwork, empowerment, partnership, and vision come across as somewhat hypocritical. What was actually happening for so many employees was a widening gap between the rhetoric of empowerment and the increasingly insecure and unrewarding reality of work.[1]

So, what do we have today? We have a large number of baby boomers, many of them well educated, coming of age. At the same time the number of opportunities for them at the middle and top levels of corporate America is dwindling. It is these two conflicting trends which have created a significant moral conundrum for corporate America, in terms of who is to get the openings that do exist. And it is these which are creating so much frustration and uncertainty for so many employees, as they decide that their failure to cash in on well-deserved opportunities has something to do with race, gender, or other subjective criteria rather than with the bloated number of qualified, competent people. When one also recalls the evolution of flatter organizational structures, as well as corporate America's inability to admit that regardless of the issues of race and gender, it does a poor job in selecting and equipping managers with effective people skills, one can hardly be surprised that employees are feeling frustrated.

Two additional factors have greatly hindered corporations in their efforts to integrate women and people of color into the workplace and to beef up their ability to attract and retain a diverse customer base. One of these is the perversely bizarre makeup of bureaucracies, the other the equally perverse makeup of the human mind.

Bureaucracies: Bulky and Out-of-Date Behemoths

We'll have more to say about bureaucracies in Chapter 7, but for now we'll just note that in its heyday—early and mid-20th century—the bureaucratic, hierarchical structure that still typifies most U.S. corporations actually worked. Or at least, it worked better than did the nepotism and the fiefdoms that had preceded it. Indeed, it seems likely that without the bureaucratic organizational structure, the Industrial Revolution would not have occurred.

At any rate, the ideal bureaucracy was a hierarchy structured around a rational division of labor. Activities were supposed to be governed by a set of policies and procedures and administered by an objectively evaluated, recruited, and promoted (not elected) group of people who were loyal to the organization and clearly understood both their limited roles and the organization's values and culture. Two of the chief values were that bureaucratic authority resides in the office, not the person, and that personal and professional life must be strictly separated. The result was the relatively smooth functioning of the organization.

In today's more highly educated, diverse work environment, however, such a bureaucratic structure and value system is as out of date as slide rules and computer punch cards. Our data tend to show that the old bureaucratic structures and values now only serve to pit people against one another and to eventually condemn all but a few to failure. They discourage cooperation and risk taking, and foster empire building, inertia, and conformity. They breed fear, distrust, dishonesty, and intolerance of different races and the opposite gender. They are inefficient, and react too slowly to the changed needs of customers. Their focus is more internal than external.

One might simply say that bureaucracies employ people in the service of their own needs rather than the needs of their customers. They are inherently unfair, for although they promise to reward everyone who is deserving, in fact they have too few advancement opportunities, too few resources, out-of-date reward systems, and too many ineffective managers to deliver on that promise. And all of this can only get worse over the next two decades, as millions of baby boomers vie for limited opportunities and as organizations continue to downsize and flatten out. Then, too, as U.S. companies become even more global, the need to develop culture-specific reward systems is sure to clash ever more stridently with the old bureaucratic values.

Human Psychology: Our Shortcomings

Compounding the problem of the inherent shortcomings of bureaucracies is the problem of our frail fallible human nature. One reason accounting for the problem of racism, sexism, and the like is that we humans have evolved certain brain functions that served us better back in the Stone Age than they are doing today. For example, our Stone Age ancestors developed ways of thinking that allowed them to sense danger and to decide how to respond to it within milliseconds. Today we still make decisions within milliseconds, whether we're facing real danger or not. And that means that whether we care to admit it or not, our minds are always, consciously or subconsciously, making snap judgments about people, judgments often based upon race and/or gender.

As if to make matters worse, we humans can't process in a timely manner all of those millions of "bytes" of information that our environment is continually bombarding us with, without grouping information in some "logical" manner. That amounts to stereotyping, and it is as natural to us as sleeping. Therefore, it should hardly surprise us that throughout the history of humankind, various groups have developed stereotypes about one another that now detract from that trust and respect we so require in order to compete in a global economy. The good news is that as long as we recognize and combat our tendencies to make snap judgments based upon stereotypes, neither of those mind functions need be dangerous.

The foregoing observations apply to human beings in general. But compounding the problem is the fact that each of us has his or her own unique programming or personality, one created not just by our genes but also by the influence of socialization, our families, and institutions. And because of our widely varying genetic makeups and socializations, we are not always rational and objective, however much we might like to think otherwise. So the operative issue is not whether we can, if we try very hard, find a way to act rationally and objectively, but to what degree we can make ourselves aware of our subjectivity and irrationality. For the simple fact is that people who can acknowledge their shortcomings and sincerely resolve to work on them are much more likely to relate effectively to different races and both genders in a wide variety of markets.

Let's face it: managing personal relationships is one of the hardest tasks we can confront in life. It demands a high level of intellectual and emotional development. And interpersonal problems are sure to arise, whenever an individual feels that there is an egregious mismatch between his or her own expectations and the behavior, feelings, or motives of another. Given the omnipresence of such interpersonal problems on the job, it is no wonder that so many frustrated people see race and gender discrimination, when in fact the root of the problem is just as likely to be the unimaginative, authoritarian, bureaucratic corporate structures we have been speaking of.

Over the past 25 years of our research, we have asked employees to respond to questions about career planning, performance appraisal, reward and recognition, being valued, supervisors, teams, leadership, and their perceptions of their companies. In the bulk of these responses, the differences have arisen based not on race or gender but on the employee's level in the company, or the particular department in which the employee is working. It is when we have asked questions about affirmative action; equal employment opportunity; and the treatment of women, people of color, white males, gays, and people with disabilities, that significant differences have emerged on a clear basis of race, gender, or other key demographic variables. That seeming disparity in our findings actually only strengthens us in our conviction that corporations have to take a holistic approach, one that sees racism and sexism as being intrinsically bound up with the more traditional, hierarchical aspects of organizations. The biggest conundrum for corporate America is to figure out the real reasons behind the snail's-paced progress of women and people of color.

A Holistic Approach to Race and Gender Issues

We believe that the first step toward a solution of the race and gender problem is to get rid of the term *diversity*. It does nothing to convey an effective, ongoing business strategy, and like *affirmative action*, the term is nothing if not loaded. It compels a variety of reactions, and means vastly different things to different people, despite the fact that for most of us it does suggest something characterized by variety and heterogeneity.

In place of the simple term *diversity*, we would like to bravely substitute *constituent capitalization*. Yes, we know it's a mouthful, but listen to what it means before you make up your mind:

> Constituent capitalization is a business strategy in which the broad spectrum of people's widely varying skills, perspectives, and styles are recognized, appreciated, valued, and respected; a strategy that will integrate all of those things into a postbureaucratic organizational structure and into new organizational operating practices, so as to maximize marketplace options throughout the world.

We believe in this model largely because it takes into account the importance of *results*. It directly confronts the issue of how results are achieved, and who, or what factors, makes that possible. At the same time, it more aptly describes those sorts of organizational structures and environments that make an organization a top-flight employer and place to do business.

A step-by-step approach to implementing the constituent capitalization model would look something like this:

Step 6
Create a postbureaucratic organization that is based upon trust and respect; one in which diverse employees are valued and are integrated into all aspects of the organization's work. Work is greatly enhanced by means of a rethinking of tasks and a redefining of missions, strategies, business practices, cultures, markets, and products. And all of this is done in order to most effectively meet the needs of an increasingly diverse body of customers and stakeholders.

Step 5
Completely reshape the organizational culture by putting in place operating practices that make possible the integration of a broad range of viewpoints, this then leading to a redefinition of how work gets done and how diverse markets are to be approached and capitalized upon.

Step 4
Understand that constituent capitalization must be two things at once: a continuous learning process and a business imperative.

Step 3
Assess with complete honesty the current corporate culture, and how it enables change and creativity—or hinders them.

Step 2
Define and implement those affirmative actions which will bring the organization into full compliance with EEO laws.

Step 1
Resolve to do all that needs to be done so as to fully comply with all EEO laws.

Notice that these steps focus on changing not only structure but *behavior.* By implementing them, organizations can do more than merely *assimilate;* they can *incorporate.* That is, they can bring diverse groups together and thereby form something new, rather than merely digest one group into another and thereby enforce conformity and agreement. In the past assimilation was the norm, simply because the workforce was much more homogeneous then than it is today and companies mass-produced for mass markets. Today, those mass markets have been replaced by niche markets, and mass production has been replaced by "mass customization" production lines. In such an environment, companies can gain the competitive advantage only by harnessing the hearts, minds, competencies, and commitments of all of their employees, both domestic and international. And that means that *both the organization's structure and its environment must be changed if all employees are going to be employed to their utmost.*

Thus, what constituent capitalization is, is an organizational strategy directly linked to a company's business strategy so as to manage change, improve productivity, and increase market share. At its heart are both team building and quality-improvement efforts. Establishing trust and respect among team members is essential to this strategy, but the need to do so isn't limited to the workforce. It is just as necessary among other constituencies, including customers and other stakeholders such as government regulators, public agencies, shareholders, members of the community within which the company does business, and any group or individual who affects or is affected by the organization.

Thus, what is especially fundamental to the constituent capitalization model is the notion that employees, customers, and stakeholders are not mutually exclusive groups. After all, employees and outside stakeholders can be an organization's customers as well, and those of us who are frequent flyers find it reassuring to think that even Federal Aviation Administration regulators sometimes fly the friendly skies! Our point is that the successful business strategy will be that which acknowledges the interrelatedness of these groups, and which always thinks in terms of the success of the total enterprise. It will be keenly aware that the bottom line will always suffer if even just one of the following components of success is undervalued: rewarding and motivating employees, effectively serving customers, and fully satisfying the demands of stakeholders.

And yet, it is important to note that this strategy *is* sequential. In other words, any organization must begin by focusing on its workforce, if it is to then find favor with customers and outside stakeholders. Quite simply, the organization which fails to foster an ethos of trust and respect among its employees, will never do justice to those customers and stakeholders whose differences mirror those of employees.

We would like to stress again in closing that the constituent capitalization model takes into account the importance of both output and results, in a way that "diversity" does not. It has no real quarrel with the notion of diversity, but simply seeks to recast it in business-related terms. And therefore by necessity it lays great stress upon *process,* upon the most effective ways of achieving results. This explains why, in the remaining chapters of this book in which we outline our strategy and examine each of its components, we will be talking almost as much about *how* we do things, as *why.*

3

The United States Is Not
a Meritocracy

Introduction

If a company is going to develop strategies for ensuring the fair and equitable treatment of all employees regardless of race and gender, it must first resolve to face up to one truth: The United States and its corporations are not meritocracies. We must begin by trying to understand who gets ahead in corporate America, and why, and that is the focus of this chapter.

The *Real* Criteria for Advancement

The Horatio Alger story has become an important component of our nation's cultural values. It's a symbol of the American Dream, whereby a person from a deprived background can achieve economic success through sheer hard work and determination, and by relying solely upon his or her self. And yet in terms of today's real world, this myth's basic message—that hard work and merit ultimately win out—is flawed. For example, implicit in the notion of "hard work" is the idea that the individual has limitless power to create opportunities. If you don't succeed, so this line of reasoning goes, it's your own damn fault; you just didn't work hard enough. Indeed it *has* to be your own fault, since you and you alone are "the master of your fate, the captain of your soul," as those famous Victorian lines by the poet W. E. Henley would have it. It's mighty tough to argue with that sort of attitude, for whatever evidence may be offered to show that a particular group hasn't fared well can always be rebutted by saying that they didn't try hard enough, or spent too much time wallowing in their predicament rather than figuring out how to rise above it.[1] This is the logic invariably employed by those at the top of the social heap in many countries. "White" Brazilians use it to explain the lowly position of "black" Brazilians, non-Indian Mexicans to explain the perennial poverty of Mexican Indians, northern Italians to explain the second-class status of southern Italians, and on and on.

The logic operative in any wholehearted belief in the power of "merit" is equally flawed. It would have us believe that our pedigree, race, ethnicity, class, age, generation, gender, national origin, religion, sexual orientation, style, and the like have little or no impact on the perceptions of us held by others. But the simple fact is that even white males have to contend with these perceptions in some arenas. Think, for instance, of the disadvantaged situation of a Baptist from Arkansas who doesn't speak with the "right" accent, when compared to a middle-class, Protestant, Eastern, Republican, Ivy League-educated man.

Then, too, the notion of merit tacitly assumes not only a widespread commitment to merit-based decision making, and the existence of enough resources to reward everyone who is deserving, but also the preexistence of standards that do not unfairly favor one individual over another. But standards, of course, must and do come from somewhere, or from someone. And rare is the someone who doesn't have some point of view that may or may not equip him or her to see merit where it really does exist.

Who's Really Making It?

In American culture, one's sense of dignity, self-esteem, and worth are often directly linked to success at work. Let's face it, most of us are heirs to a cultural tradition that values winning. From an early age most of us are told, "The only thing that will hold you back is yourself. The top is yours for the taking, if you just believe you have the right stuff."

The sad truth, however, is that all but a select few make it to the top. That has been especially true in the 1980s and 1990s, an era of few openings at the middle- and upper-management levels because of downsizing, reengineering, the flattening of organizations, and the great number of baby boomers vying for fewer and fewer slots above them. It use to be the case that career moves were upward. Employees could expect regular promotions every two years, job security was an important part of the employment "contract," and success was measured by the size of the paycheck. Today, rewards are more likely to come in the form of lateral moves. And even for those who do get promoted, the time frame has widened from two to four, or even six, years. Job security is a thing of the past. All of which means that today's employees tend to measure success not by dollar figures but by the quality of their work and personal lives.

Yet our implicit capitalist ideology is continually promoting the idea that the job market is a perfect market. Work hard, get the right education and training, have the right innate abilities and talent, and the opportunities will come swarming around you as thick as the flies at the company picnic. Meet Mr. Horatio Alger, yet again. And yet the truth, once again, is that of the thousands who set out, many with the same level of ability, personality, and behavior, only one can and does make it all the way to the top. The obstacles that get in the way of all the rest may have to do with racism or sexism, but they are just as likely to be corporate-structure-based. The hierarchy is simply too narrow to accommodate everyone, particularly in some functional areas.

Let's take a moment here to look at some of our 1995 survey participants' comments, about how they perceive advancement at their companies. Notice just how varied are the opinions as to who is getting the advancement opportunities. Such drastically conflicting views can't help but detract from trust and respect in the organization. They also make it extremely tough for U.S. corporations to develop high-performance teams comprised of diverse individuals. And it is expressly because of the average corporation's inability to deflect or harness these perceptions that discrimination charges are on the increase all across the land.

> If you think like someone in the "good ole boy" club, you have a better chance to get ahead.
> *Hispanic female, lower-level manager*

> I used to think that a good job was important. But now I think it's who you know, or if you are a part of the "good old boy" network.
> *Black male, lower-level manager*

> Merit is not as important as how well you know key people.
> *White male, lower-level manager*

> Women are 65 percent of this company but only 7 percent of senior management—i.e., one person! Tell me who has the advantage. It certainly isn't women!
> *White female, middle-level manager*

> White men are still the privileged class.
> *White female, occupational**

> Tall, Aryan-looking men do well in this company.
> *White male, upper-level manager*

We use the term "occupational" rather than "nonmanagement."

When you talk about people of color, the first thing that comes to mind is merit. And people forget that prior to this, we didn't always hire on merit in the old days.

Black male, middle-level manager

Being a minority or being female will help you get ahead.

White male, occupational

You have to be a white male to get ahead, especially in the marketing department.

Black female, lower-level manager

White males are an endangered species.

White male, middle-level manager

Asians are not seen as management material in this company.

Asian male, lower-level manager

Clearly, not one of those employees we have just heard from believes that his/her organization is a meritocracy. In fact, the suggestion is that the higher one goes in a bureaucracy, the more likely one is to be "elected" on the basis of personality-fit, and adherence to the norms of the organization, rather than "selected" on the basis of merit. And such an election approach can't help but create a stressful, hostile, uncooperative, competitive environment, one that extends special privileges to higher-level managers while leaving most employees out in the cold, or at least *feeling* like they're out in the cold. Rather than encouraging cooperation, teamwork, and open communication, that approach fosters divisiveness, conflict, and poor communication. The resulting lack of trust and respect leads to perceptions, whether well founded or not, that race and gender discrimination are rampant.

Conformity, Ambition, and Education

The bureaucratic structure not only condemns practically everyone to failure, it also has a depressingly bad effect even upon those who succeed. Harry Levinson, for instance, talks about how a constant pressure is exerted upon corporate managers to be "methodical, prudent, disciplined," as a way of ensuring that they will remain wholly predictable and conforming.[2] And it certainly is the case that employees who want to be promoted tend to behave however the corporation asks them to behave, right down to the pattern of their ties. The arms of the corporate octopus reach out to envelop the lives, actions, and thoughts of employees in direct proportion to the extent of their ambition.

Now, one can't help but ask, given the odds against reaching the top and the high price exacted upon those who try, "Why do so many people, regardless of race or gender, still strive so persistently?" For although in recent years some have been voluntarily stepping off the corporate fast track, society still largely weighs self-esteem and self-worth on a scale that is calibrated in terms of career advancement and material success. Promotions not only bring financial rewards and status; they gratify the ego and validate one's feeling of self-worth. And who can doubt that once we have based our sense of self-esteem on status, our hunger for ever higher status tends to grow both morally and practically, with what it feeds on?

Just as the incentive of promotions is a mixed bag, so too is personal ambition. Sure, the desire to "move on up" can make an employee work harder, and competition can bring out the best in us. When it is untempered, however, personal ambition is destructive both to the person and to his/her corporation. When goals become too important in a person's eyes, or are too hard to reach, failure can be devastating. Moreover, employees who are deeply committed to reaching certain goals can lose sight of human concern for family and for other workers, as well as of the broader goals of the corporation as a whole. Such persons believe that anything which stands in the way of their own advancement must be ruthlessly trodden down. This tends to be particularly true in the context of diverse rather than homogeneous groups, for there the competition for rewards generally *seems* more intense. In such diverse groups, stereotyping and labeling rather than trust and respect can all too quickly become the norm.

Let us make it clear that the drive toward conformity begins before the employee has even walked through the door. Employees selected for interviews always have the education, job experience, and technical skills needed to do the job. Then at the interview stage, nontechnical and subjective factors such as presentation, appearance, and mannerisms come into play. The interviewer is drawing upon these factors in order to make a subjective judgment as to whether or not the candidate will fit into the organizational culture. Such obvious subjectivity leads many women and people of color to feel ill at ease and at a disadvantage; they don't "fit the norm" that seems to have been predetermined by the interviewer, especially at the higher levels of management, a white male. In the absence of any systematic interview process, the interviewer tends to make decisions on the basis of gut reaction. If the interviewer "feels comfortable" with the candidate, then he or she is more likely to view that candidate in a positive light. For the simple fact is that interviewers are people, and all of us tend to feel most comfortable when in the presence of those who look and act most like ourselves.

It is true that, more and more, traits such as responsibility, accountability, leadership, positive attitude, team orientation, and strategic-thinking ability are the chief criteria being taken into account in interviews, performance appraisals, and promotion decisions. And yet traits like those can mean very different things to different people. Does having "a positive attitude" mean that you readily agree with another's point of view just to avoid unpleasantness? That you are always "up"? That you never question the corporation? It is precisely because the assessment of these traits is so subjective a matter, that this subjectivity can do genuine damage to the careers of women and people of color who are trying to move higher in middle and upper management.

By the way, a Labor Department study of employers has revealed that attitude is the most important factor in any decision to hire; academic qualifications came in at the bottom of the list. And yet the very same study shows that an across-the-board increase of one year of education increases a company's productivity between 5 and 8 percent in the manufacturing sector. Such a finding would seem to suggest that the emphasis on attitude is misplaced. Companies that want to improve performance would do better to look closely at a candidate's educational background rather than rely so heavily on the "gut reaction."

The Peter Principle

Once a person has finally landed a job, her/his troubles may have just begun. The promotional process itself can have disastrous effects both on individuals and on the company at large. Since many promotions are based upon present performance, conformity, likability, and the approval of key people (rather than upon skills and the potential to perform the next higher task), many employees are promoted until they reach positions in which they can no longer perform competently. And to the corporation's detriment, such employees are likely to *stay* in those positions. In other words, the well-known Peter Principle has here come into play.

One reason accounting for the Peter Principle is that it's mighty hard to define and to quantify job qualifications at the managerial level. Most corporations rely largely upon "soft skills." But exactly how is one supposed to go about defining and measuring such soft skills as leadership, negotiating skills, organizing and planning, visioning, strategic thinking, reasoning, and communicating? As a person moves up the ladder these skills grow even more abstract, thereby implicitly encouraging decision makers to give subjectivity an even greater role in determining who will be promoted. The result is that the higher one goes the more important "image management" becomes, and the more one is forced to bring oneself into line with criteria not related to ability, including those of race and gender. In other words the higher one goes, the more (or less) likely it is that a person with certain identifiable characteristics—race, sex, dress, language, style, height, weight—will be seen as being "the right kind of person" and therefore granted access to positions of discretion and power.

Conformity and Stereotyping

Stereotyping only exacerbates the "soft skills" dilemma, for women and for people of color. Our data show that white men perceive various racial and ethnic groups, and women, as being deficient in these soft skills, regardless of their level of education or the extensiveness of their experience. And at high levels in an organization, very similar behavior in different persons is perceived in very different ways, again as a function of stereotyping. Thus a white man who is a "screamer," is merely "having a bad day," or "that's just his way." But a woman who screams at her employees is "hysterical," or a "bitch." If a Hispanic male is a screamer, he is "militant," "aggressive," or "has a chip on his shoulder." White men "network" at the drinking fountain, whereas women merely "chit-chat." And the beauty of this "system," in the eyes of those determined to deny promotional opportunities to women or to people of color, is that one day you can tell someone she's aggressive, the next day that she's not aggressive enough—and so on. In other words, these subjective criteria as they are involved in the cases of women, of people of color, and even of nonconforming white males, constitute a kind of Catch-22. Members of these groups are unable to align themselves with these shifting perceptions, alter their conduct as they may.

Back in 1941, C. Barnard, a former president of the old Bell System, said that the smooth functioning of an organization depends upon the homogeneity of its employees. And surprisingly, many corporations still buy into Barnard's proposition. Being "a team player" really boils down to conforming—in choice of housing, automobile, food, entertainment, school, ritual of greeting, behavior at meetings, mode of socializing. Among managers such a homogeneity leads to a fear of uncertainty and therefore to an impulsive desire to *control* by means of exclusion of strangers and insistence on unbounded loyalty, and to a preference for comfortable communication with those who seem to be "like me."[3] The tragic aspect here is that it is precisely those kinds of managerial impulses that cause corporations to lose their creativity and the opportunities that come along with risk taking. What they get from their employees is mere fawning agreement, and what they lose are the valuable suggestions and the feedback that only independent, secure employees can contribute.

Since it is one's comfort level with one's "networks" that largely eases the progression to higher levels in a corporation, and since that comfort comes to many people through their interactions with others who seem to be like them, a major obstacle to the advancement of women, people of color, and nonconforming white males is their exclusion from powerful networks. Sometimes they are excluded because of raw prejudice, sometimes not, but as we have noted, the liking of "like for like" is a common feature of our humanity. Most people simply prefer to associate with those who resemble themselves. And let's be honest and admit that when two parties do share the same culture, customs, background, and language, it generally *is* easier to operate at a high level of understanding and agreement. "Constituent capitalization" at least at first—does tend to violate the similarity principle. It's messy. It disrupts clear communication and efficient problem solving. But it's important to note that it does so for reasons which may have little to do with prejudice.

The Role of Racism and Sexism in Hindering Advancement

All employees are confronted by the problem of employers' subjectivity with regard to promotion decisions. But race and gender continue to be major factors in those decisions. Over the decades, researchers have looked closely at the role which race and gender play in employees' perceptions of the ideal image of a promotable manager. Let's review some of the results.

In 1964, Garda W. Bowman studied 2000 corporate employees, almost exclusively white, and found that 77 percent believed that being black constituted a hindrance to advancement; 71 percent believed this was true for Chicanos (Mexicans), 68 percent for Asians. In 1972 we found that those numbers had been substantially reduced; 68 percent of blacks and 58 percent of whites believed that being black was an obstacle to advancement.

In 1978 we changed the wording of our questions, to make it focus on the employee's own race rather than race in general. That year, 46 percent of black employees and 45 percent of white males told us that their race would harm their chances. In 1988, the percentage of white men who believed their race would harm their chances had gone down to 39 percent, whereas that of black employees had gone up to 50 percent. In 1992 that same depressing trend was in place, such that the disparity had grown truly troubling: only 20 percent of white males but a whopping 60 percent of black employees believed their race to be an obstacle to career advancement.

Then, in 1995, we asked a different question: "How do you feel that emphasizing diversity will impact your personal career opportunities and your career?" Among white males, 34 percent believed that such an approach would cause their opportunities to worsen, compared to 15 percent of white women. In contrast, fewer than 10 percent of people of color, regardless of race, believed their opportunities would worsen.

A number of studies have confirmed the existence of race and gender discrimination. A 1996 study by Arthur Brief, a professor of organizational behavior, asked 76 business students, almost all of them white and none black, to choose three candidates from a pool of applicants for a vice presidential position. One group of students was encouraged to select a black; a second group was urged to select a white; a third group, the control group, was given no instructions as to whom they should select. Four applicants, two of them white and two black, clearly were superior, and equally qualified. The first group recommended two blacks and one white; the second, two whites and one black. But the control group, the one given no instructions, selected whites and blacks in the same proportion as the group urged to hire a white; that is, two whites and one black. The point here should be obvious: An unbiased control group would have picked two blacks half the time and two whites half the time; as it was, the control group selected a black only a quarter of the time.[4]

A second study focused on women. In "Managerial Promotion: The Dynamics for Men and Women," the Center for Creative Leadership (CCL) analyzed the promotion decisions made at three progressive *Fortune* 500 companies. CCL found that for both women and men, factors frequently cited as accounting for promotion included credentials, experience, track record, skills, work ethic, ability to work on a team, interpersonal skills, and growth potential. And yet on closer inspection, it became clear that there were some considerable differences in terms of what caused executives to have confidence in a particular candidate. In the selection of managers, the executives doing the promoting spoke of having a high level of comfort with 75 percent of males; executives promoting women felt comfortable doing so only 23 percent of the time. Also playing a role here was the candidate's familiarity with the tasks of the new job. A tendency to promote women to jobs they already are familiar with was evidenced by the degree to which continuity—a knowledge of the new job—was expressly mentioned as a reason for promotion: 38 percent of the time in the case of women, only 6 percent of the time in the case of men.[5] Again, the conclusion seems clear: Women get promoted if they can show prior familiarity with their new job; men get promoted if they are "one of us."

Conclusions

We have all been fed a great deal of propaganda, explicit and implicit, about advancement opportunities, who gets them, and why. But an honest look at the structure of corporate America reveals that it remains very much a rigid hierarchy, with few opportunities at the top and only limited opportunities in the middle. Sad to say but true nonetheless, the vast majority of employees still fail to reach their goals, regardless of race and gender.

And those who do succeed will do so, in large part, not on account of merit and ability but of subjective criteria such as race, gender, schools attended, and the like. Above all, the more closely they resemble their corporate leaders, both physically and mentally, the greater will be their chance of advancement. As Merton has so trenchantly observed, the main purpose of promotions, salary increases, bonuses, and so on, is "to provide incentives for disciplined action and conformity to the corporate way of doing things."[6] Since the vast majority of employees do want to move up, and since it is true of us humans that "our reach always exceeds our grasp," the reward of promotion for company-authorized behaviors will always be a strong motivating factor.

Corporate executives must understand that bureaucracies are social structures. They are characterized by a whole set of acceptable behaviors, mannerisms, dress codes, lifestyles, and other such factors, all of them tending to control employees and to maintain the "bureaucratic social system" that—so it is believed—is vital to the efficient production of goods and services. Employees who do their bit to maintain the status quo are rewarded for their effort; the heads of nonconformists are the first to roll, when the downsizing guillotine comes down. As M. J. Gannon has said, "In technical society, the rhetoric of merit provides a thinly veiled rationale for a process of organizational cloning."[7]

4

To Stereotype Is Human— But Dangerous

Introduction: Take the Objectivity Test

Take a moment to picture in your mind each of the following individuals: a successful corporate executive; a great artist; a renowned heart surgeon; a master burglar; a secretary; a classics professor; a migrant farmworker; a welfare recipient; a nurse; a drug dealer. What does each of them look like, in your mind's eye? If you are like most people, your visual images fit into various stereotypes, some of them based upon race and gender. You're a rare bird indeed if your nurse wasn't a woman, your classics professor a tweedy white male—or your welfare recipient a portly black or Hispanic woman.

Our point here is that the instant perceptions we form of others often determine the course that all of our future interactions with them will take, and even before a single word or handshake has been exchanged. And if that is the case, how could it fail to have major implications regarding the attempt to establish fair and equitable treatment for all employees, especially women and people of color? Regarding the ability of employees to see clearly and compassionately, and thereby to influence, a broad spectrum of stakeholders? Regarding how fully these employees will be able to contribute to the bottom line, by providing top-quality products and services to a very diverse customer base?

In other words, judgments based upon racist and sexist stereotypes clearly do inhibit successful interactions among employees, customers, and stakeholders, because they undercut trust and respect. None of us can hope to build up trust and respect on the basis of incorrect or incomplete information about the people we are trying to interact with. In such a situation each party to the interaction feels that the other is condescending or not really listening, and the result is miscommunication, misunderstanding, resentment, low morale, rampant mistake making, inferior productivity and product quality.

Thus, if corporate managers are going to gain a comprehensive understanding of how people actually do tend to interact, it is vital that they become students of psychology and human nature. As Harry Levinson has written:

> Managers must know and understand . . . psychology [and] . . . motivation with the same degree of proficiency as . . . marketing, manufacturing, economics, sales, engineering, and so on. Not every manager must be a master of all these, but each must have a basic knowledge and understanding of people or he/she will be unable to meet the demands inside and outside of the organization that are inevitably to come.[1]

It is when one seeks to apply Levinson's prescription to race and gender issues not only in the United States but throughout the world, that the challenges confronting organizations begin to look truly daunting.

Reason and Emotion

Business and organizational practices are commonly premised on the notion that we humans are rational creatures, able to keep our thoughts entirely separate from our emotions. Such a model would have us believe that success in human enterprises derives solely and strictly from the use of rational processes in the service of building up institutions, laws, and organizations.

But even though race and gender problems in organizations usually are approached in the belief that company employees are especially capable of acting rationally, the fact is that they aren't—at least not always, or consistently. Rather, it is the case that complex emotions, neuroses, psychological processes, and even our genes all come together to define who we are and why we think and behave as we do. Complicating this process is the fact that the sharp distinction we love to draw between reason and emotion is very likely a false one. In his book *Emotional Intelligence*, Daniel Goleman correctly points out that in fact our emotions and our rationality must work hand-in-hand:

> In the dance of feeling and thought, the emotional faculty guides our moment-to-moment decisions, working hand-in-hand with the rational mind, enabling—or disabling—thought itself. Like-

wise, the thinking brain plays an executive role in our emotions . . . In a sense we have two brains, two minds—and two different kinds of intelligence: rational and emotional. How we do in life is determined by both—it is not just IQ, but *emotional* intelligence that matters.[2]

If we are to deal effectively with the issues of race and gender we have no choice but to acknowledge the truth of this view, for many human prejudices and biases clearly are brought on by neuroses and a low level of emotional intelligence. No strategy that seeks to create an effective, variegated workforce will succeed over the long term if it is not formulated with this truth in mind. And by the way, when we use terms like "neuroses" and "low emotional intelligence," we're not making any sort of value judgment. We're merely suggesting that although to be human is to be afflicted with such ills, nonetheless all of us can develop strategies that will override our neuroses and help us to boost our level of emotional intelligence. It is by seizing these opportunities that all of us can reduce misunderstanding and conflict, particularly in those multicultural environments where each person has his or her own values, beliefs, and assumptions, and rightly considers them to be just as "correct" and "rational" as anybody else's.

Stereotyping and Cultural Differences

If we combine our earlier comments about the judgmental human brain with the foregoing reflections on cultural differences, we arrive at this conclusion: that while the processes compelling us to react to others in a certain way may be innate, nonetheless the content and meaning of those processes is purely social. That means that none of us is biologically predisposed to dislike anyone possessing a certain characteristic. It also means that even though we are indeed drawn to those who are similar to us and repelled by those who are different, such similarities and differences are relative to the meanings we attach to them, and are largely shaped by sociocultural processes. A recent study brings home this point.

The purpose of the study was to evaluate children's attitudes toward two teachers—an attractive but inexperienced teacher, and a less attractive but highly experienced one. The less attractive teacher performed objective tasks better than the attractive one; for example, she was much more attentive to the children's needs. And yet it was found that the children overwhelmingly preferred the attractive teacher, reporting that they liked her better and that she more effectively carried out such work-related tasks as spending time helping them with their work. Even at their early age, these children already had developed a stereotype: that attractive people are more cooperative, competent, and likable. The same study revealed that attractive women tend to get more job offers, and higher salaries, than equally qualified "unattractive" ones.

Learning to Appreciate Cultural Differences

One particularly common yet self-defeating and erroneous perception, is that all persons of a given race, gender, or ethnic group are the same, that they share a common set of values, beliefs, and outlooks. The following examples should serve to give the lie to that trust-and-respect-destroying attitude.

A Mexican American with ties to Northern Mexico, and a Cuban American, may share a generalized Hispanic cultural identity. And yet, ethnically, as Mexicans and Cubans, they are as different as can be. For instance, the Cuban diet has been heavily influenced by its island geography, whereas the Mexican diet is a product of that nation's system of irrigated agriculture; Cuban music has been more influenced by African rhythms, whereas Mexican music reflects some European, polka influences. Both the Mexican and the Cuban do speak Spanish, but in different idiomatic forms; both practice Catholicism, and yet in fact different indigenous religious attitudes underlie the same European veneer.

Similarly, a Mexican living in Los Angeles and another living in Mexico may share a common identification as Mexican, or Hispanic, or Latino, and nonetheless have very dissimilar experiences and ways of looking at the world, with the inevitable resulting differences in terms of cultural identity. For the Mexican American, minority status and ethnic distinctiveness in an urban environment play a relatively leading role; for the Mexican, both the Spanish language and living in Mexico themselves loom more large.

We see, then, that Hispanic culture, like other cultures, transcends race and ancestry. One historical reason for this is that Hispanic culture was imposed by Spanish explorers and settlers upon the indigenous peoples of Central and South America, just as African slaves were brought to the new world by their Spanish owners. This Hispanic culture was later adopted by immigrants from areas as widely varied as Italy, Japan, China, and Portugal. Therefore, while those who share similar customs, language, and/or religion may perhaps have similar social or ethnic backgrounds, they are just as likely to have very different racial/ethnic backgrounds despite the fact that they are linked by a common cultural bond.

One more illustration. In a seminar we conducted at the Centers the Disease Control, we were using a cultural assessment to provide the participants with a better understanding of their cultural similarities and differences. We paired a young black woman who had a master's degree in public health, with a fiftyish white male doctor. And what these two discovered, to their great surprise, was that despite the obvious differences in key demographics such as race, gender, and age, their cultural values as measured by the assessment were similar throughout. They found that they were both born and raised in suburban Indiana towns. The parents of both were well-educated professionals who worked outside of the home. Both had attended the University of Indiana, and one was Presbyterian while the other was Episcopalian. It was clear to all of us that these cultural factors had had an even greater impact upon these two individuals than had their race, gender, or age.

These historical processes suggest that we can have a cultural identity that is defined by two or more distinct cultural influences. These influences might be family structure, geographic location, experience living in other countries, and so on. Those of us who are bi-cultural or multi-cultural may feel ourselves drawn to one of our cultures at some times, to another at others. And indeed almost all of us, as human beings, have an ability to adapt to and to operate in more than one socio-cultural context. Thus, if employees are consciously bi-cultural or multi-cultural, the functioning of the two or more cultures need not be a hindrance to the organization; however, if they are only subconsciously so, or are consciously racist, tremendous conflicts can and will occur. The personal values that grow out of these varying cultural influences may serve to build character, support one another, or to create conflict.

For example, an individual's socioeconomic status and place of origin may produce values, beliefs, and assumptions that are consistent with one another, and yet influences such as political affiliation or educational attainment may still cause the individual to question these values, beliefs, and assumptions. Our point is that every individual's culture is a complex network that mightily influences the way he or she behaves and perceives the behavior of others. Thus, an African American who was born and raised in a working class, religious culture, yet who as an adult went to Harvard and now works in a major investment banking company, in all likelihood has retained her African American, working-class, religious norms and values, and draws upon them freely when she is in her "home" environment. And yet it is quite certain that she also has adopted some values and norms from the Harvard and investment banking communities, and can make use of those when she finds herself in the latter two environments.

Person versus Culture

A person's stereotypes and his or her personal beliefs are two very different things, and each may tell us something quite different about the person or group to which we're responding. For one thing, we begin to learn our culture's stereotypes, without questioning them, at a very early age, whereas our personal beliefs come to us only much later, as a result of more sophisticated cognitive tasking. It is precisely because stereotypes develop early, and we access them more often, that they tend to be automatically activated whenever we encounter a member of a stereotyped group. And yet ironically, and hopefully, many people who hold stereotypes don't really believe in the content of those stereotypes. This contradiction seems to tell us that it isn't stereotyping per se that is harmful, but rather the content of those stereotypes and how we choose to act upon them.

Alas, most cultures actually encourage the acceptance of stereotypes. At the beginning of the chapter we asked you to visualize a number of individuals. If you were to share those spontaneous images with others from your own cultural group(s), you would almost certainly discover some similarities in your perceptions. And of course that is explained by our point that stereotypes are socially and culturally produced—we learn them from our families, schools, media, and a host of other influences. This also explains why people are so reluctant to admit out loud that they don't agree with a widespread cultural stereotype—because they are reluctant to set themselves apart from their own cultural group. The price of remaining loyal to one's own cultural group can be an expression of antipathy for another one, especially when there is a long history of enmity between the groups.

As if to make matters worse, when people are uncomfortable with something about themselves but can't admit that to themselves, they often project this hidden and feared characteristic onto other groups. When such characteristics are widely shared by a group, they can subtly be converted into stereotypes that are then employed by that group (or society or culture) in its war with other groups.

Perhaps American attitudes toward people from the Far East provide us with a good case study here:

> In 1935, most Americans thought of Japanese as "progressive," "intelligent," and "industrious"; by 1942 they were "cunning" and "treacherous"; and by 1950 the image had changed again. When there was a need for Chinese laborers in California, they were portrayed as "frugal," "sober," and "law abiding"; when labor was plentiful and they competed with White workers, they became "dirty," "repulsive," "unassimilable," and "dangerous."[4]

By contrast, more specialized attributes are given to Jews in the United States—e.g., they are "defensive," "aggressive," "shrewd," and so on.

Many of us like to believe that such vile ways of thinking no longer exist. It would seem almost outlandish of us now, to think of Chinese people as dirty, Japanese people as treacherous, or Jewish people as aggressive, like some antiquated holdover from our grandparents' generation. But the truth is that in many respects they are still with us. It's just that we have found ways to inwardly change the content of our stereotypes while outwardly talking about "old prejudices." Over the years, for example, we have found new ways in which to subtly disparage African Americans. Today we don't expect to hear a manager admit that "We don't hire blacks." But we do hear that "many blacks don't have the proper qualifications." In other words, while the attitudes of American whites toward blacks really have become more tolerant over the past forty years or so, more subtle forms of bias persist. People openly disavow racist attitudes, but still act with covert bias. Such bias can take the form, say, of a white male senior manager, who is convinced that he has no prejudices, rejecting a black, Hispanic, or Asian job applicant, ostensibly not because of her race but because her education and experience are "not quite right" for the job—then hiring a white applicant with the same credentials. Or it might take the form of giving helpful tips to a white salesperson as to how best to make a call, while neglecting to do the same for a black or Hispanic salesperson. Ironically, our research has shown that when it comes to both women and people of color, it tends to be those who say they believe these groups are no longer viewed in a stereotypical light, who are the very ones also to express a belief in the highest number of stereotypes.

So too, while much of the overt stereotyping of women has left us, new and more subtle biases are evolving as we speak. For example, one female attorney has told us that when she appears in court, judges initially will turn to her male clients with their questions, assuming that she is the client, the client her attorney! "Typically," she reports with enviable good humor, "corporate lawyers . . . are not little chubby black women who have white-haired, three-piece-suit-wearing gentlemen as their clients."[5]

Conclusions

It would be folly for any of us to assume that stereotypes cannot and do not damage work relationships and work teams. However, *the fact that we can develop beliefs that are based on more conscious thought processes than stereotyping—and that even stand in defiant contradiction to our stereo-*

types—indicates that through self-awareness and education, we truly can gain a better understanding of ourselves and of others. This, in turn, will help us strengthen our relationships within the workplace, with our customers and stakeholders, and in our personal lives.

In other words, although our brains do innately form instant perceptions of others, they do so only within a sociocultural context. Both our perceptions and what we do with them are greatly and inevitably influenced by the norms and rules of the culture we live in. It is by becoming fully conscious of our culturally based stereotypes, and by questioning their content, that we greatly diminish their damaging effect upon our souls and our relational lives.

5

Stereotyping and Discrimination in Corporate America: A 25-Year Perspective

Despite all the affirmative action and diversity training efforts that corporate America has undertaken in the past three decades and especially in the late 1980s and the 1990s, stereotyping and its spawn, discrimination, remain alive and well in boiler rooms and board rooms alike. In this chapter we'll be taking a detailed look at the data we've gathered in surveys which strongly support this assertion. We will begin by examining some of the persistent stereotypes that continue to dog people of color, women, and white men, and then we will see the discrimination that these stereotypes continually give rise to.

25 Years of Stereotyping

Stereotyping and People of Color

In 1992, the ABC network conducted a hidden-camera investigation called "True Colors" which clearly showed its viewers those real-life situations in which racist stereotyping persists. No one who was watching *20/20* that night could have denied that on a day-to-day basis, a black, single male faces racist discrimination that his white, single male counterpart does not, despite their possessing equally good qualifications and similar personalities and styles.

For a long while now, our research has been telling us more or less the same story. In the 1970s and early 1980s we learned that most racist people tend to be older, less educated, and more traditionally religious. They also tend to have lower self-esteem and higher anxiety levels, and to be more authoritarian and likely to conform to group pressure, less empathetic and tolerant of ambiguity. Our survey data dating from the late 1980s and 1990s yielded some different results regarding the role that age, education, and religion play in discrimination. What we decided we were seeing was a heightened level of stereotyping due to the increased intensity of competition for more limited opportunities in the late 1980s and 1990s. But whatever the reason, it was clear that many younger, educated whites had developed negative stereotypes about people of color.

Let's begin by looking at some of the racist stereotypes about people of color that employees in our studies of the 1990s gave vent to. These remarks—and our list could go on and on, if we had the space and our readers the patience—were made in response to neutral, open-ended questions relating to the issues of diversity, affirmative action, and people of color as these were operative within the respondents' companies.

I have had problems with people of color, and nothing gets done about it, and I believe it is because of their color. They are also getting away with things that others cannot.

White female, occupational

Some employees of color hide behind their race and give their race an unfair perception.

White male, upper-level manager

In my heart, I truly feel if employees of color would quit whining and just do their job, there would not be so much of it [discrimination] here as I've experienced.

White female, occupational

There is a lot of subtle prejudice. . . . I don't think African Americans are thought of as being the same quality or needing to be of the same quality.

White male, middle-level manager

The talent pool is small. It's hard to find a qualified black person.

White male, middle-level manager

You would have a better chance for advancement if you were a minority or a woman.

Asian male, lower-level manager

Some [blacks] are very lazy.

White male, lower-level manager

Many employees of color are some of the most racist, and view the actions of a few people 100-plus years ago as just cause for their views of all white people today.

White male, occupational

My co-worker stated "I have never met a Mexican that wasn't worthless." I reminded her that my son-in-law was Hispanic, and she reiterated "I have never met a Mexican that wasn't worthless."

White male, lower-level manager

I think employees of color are chosen for jobs over white people because of color, not ability.

White female, occupational

All promotions in our area have gone to People of Color, and are undeserved!

Native American, female, occupational

African Americans . . . get followed by security. I bought something in the company store and I made sure to keep the receipt because security accused me of stealing it.

Black male, lower-level manager

Going to black schools is held against minorities.

Black male, middle-level manager

I do not consider myself to be very prejudiced; however, I have experienced firsthand the problems that result from affirmative action when a person is hired/promoted because of their race rather than their abilities.

Hispanic male, middle-level manager

Stereotypes are held by people at this company. Blacks at this company are thought of as exceptions from the norm of the stereotype.

Black male, upper-level manager

I recently overheard a HR employee telling obviously racial "jokes," including the use of "coon" and "jungle bunny"—disgusting!

White female, lower-level manager

Back in the 1970s and 1980s, openly racist comments were very common in our surveys. With some exceptions, people in the 1990s have become more subtle and sophisticated in expressing their biases; they would say, for example, that Hispanics are unqualified for positions rather than that Hispanics are lazy. Such subtlety of the new racist stereotypes causes many to conclude that racism is much less prevalent today than it was "back then." Our research indicates that this isn't true; what has changed is not the reality of racism, but merely the language used to express it.

A review of our historical data on specific stereotypes about people of color will further support us in this position. In the following tables except for the question "What is your position on Interracial Relationships?" the numbers represent the percentages of those who responded "strongly agree" or "agree" to the statements in our surveys. For the interracial relationship question, the responses are of those who are very supportive or supportive. Note that over the years, significant percentages of white employees have believed in these stereotypes; even more sadly, a rather high percentage of people of color have concurred.

Table 5.1
Stereotypes about People of Color

In general, people of color use race as an alibi for difficulties they are having on the job:

	1972	1978	1984	1985	1986	1988	1995
Whites	—	15	30	43	36	42	44
Blacks	—	13	22	30	20	26	11
Hispanics	—	9	26*	23*	29*	33	11*
Asians	—	8	26	23	29	21	11
Native Americans	—	16	26	23	29	44	11

*Because of the small numbers and the similarity of responses among these groups, the data have been collapsed into one category, that of other people of color.

In general, an employee of color, if demoted even if inadequate in his/her role, will make undeserved charges of discrimination:

	1972	1978	1984	1985	1986	1988	1995
Whites	56	—	56	58	58	58	59
Blacks	27	—	19	15	12	9	27
Hispanics	—	—	42*	39*	36*	40	51
Asians	—	—	42	39	36	24	48
Native Americans	—	—	42	39	36	38	47

In general, people of color obtained their current position only because they are people of color:

	1972	1978	1984	1985	1986	1988	1995
Whites	31	—	55	—	67	56	43
Blacks	7	—	10	—	19	28	12
Hispanics	—	—	28*	—	30*	24	15
Asians	—	—	28	—	30	35	17
Native Americans	—	—	28	—	30	67	21

Many people of color come from backgrounds which are not conducive to success in your department:

	1972	1978	1984	1985	1985	1988	1995
Whites	17	37	25	28	34	31	29
Blacks	0	38	41	31	25	35	37
Hispanics	—	35	38*	29*	45*	27	28
Asians	—	34	38	29	45	38	38
Native Americans	—	36	38	29	45	55	37

In general, people of color are just as dependable as whites:

	1972	1978	1984	1985	1985	1988	1995
Whites	—	—	92	99	87	90	83
Blacks	—	—	98	84	98	91	93
Hispanics	—	—	94*	95*	94*	97	91
Asians	—	—	94	95	94	95	86
Native Americans	—	—	94	95	94	78	75

People of color are more frequently suspected of having committed a crime than are whites:

	1972	1978	1984	1985	1986	1988	1995
Whites	—	—	—	—	—	—	39
Blacks	—	—	—	—	—	—	78
Hispanics	—	—	—	—	—	—	58
Asians	—	—	—	—	—	—	59
Native Americans	—	—	—	—	—	—	42

What is your position on interracial relationships (very supportive or supportive)?

	1972	1978	1984	1985	1986	1988	1995
Whites	—	—	—	—	56	52	65
Blacks	—	—	—	—	83	73	77
Hispanics	—	—	—	—	75	86	75
Asians	—	—	—	—	75	80	78
Native Americans	—	—	—	—	75	62	70

Table 5.1 tells us that whites hold stereotypes about people of color fairly consistently. For example, about 55+ percent of whites believe that people of color cannot be demoted without bringing undeserved charges of discrimination—a view that about 1 in 3 people of color supports. The percentage of whites who believe that people of color use their race as an excuse for the difficulties they face has increased from 15 percent in 1978 to 44 percent in 1995. The table also makes it clear that while there have been some fluctuations up and down, there has not been any consistent downturn in the prevalence of stereotypes about people of color. This, despite all the growing awareness of racism in our society over the past 30+ years, and the progress that has been made in employing people of color, especially in non-managerial and lower-level management jobs. It was in 1995 that we started to ask about people of color being suspected of crime more often than whites; 39 percent of whites and 78 percent of blacks believe this to be the case. This is a new stereotype that has emerged only in the past 10 years, thanks both to the news media's distorted coverage and to conservative politicians who succeed in turning crime committed by people of color into a divisive issue.

Finally, note that while significant percentages of people of color have their own stereotypes about people of color, generally they do not with their own color group but with another. In fact, and hard as it may be to believe, we have found that people tend to hold stronger, more ardent racist stereotypes than do whites. A 1993 Harris poll has confirmed us in this,[1] for it revealed the following:

- *46 percent of the Hispanics and 42 percent of the African Americans polled agreed with a description of Asians as being "unscrupulous, crafty, and devious in business"; in contrast, only 27 percent of whites agreed with that assertion.*

- *68 percent of Asians and 49 percent of African Americans agreed that Hispanics tend "to have bigger families than they are able to support"; the figure here for whites was 50 percent.*
- *33 percent of Hispanics and 22 percent of Asians believed that African Americans, "Even if given a chance, aren't capable of getting ahead." Only 12 percent of whites agreed.*

There are several possible explanations for these views. One is the historical tensions between certain color groups, brought on by disparate opportunities and treatment. Another is that individual people of color have generalized the negative experiences they have had with people of other color groups so as to include those groups as a whole. And finally, some people of color may be adopting the views of whites as part of their attempt to assimilate. In effect they are saying, "I am different from those other people of color. I understand why whites hold these views."

While significant numbers of white employees have told us over the years that they hold negative stereotypes about people of color, only a few have spoken of frequently or very frequently hearing racist remarks at work. In the early 1980s, the percentages who reported hearing these types of remarks very frequently or frequently were 46 percent of black and 14 percent of white employees. In 1988 the numbers were holding steady: 46 percent of blacks and 16 percent of whites. In 1995 the percentage of blacks was down to 33 percent, while the percentage of whites held at about 15 percent. Note that, over the years, only about 1 out of 5 whites has told us that he/she never hears any racist language at work.

The upshot of all this is that even though there has been a significant decrease in people admitting to hearing racist language, let's not over-repeat: the belief in stereotypes about people of color has not significantly decreased. We attribute this situation, in large part, to the politically correct environment we now live in both corporate America and in society in general. It simply isn't "politically correct" to admit to hearing racist language—"Our company is not racist!"—but it *is* "politically correct" to question people of color's ability and to believe that they use their race as an alibi for their mistakes and their poor overall performance.

Stereotyping and Women

Despite a widespread perception that the United States is far ahead of other nations when it comes to rooting out sexist stereotypes, a recent Gallup poll that covered 22 nations has shown us that we still have a long way to go. In the United States as well as in Chile, France, and Japan, about half of the respondents believed the ideal family to be one in which the father works and the mother stays at home. In countries such as Germany, India, Lithuania, and Spain, only about a quarter of the respondents held this view. In addition, about one half of U.S. citizens said that they prefer to have a male supervisor rather than a female one.

Another study which asked U.S. senior executives to explain why women are not likely to become CEOs sooner, confirms the prevalence of gender stereotypes, particularly those that question women's experience, skills, and commitment to the job. Women lack enough experience (64 percent); they are too concentrated in those areas of the company that don't lead to the top (50 percent); they don't have broad enough experience (45 percent); they have not built up a solid enough network of connections and support (31 percent); their personal lives and their obligations to their families get in the way (29 percent).

Alarmingly, our research of the 1980s revealed an increasing trend toward stereotyping women. For example in 1978, only 16 percent of men and 7 percent of women agreed with the proposition that women are not serious about their professional careers. In 1988, 20 percent of women and 25 percent of men agreed, a significant increase. We're glad to report, however, that in 1995 we saw a significant reversal in such openly sexist stereotypes as women being too emotional to be effective managers and not being serious about their careers; only 3 percent of the women and 6 percent of the men agreed with the latter proposition. And yet a key area in which there has been a steady increase in stereotypes has been that of women lowering hiring and promotion standards. Notice in Table 5.2 how in 1985, only 18 percent of the women and 38 percent of the men believed this; in 1995, the percentages had risen to 39 and 48 percent, respectively. Table 5.2 shows a significant decrease in the responses in almost all areas of stereotyping about women over the years. And yet it also shows that at least 1 out of 3 men, and 1 out of 4 women, either strongly agree or agree with 3 out of the 5 more common ("acceptable") stereotypes about women. That consistently over the years a higher percentage of men than women should concur with these stereotypes is no surprise; however, that at least 25 percent of the women agree with the more subtle, politically correct stereotypes *may* come as a surprise to some. Still, it shouldn't; after all, men hold no monopoly on stereotypes about women. Both men and women go through basically the same socialization process: both are bombarded with the same stereotypes. Just as we saw some people of color believing in stereotypes about people of color, so do some women come to believe in the stereotypes about women.

Table 5.2
Stereotypes about Women*

Diversity will force us to lower our hiring and promotion standards:

	1972	1978	1984	1985	1986	1988	1995
Women	—	51	28	18	18	25	39
Men	—	62	51	38	25	40	48

*Numbers represent percentage of participants who strongly agree or agree.

In general, women received their present positions because they are women:

	1972	1978	1984	1985	1986	1988	1995
Women	46	—	—	—	42	32	25
Men	64	—	—	—	62	43	39

In general, women use their gender as an alibi for difficulties they experience on the job:

	1972	1978	1984	1985	1986	1988	1995
Women	—	6	18	23	17	22	11
Men	—	18	33	39	34	27	21

In general, women are not serious about their professional careers:

	1972	1978	1984	1985	1986	1988	1995
Women	—	6	8	22	18	20	3
Men	—	17	19	32	25	25	6

In general, women are too emotional to be competent employees:

	1972	1978	1984	1985	1986	1988	1995
Women	—	—	13	8	7	9	2
Men	—	—	21	19	15	8	4

The increasing employment of women has led to the "breakdown" of the American family:

	1972	1978	1984	1985	1986	1988	1995
Women	—	—	38	—	23	29	32
Men	—	—	55	—	45	49	33

Now let's take a look at some of the comments we were given in our most recent surveys about women in the workplace.

> Women of color [are] . . . not as easy to work for, and are much more demanding and lack understanding.
>
> *White female, occupational*

> Far too often women are promoted because they are women, not because they are competent.
>
> *White male, occupational*

> Women should stay at home with the children until they are in school.
>
> *White male, middle-level manager*

> Women seem rather petty.
>
> *White female, occupational*

> Sometimes men still think we work for a hobby.
>
> *White female, occupational*

> If in a position of authority they are expected to act as a man, but if they do, there is something wrong with that.
>
> *White female, occupational*

> The woman I work for is one of the biggest sexists I've ever seen.
>
> *White female, occupational*

> A strong woman is a threat to most men.
>
> *White female, occupational*

> They are given jobs not because of ability, but to fill a quota.
>
> *White male, occupational*

> Men look at women as if they were meat.
>
> *White female, occupational*

> I am a woman, and I have seen women use their gender as an excuse not to work efficiently.
>
> *White female, occupational*

> Women seem to get their way easier than men.
>
> *Hispanic male, occupational*

Women should stay at home and cook and keep their kids off the street!

Asian male, middle-level manager

I feel men think women are too emotional; therefore, they do have to try harder to make it.

Asian female, occupational

I believe that the area I work in is very cognizant of diversity; however, it is predominantly women in management and unfortunately women haven't been trained to work well together and tend to want to control individuals to the extreme.

Black female, middle-level manager

They, in general, do not have the same background experience [in sales] as men, which makes their possibility of success less likely.

White male, middle-level manager

This perspective is from my department only—a generalization—but I think some women do perpetuate stereotypical thinking about women as much as men do.

White male, middle-level manager

Most women in our immediate work area are poor examples of team workers and do not do their responsibilities. I say this honestly from the best example I have—my wife.

Asian male, occupational

Stereotyping and White Males

As is to be expected, people of color and women look at the generally dominant position of white men in the workplace from a very different perspective than do those white men themselves. It is not at all unusual to hear the employees in our seminars describing white men as "unaware," "arrogant," "crazy," "ignorant," "insensitive," "out of control," "spoiled," "selfish," and "out of touch." The more positive descriptions are "privileged," "shrewd," "in control," "dominant," "powerful," and "smart." Table 5.3 summarizes the responses which surveyed employees have given us to several questions we asked about the stereotyping of white males. The table reveals that between 1988 and 1995, perceptions have not become any more consistently positive or negative. However, significantly higher percentages of all races and genders believed in 1995 that a white male cannot be demoted, even if he was inadequate in his role, without his then making an undeserved charge of discrimination. And when it comes to the stereotype about white males using their race/gender as excuses to account for difficulties they are having on the job, significantly higher percentages of African Americans, Hispanics, and Asians believed in this one in 1995 compared to 1988. Interestingly, in 1995 rather than in 1988 a lower percentage of all groups across the board believed that white men received their current position because they *are* white men.

What these data suggest is that the tremendous attention which white males have received over the past four to five years, vis-à-vis reverse discrimination charges, is translating into more hardened stereotypes about white males. And it is clear that in both years, significant differences of outlook exist between white males and people of color, more so than those between white men and white women. As for white men themselves, in 1995, only 9 percent of them, as opposed to 29–68 percent of other groups, believed that white men had received their present positions just because they *are* white men.

Table 5.3*
Stereotypes about White Males

In general, a white male employee, if demoted, even if inadequate in his role, would make an undeserved charge of reverse discrimination:

	1988	1995
White Male	8	29
White Female	15	30
African American	26	53
Hispanic-Latino	26	48
Native American	20	43
Asian	17	37

*Numbers represent percent of participants who strongly agreed or agreed.

Many white men use their race/gender as an alibi for difficulties they have on the job:

	1988	1995
White Male	10	11
White Female	17	9
African American	29	46
Hispanic-Latino	21	32
Native American	20	21
Asian	23	33

In general, white men come from backgrounds which are not conducive to their success in the new, "diverse" environment:

	1988	1995
White Male	27	39
White Female	49	45
African American	54	47
Hispanic-Latino	42	38
Native American	46	56
Asian	40	46

In general, white men received their present positions because they are white men:

	1988	1995
White Male	23	9
White Female	49	29
African American	79	68
Hispanic-Latino	60	42
Native American	55	32
Asian	48	39

Now let us turn to some of the comments shared with us by employees in our surveys, as to their perceptions of white men in the workplace.

This place is the last refuge of the classic male-chauvinist.
White female, middle-level manager

I'm so sick of their whining—white guys blame everyone else!
White male, lower-level manager

Most think they are better than others and know more.
White male, occupational

The "white" male population has been blamed for nearly all problems at our company.
White male, lower-level manager

I think they are scared. Some do get hurt by Affirmative Action. They arc the ones who primarily built this country. . . . Just look at countries where there is *little* white influence and where they are at.
White female, middle-level manager

They fear being perceived as a bigot, if they complain about some inappropriate effort at achieving diversity.

White female, lower-level manager

I've often heard the comment that white men think more logically than women or people of color, and therefore they get promoted.

Black female, lower-level manager

Our company is run by white men. They don't have a problem doing anything they want. It's all about who you know. White men in this company have the greatest opportunities.

Hispanic female, lower-level manager

White men face few problems with promotions, and more problems with stress. They tend to bond with their own sex and color, and are not very social or motivators in the work environment.

Asian female, occupational

A fact is that white men are the winners of the world as far as the job market. If a white man is unemployed that is a personal problem, because the jobs are available just because of being white.

Black female, lower-level manager

I don't know what a white male feels. He has more advantages than any other individual.

Black female, lower-level manager

One thing that is interesting about many of these comments is that the employees who made them lumped all white men into a single category. But as we noted in Chapter 3, the truth is that only those white men who fit some very narrowly defined criteria are indeed the favored ones—not only over women and people of color, but also over other white men who do not fit the criteria.

25 Years of Discrimination

We could dismiss stereotyping as unimportant, if it didn't give rise to specific behaviors in the form of discrimination which undercut trust and respect, and which cripple efforts to form high-performance teams capable of offering top-quality products and services to diverse markets. What we will now be showing is that the stereotypes we heard being aired in the previous section are in fact continually being translated into both discriminatory actions and clear-sighted perceptions of discrimination. And this, despite the fact that hundreds of millions of dollars have been spent on equal-employment-opportunity and diversity-training programs. It is clear to us from both our survey data and the consulting work we do at all levels of organizations, that the various race and gender groups hold notably different views as to discrimination, and that it is these disparities which are doing so much to undermine trust and respect and to foment discord.

Discrimination against People of Color

While the debate rages on as to the extent of racial discrimination in corporate America, the reality is that after 34 years of equal employment opportunity, the number of people of color whom one will find happily ensconced in middle- and upper-management positions, and in the key areas of organizations, remains pitifully small. Granted, some progress has been made in some companies, when it comes to providing employment opportunities at nonmanagement and lower-management levels. But above those levels, progress has been only of the token sort at best. People of color still account for less than 1 percent of all boards of directors, for only about 2 percent of all senior positions, and for only about 5 to 6 percent of middle-level managers.

In addition, there is a clear trend at work for people of color to be steered directly into certain job categories. Thus, particularly above the lower levels of management, most blacks and Hispanics seem to be placed in such areas as human resources, public relations, and marketing/sales jobs related to their communities. In essence all of these constitute corporate "ghettos," and fortunate is he or she who can break free from them and find a way to move laterally, much less up to the next higher level. Similarly, many Asians are seen as being technically skilled but lacking managerial savoir faire. The sad reason behind all of these sad facts is of course the very one we have been examining here: Stereotypes relating to the abilities of people of color simply have not changed much over the past 25 years. And given our earlier frank appraisal of the intrinsically judgmental nature of the human brain, none of us should be so naive as to doubt the fact that these stereotypes play havoc with decision makers' objectivity when they evaluate people of color.

Once again, let's turn to the data. Table 5.4 presents you with some responses to specific questions we've been asking about discrimination against people of color over the past 25 years.

Table 5.4

Responses by Race to Questions about Discrimination against People of Color

To what extent do you agree or disagree with each of the following statements about people of color employed in your company? (Numbers represent percentage of participants who strongly agree or agree.)

In general, people of color have to be better performers than white people to get ahead.

	1972	1978	1984	1985	1986	1988	1995
Whites	33	17	33	—	25	32	30
Blacks	88	82	92	—	94	87	89
Hispanics	—	46	51	—	67	53	55
Asians	—	45	51	—	67	58	71
Native Americans	—	16	51	—	67	67	31

In general, people of color are more severely penalized for mistakes than are white people.

	1972	1978	1984	1985	1986	1988	1995
Whites	—	9	—	—	—	14	15
Blacks	—	53	—	—	—	80	74
Hispanics	—	23	—	—	—	30	39
Asians	—	20	—	—	—	23	45
Native Americans	—	6	—	—	—	44	28

In general, employees accept the authority of a person of color as readily as they accept that of a white person in a similar situation.

	1972	1978	1984	1985	1986	1988	1995
Whites	—	—	78	84	77	56	83
Blacks	—	—	30	35	27	32	45
Hispanics	—	—	67*	70*	59*	38	55
Asians	—	—	67	70	59	33	65
Native Americans	—	—	67	70	59	33	61

In general, it is true that people of color often are excluded from their informal social networks by white people.

	1972	1978	1984	1985	1986	1988	1995
Whites	—	29	32	29	41	36	27
Blacks	—	65	67	75	83	87	70
Hispanics	—	30	36*	44*	52*	42	50
Asians	—	25	36	44	52	42	51
Native Americans	—	22	36	44	52	44	49

People of color do not have the same advancement opportunities as white people.

	1972	1978	1984	1985	1986	1988	1995
Whites	—	—	—	—	—	—	15
Blacks	—	—	—	—	—	—	70
Hispanics	—	—	—	—	—	—	39
Asians	—	—	—	—	—	—	55
Native Americans	—	—	—	—	—	—	42

In general, people of color have a harder time finding a sponsor or mentor than white people do.

	1972	1978	1984	1985	1986	1988	1995
Whites	—	28	37	35	41	35	30
Blacks	—	72	85	92	92	87	78
Hispanics	—	39	51*	65*	64*	54	55
Asians	—	32	51	65	64	57	61
Native Americans	—	23	51	65	64	44	55

*In these surveys, the number of Hispanics, Asians, and Native Americans were small and their responses quite similar; therefore, their responses were collapsed into a category called "other people of color."

The data presented in Table 5.4 give rise to five basic observations:

1. Over the years, blacks have been the employee group most vocal about discrimination, and by a good measure. Back in 1978 Hispanics/Latinos were slightly more critical of discrimination than were Asians and Native Americans, but by 1988 the responses of Hispanics/Latinos, Asian Americans, and Native Americans were no longer significantly different in many areas, although there remains a tendency for Native Americans to be the least critical. What is of greatest significance here is that the responses of all three of these groups grew significantly more critical during this 10-year time frame, so as to move them collectively closer toward the responses of blacks—not a good omen, when one recalls that Hispanics/Latinos and Asians are the fastest-growing racial groups in the United States. As if in confirmation of the trend, whites too perceived more discrimination in 1988 than in 1978.

2. In the 1990s, we found there to be considerably more agreement about discrimination in corporate America among all people of color. For although in 1995 both blacks and whites perceived slightly less discrimination, people of other color groups perceived more. Several possible reasons might be adduced in explanation of this convergence of the responses of people of color. One is that as the Hispanic/Latino population has grown, whites have begun to perceive them as constituting more of a threat to their own careers; thus, Hispanic/Latinos are more frequently targets of the discrimination and are fully aware of that fact. Another is that so much national attention has been focused on illegal Hispanic/Latino immigrants that this has generated more anti-Hispanic hostilities, which are then carried over into the workplace. A third explanation pertains to a kind of "infighting" within the Hispanic/Latino group. Under the umbrella of "Hispanic/Latino" are gathered five distinct groups: Mexicans, Puerto Ricans, Latinos from Central and South America, and "others," hailing primarily from Spain and its colonies. When we analyze the responses to our surveys, we consistently find that Puerto Ricans, many of whom have some black ancestry, respond more like blacks than do other Hispanic groups. By the same token, "other Spanish" usually are white and respond more like whites. "White Latinos get treated more like whites and dark Latinos get treated more like blacks," says a Hispanic, lower-level male manager. The implication here is that the skin color of Hispanic/Latino group members strongly influences their responses, thereby mimicking the pattern that exists in black society of light-skinned blacks facing less discrimination than dark-skinned blacks.

3. As the total number of Asian Americans in corporate America burgeons, and as anti-Asian attitudes grow because of both increased immigration and the perceived economic success of Asian countries, so has the amount of discrimination they face in the workplace. Non-Asian Americans, especially whites, fear that Asians are taking over because of their numbers and economic influence. (Witness the 1997 flap over Democratic fund-raising and "the Asian connection.") Thus, Asians who once were quite confident they could assimilate are becoming more and more aware of their race and of the problems their race creates for them.

4. The higher level of resentment among whites against Native Americans is perhaps a result of the latter's more aggressively fighting for their legal rights, and of their successes in the gaming industry. These have released them from dependence upon the government and consequently upon the goodwill of others.

5. As one might expect, white men are the group least likely to perceive discrimination against people of color. What is rather shocking, however, is the way in which white women, who saw more discrimination against people of color than white men did in the 1970s and 1980s, are responding in the 1990s much like white men, as they perceive people of color taking advantage of opportunities to the seeming detriment of white

males. Many white women seem never even to consider the reality here, which is that many of the opportunities that are not going to white men are going to *them!*

Now let's look at some comments from the surveys:

> We don't have any [people of color] in our office.
> *White female, middle-level manager*

> The area that you are in won't let you go, because you are the "one" minority.
> *Black female, lower-level manager*

> I have been an assistant manager, and they will not consider me for a manager position. They expect you to just work here and do your job and tell other black people how great it is.
> *Black female, lower-level manager*

> People of color cannot get above a certain level that is reserved for white males, and I don't see that changing.
> *Black male, middle-level manager*

> Whites have it all, people of color have nothing.
> *Hispanic male, occupational*

> White men . . . receive higher salaries for equal positions. White men are fearful of diversity because they feel it excludes them.
> *Hispanic female, lower-level manager*

> I have a hard time convincing a few of my peers to look at people of color constructively.
> *White male, upper-level manager*

> This company (traditionally) has been a good old boys' management structure of white males. Women and minorities are excluded from promotional opportunities, mentoring, and networks.
> *Hispanic female, middle-level manager*

> Let's face it, we have a long way to go. Minorities do have to be better in many cases, but not all.
> *White male, lower-level manager*

> I feel that white males still have far better employment and advancement opportunities than people of color or women.
> *Asian female, lower-level manager*

It makes me mad that the person best for the job isn't necessarily the one chosen for it just because he's not a minority.

White female, middle-level manager

To be equal, I have to be twice as good and produce twice as much.

Black female, lower-level manager

I am the only one [black]. I deal on the phone a lot, and when people finally meet me they look and say, "Oh, so you're black."

Black male, lower-level manager

There is conscious behavior to set black people up to fail.

Black male, occupational

As some whites look at the data in Table 5.4, they are likely to say that blacks and other people of color are paranoid, that they have foolishly adopted the mentality of victimhood. But in three of the five areas of discrimination we are discussing, about 30 percent of the white population actually supports people of color in their views. At any rate, what is just as clear is that white employees do hold stereotypical attitudes about people of color and their abilities—for example, that they are more likely to "cry discrimination" unfairly—and that discrimination does exist—less so, perhaps, than blacks believe it does, but certainly more than most whites believe it does.

Discrimination against Women

So, you still think gender discrimination is a thing of the past? Well, take a look at these statistics:

- *While women have come to constitute a full half of the workforce, one report has found that less than 0.5 percent of the highest-paid officers and directors of the top 1000 U.S. companies are women.*
- *Women hold only 2.6 percent of the top executive positions at Fortune 500 companies.*
- *Of the few women who have made it to the highest positions, fewer still are in line or sales jobs. Most are trapped in the "ghetto" of the traditionally female jobs: human resources, research, marketing, public affairs, or administration.*
- *In 1979, women earned 62 cents for every dollar earned by men. In 1990 they earned 74 cents; in 1995, 76 cents.*
- *Several jobs in the computer field paid better for men than women in 1993. The average salary of a male mathematical and computer scientist was $8060 higher than that of a woman in the same position.*

> *The differential for computer systems analysts and scientists was $5304, in favor of men. Men also earned more as operations/systems researchers and analysts.[2]*
> - *Female managers work about 52.5 hours per week, to men's 52. They earn, on average, $44,000 to men's $50,000.*
> - *Women hold managerial positions a half-level lower than those held by men, despite their greater likelihood of being in possession of a four-year rather than a two-year college degree.*

All of the data we have collected since 1970 bespeak a stubborn persistence of sexist attitudes. And make no mistake, such beliefs as "Women are too emotional to be effective managers," "Women are not really interested in a professional career," and "Working women lead to the breakdown of the American family" do directly translate into discrimination on the basis of gender.

Table 5.5*
Discrimination against Women

In general, women have to be better performers than men in order to get ahead:

	1972	1978	1984	1985	1986	1988	1995
Women	—	72	81	85	84	75	77
Men	—	27	30	32	31	25	31

*Numbers represent percent of participants who strongly agree or agree except for the last question.

In general, women are penalized more for mistakes than men are:

	1972	1978	1984	1985	1986	1988	1995
Women	—	38	—	—	—	45	51
Men	—	17	—	—	—	93	13

In general, women often are excluded from informal work networks by men:

	1972	1978	1984	1985	1986	1988	1995
Women	—	67	71	68	75	71	65
Men	—	59	52	43	53	43	35

In general, women have a much easier time finding a sponsor or mentor than men do:

	1972	1978	1984	1985	1986	1988	1995
Women	—	54	83	77	82	81	76
Men	—	37	44	43	45	55	40

In general, women are faced with some type of sexual harassment:

	1972	1978	1984	1985	1986	1988	1995
Women	—	—	73	64	71	62	59
Men	—	—	55	45	51	47	47

In general, internal clients/customers accept a woman's authority as much as they accept a man's in similar situations:

	1972	1978	1984	1985	1986	1988	1995
Women	—	—	—	—	9	—	—
Men	—	—	—	—	25	—	—

In general, women have a difficult time initiating informal, work-related activities such as lunch and socializing after work, because men misinterpret their behavior as a "come-on."

	1972	1978	1984	1985	1986	1988	1995
Women	—	47	—	—	—	50	47
Men	—	43	—	—	—	34	31

How frequently do you hear language in your organization which you consider sexist? (Very frequently or frequently)

	1972	1978	1984	1985	1986	1988	1995
Women	—	—	48	—	—	34	30
Men	—	—	37	—	—	22	23

Four observations in particular must be made with regard to the responses in Table 5.5.

1. Apropros of all the questions except that about hearing sexist language, about a majority of women consistently perceive discrimination against women.
2. In 1995, at least 3 out of 10 men—often more—supported many of the positions of women as to widespread gender discrimination.
3. The largest percentage difference between men and women came in response to the question about women having to be better performers; the smallest, remarkably enough, to the question about sexual harassment.

4. There has been no overall, consistent decrease in men's and women's perception of discrimination against women in the past 20 years, except in the areas of sexual harassment and sexist language.

Now let's turn to some of the actual comments we heard from the participants in our surveys.

> Women at this company are advanced ahead of more qualified males.
>
> *White male, middle-level manager*

> I believe they are not treated equally for the same work.
>
> *White male, middle-level manager*

> It's sad that we [men] have trouble communicating with women.
>
> *Asian male, occupational*

> The old-boy network prevents women from holding positions such as director.
>
> *Hispanic female, occupational*

> Older men are culturally conditioned to treat women differently; younger ones are self-absorbed, and don't know how to treat women as human beings, as equals.
>
> *Hispanic female, lower-level manager*

> Little to nothing is planned to bring together women of all colors (white included) to talk or socialize or educate one another.
>
> *Asian female, lower-level manager*

> In my area, if you are a woman, you will be chosen to do clean-up before a man will. Doesn't matter what color or sexual preference! A man will talk to a man first, before approaching a woman standing or sitting next to a man. Every day *for 17 years.*
>
> *White female, occupational*

> If anything, women may have an advantage over men at our company.
>
> *White male, lower-level manager*

> I see sexual harassment at some level almost every day at work.
>
> *White male, lower-level manager*

> We are politically correct, culturally sensitive, but gender bias is rampant!
>
> *White female, lower-level manager*

Ironically, many female supervisors treat support staff women more unfairly than male supervisors treat female support staff.

White female, occupational

Women are looked over and excluded from promotions in our department.

Asian female, occupational

White women are accepted very well, but black or women of color are not very well accepted in the company's workplace.

Black female, lower-level manager

Women are promoted because they are women.

Hispanic male, lower-level manager

Women get away with everything.

White male, lower-level manager

I hear sexist language by both males and females.

White male, middle-level manager

I think issues around this have been blown out of proportion, and unduly hinder normal working relationships. Men and women need to grow up and act like adults.

White female, lower-level manager

Sexual harassment is something that this company does not deal well with. Most supervisors choose to ignore it.

White female, lower-level manager

When taken jointly with the data, given in Table 5.5, these comments present us with a picture of women in U.S. corporations working in a hostile, discriminatory environment. How much longer can American corporations avoid facing up to the fact that women in many cases represent over half of their workforces, and that for them to fail to fully utilize these resources, because of discrimination, is simply to commit (business) suicide?

Discrimination against White Men

Not until 1988 did we begin to ask the participants in our surveys questions about stereotypes of, and discrimination against, white males. One fact has always been too clear to us, however: that white males can be and often are the victims of discrimination. For over 80 years, studies consistently have shown that white males who are six feet to six feet four inches in height, Protestant, and conservative Republican, who come from middle- to upper-middle-class families, and who have attended Ivy League schools, have far more opportunities of advancement available to them than does the average or below-average white male.

Table 5.6 summarizes the responses of employees to questions relating to discrimination against white men. When comparing 1988 and 1995 data, please be sure to note the significant jump upward in the percentages of white men, rather than of women and people of color, who perceived in 1995 that they were having a more difficult time finding mentors than women and people of color. And when it comes to a similar assertion, relating to white males having a harder time finding mentors than women, again only white males were significantly more likely to believe this in 1995 than in 1988.

Note the high percentage of employees, at least 66 percent, who believe that white males perceive diversity efforts as being a form of reverse discrimination. But note too the wide differences in views about white males being bypassed for promotion.

Table 5.6*
Discrimination against White Males

In general, white men often are passed over for promotions because they do not help the company to meet its Affirmative Action goals.

	1988	1995
White Males	57	63
White Females	48	47
African Americans	17	23
Hispanics	20	21
Asians	28	34
Native Americans	42	32

*The numbers represent the percent of participants who strongly agree or agree.

In general, white men have the same advancement opportunities as women.

	1988	1995
White Males	—	51
White Females	—	49
African Americans	—	54
Hispanics	—	46
Asians	—	58
Native Americans	—	43

In general, white men have the same advancement opportunities as people of color.

	1988	1995
White Males	—	46
White Females	—	44
African Americans	—	44
Hispanics	—	52
Asians	—	41
Native Americans	—	40

In general, white men perceive diversity efforts as being a form of reverse discrimination.

	1988	1995
White Males	67	67
White Females	67	69
African Americans	75	66
Hispanics	65	66
Asians	79	75
Native Americans	70	76

In general, white men have a harder time finding a sponsor or mentor than people of color.

	1988	1995
White Males	34	53
White Females	13	20
African Americans	5	7
Hispanics	10	15
Asians	10	21
Native Americans	15	27

In general, white men have a harder time finding a sponsor or mentor than women.

	1988	1995
White Males	39	48
White Females	10	9
African Americans	6	3
Hispanics	13	12
Asians	10	13
Native Americans	21	18

Some of the comments made by employees about discrimination against white men are highly revealing.

> I know from talking to white men at this company that many of them feel like targets for reverse discrimination from women and minorities. This discrimination ranges from insults in the press, to loss of job security, to frivolous harassment suits. . . . As a rule, in this company, "diversity" seems to mean that if you are an average white male, you better keep your mouth shut . . . and tolerate reverse discrimination without any objections, otherwise face the accusation of [being] sexist or racist.
>
> *White female, middle-level manager*

> White men have much better advancement opportunities than women and people of color.
>
> *Hispanic female, lower-level manager*

> The best chance for promotion generally goes to 1) minority women 2) minority men 3) white women 4) white men. Yes! There is reverse discrimination! What is wrong with just going by best *qualifications?*
>
> *White female, lower-level manager*

> I feel it is extremely difficult for white males to gain employment or to be advanced, as 95 percent of all positions posted are underutilized for minorities and about 40 percent also underutilized for women as well.
>
> *White female, middle-level manager*

> The white man has now become the minority—thanks to this diversity *bull!*
>
> *White female, lower-level manager*

> A white male must be more qualified than a minority to be hired for a job.
>
> *White male, lower-level manager*

> If a white man has a problem here, he has brought it on himself.
>
> *Hispanic male, occupational*

> If you are white, you are doomed.
>
> *White male, occupational*

> I really do not perceive white males as having a problem with promotions, raises, etc.
>
> *Black female, lower-level manager*

I feel that white males still have far better employment and advancement opportunities than people of color or women.

Black female, lower-level manager

When I first applied for a permanent position, I was beat out of a job by three women and one black man for four jobs. I do not blame these people, only the system. *I had to train them after they were hired!*

White male, occupational

It's part of our country's history—white-male privileges, rights they are born with, where women and people of color are historically not placed on the playing field with all the same skills to help move them along.

Black female, middle-level manager

I believe many of the reverse discrimination issues of white men are really those of experiencing the change of having to share more equal opportunities with women and people of color, especially at this company.

Black female, lower-level manager

In 1990, we noted that if one wishes to understand the negative impact of racism and sexism upon white males, one must look closely at the issues and concerns of white men in corporate America. Beginning as early as 1964, and especially in recent years, numerous articles have been written about white males' fears about their position in society. Many now believe that it is they who are in the disadvantaged group. They feel that they are facing discrimination and stereotyping because of their whiteness and maleness, and that makes them angry, defensive, stressed, and generally unhappy.

Conclusions

Although some progress has been made in overcoming workplace discrimination over the past decades, many women and people of color, and many white males, still believe—rightly—that a great deal of racism and sexism still exists in corporate America. It also remains the case that people of color and women are faced with a whole host of problems that many, *but not all,* white males do not have to face. These range from the ongoing battle to combat stereotypes about their abilities, to the daily need to be better performers than white males in order to get ahead. And they must strive to fight that battle, and fulfill that need, under the additional handicaps of not having sufficient power and authority, of being excluded from informal work groups, of having more difficulty finding mentors, and of having to deal with white men and women, especially at senior levels, who often support white men in their criticism of people of color regardless of the merit of their views.

As for Affirmative Action, much of the antagonism toward it is based upon the belief that standards have had to be lowered in order to admit "less qualified" women and people of color to entry positions over "more qualified" white males. And yet the sheer historical fact of the matter is that people of color and women have had to be *overqualified* in order to obtain their opportunities.

Why so? Simply because *as a group,* and regardless of the many individually justified cries of "Reverse discrimination!" coming from particular white males, white men do continue to dominate the U.S. workplace. They set the cultural tone, the standards, and the criteria for advancement. And our seminars and research have conclusively shown that favoritism toward in-group members tends to dominate all other factors during the hiring process.

The overall impact of excluding women and people of color from positions of power and influence, and thereby robbing them of self-esteem, is to render some of them unable to function effectively in high-performance teams within their organizations. And that of course is directly detrimental to corporate well-being, because it means that companies are in effect letting over half of their workforce lie fallow. As for white men, we must always remain cognizant of the fact that white males in positions of power clearly do discriminate against white males who fail to correspond with their image of the promotable manager. Thus, it is by no means true to assert that all white males have it made, and that none is a victim of discrimination. To the contrary, in a small but growing number of cases, white males at lower- and middle-management levels are working in organizations dominated by white women and even by people of color. Stereotyping in such organizations can certainly lead to discrimination against white males.

So, what is the proper balance here, between all of our understandable concerns about *both* discrimination *and* reverse discrimination? Each of us must be his or her own judge of that, but let us at least leave you with one final piece of food for thought. In our seminars of senior executives, we have noted a clear tendency for both white men and white women to support white males, regardless of the "rightness" or "wrongness" of their positions, and to be very critical of people of color, especially blacks.

6

Beyond the Rhetoric of Race and Gender: Two Immodest Proposals

W E WOULD LIKE TO WRAP up Part I of this book by offering our readers two related proposals for getting beyond the rhetoric of race and gender and bringing some real change to their organizations. The first seeks to create a zero-tolerance environment for race and gender discrimination. The second provides ways of promoting that individual self-awareness, without which a zero-tolerance environment will never bloom and flourish.

Proposal One: Zero Tolerance

Stereotypes and discrimination clearly inhibit an organization's ability to form high-performance teams, composed of diverse people, with a goal of delivering quality products and services to global customers. Yes, we know we keep saying it, simply because it is our bedrock belief. That's why we're going to keep on saying it, throughout this book. They lead to miscommunication, conflict, inordinate self-interest, conformity, and fear.

We realize that in an age that has grown to distrust all hyperbole, a phrase like "zero tolerance" is bound to elicit some people's cynicism. So let us clarify exactly what we mean by this term.

A zero-tolerance environment is all about that threshold at which personal behavior passes from the realm of the acceptable to that of the unacceptable. And what we're saying here is that *any* form of racism and sexism, whether overt or covert, is unacceptable. In a zero-tolerance environment, people are held to a high level of personal accountability for their behavior, including their stereotypes, their language in the workplace, their commitment to honest and open dialogue, and their positive treatment of others regardless of race or gender. The values that bloom in such an environment are mutual trust and respect; placing a high value on differences, but also on cooperation and teamwork; and a desire to expand market share and grow the organization's business.

A zero-tolerance policy is enforced through several means. The most important of these is everyone's commitment to create and maintain an environment in which every employee, regardless of race or gender, can feel safe, respected, and empowered to contribute to his or her fullest potential. It is the officers of the corporation—vice presidents through board members—who have the lion's share of the responsibility for creating this kind of environment. For in the postbureaucratic organization, the primary role of leaders is to partner with employees so as to set a clear course for the organization's teams and thereby grow the business. The need for officers to be role models, when it comes to upholding the appropriate race and gender values and behaviors, should be made an explicit part of the package of expectations during their performance evaluations. Holding our leaders accountable in this way raises the likelihood that others will follow by holding *themselves* accountable for creating a zero-tolerance environment. Of course some employees will resist; they won't respond to leadership from above. Those that continue to resist should be let go. To allow them to remain on in the organization would be duplicitous, and would send the wrong message throughout the company.

At the team level, members must hold one another accountable for creating and maintaining this environment. Every team member has an obligation to speak up when she or he observes behavior or language that is inconsistent with zero-tolerance. At this level, an employee must serve as his or her team members' coach, and show a real commitment to the personal growth and development of all teammates regardless of race or gender. Such a commitment cannot coexist with the arrogance of those who deny they have anything to learn from adopting the viewpoints of other racial groups or the other gender. It also allows no room for the mistaken belief that anyone who needs coaching must be inherently ignorant, and/or incapable of learning or changing.

Proposal Two: Know Thyself

We hope you're intrigued by Proposal One, but it does beg the question, "How does an organization go about *creating* an atmosphere of zero tolerance for stereotyping and discrimination?" Part II of this book will provide you with some of the *systemic* changes that your organization can make to further this end. But the first and most important step lies with the *individual*. Therefore, the purpose of this section is to help you better "know thyself." Specifically, our goal is to offer some concrete suggestions to those who sincerely desire to increase their self-awareness and improve their ability to operate in a diverse, multicultural environment.

In the multitude of conversations we have had with employees over the past 25 years, they frequently describe each other and their work environment in unflattering ways, speaking of poor management, petty politics, and unfair treatment based on race and gender. They complain about rigidity, about how that disempowers them to service customer needs effectively. While many of these perceptions are no doubt accurate, many probably are not. Therefore, we have gotten into the habit of asking ourselves to what extent these employees are sidestepping, ignoring, or misinterpreting their actual situation, and to what extent such less-than-honorable behavior reflects the thoughts and attitudes of their managers as well.

Emotional Intelligence

Besides the traditional bureaucratic structure, we firmly believe that many of the problems in organizations related to racism and sexism, as well as to low morale, conflict, and lack of trust and respect, are the result of low emotional intelligence, which in turn reflects a lack of self-awareness and cultural understanding. Understanding our culture, our strengths, and our weaknesses and how they influence our interactions is the critical first step in our holistic strategy for solving the race and gender problem.

Few of us indeed aren't interested in gaining greater self-awareness and understanding. And yet today's employees are hindered from achieving it by two obstacles. First, each of us tends to believe that our own norms, values, assumptions, and behaviors—that is, our culture—is superior to that of others. Second, in this era of political correctness, many of us are weary of continually engaging in this form of self-examination, and then being forced to admit that we do have unresolved race and/or gender issues. As a result, we defiantly deny, right up front, that we hold any racist or sexist values whatsoever.

But while all of us may be part of the problem, we at ARMC believe that we all can become part of the solution by changing our attitudes and behaviors—that is, by exhibiting a high level of emotional intelligence. As Geert Hofstede has observed: "Awareness is where it all starts: the recognition that I carry a particular mental software because of the way I was brought up, and that others, brought up in a different environment, carry a different mental software for equally good reasons."[1]

Only recently have corporations begun to understand and to accept the fact that their employees bring a lot of personal biases and prejudices into the workplace. From the 1950s through the 1980s, the prevailing attitude was different: "Don't bring your personal issues to work; leave them at home." But it simply isn't possible for human beings to do that, as a small but growing number of corporations is beginning to recognize. These are the very same corporations that are seeing the bottom-line benefits associated with having an emotionally intelligent workforce, one that knows how to deal with people empathetically and compassionately. As Goleman notes:

> On the positive side, imagine the benefits for work of being skilled in the basic emotional competencies—being attuned to the feelings of those we deal with, being able to handle disagreements so they do not escalate, having the ability to get into flow states while doing our work. Leadership is not domination, but the art of persuading people to work toward a common goal. And, in terms of managing our own career, there may be nothing more essential than recognizing our deepest feelings about what we do—and what changes might make us more truly satisfied with our work.[2]

We agree with Goleman that emotional competency is a vital employee trait, and further suggest that to achieve such competency, each employee must conduct an honest self-assessment. But he/she can't be expected to do so without some guidance.

Skills Needed in a Multicultural Environment

The first step that must be taken, in the course of personal self-assessment, is to evaluate how proficient I am in the skills I will need to operate effectively in a multicultural environment. Luckily for all of us, the Society for Intercultural Education, Training and Research (SIETAR) has identified 14 of those skills. In effect these 14 are building blocks; we must develop the first one in order to address the second one, and so on. In addition, the first 7 of these 14 skills are internal; they have to do with our awareness of ourselves, including our ability to understand and to acknowledge our stereotypes. Only after we have developed these seven self-awareness skills can we then go on to the next seven, which are external and enable us to interact effectively with people of different cultural and race/gender backgrounds. Interestingly, when we administer this instrument to senior executives and ask them to rank-order these 14 skills, almost all of them tell us that the communication and listening skills simply have to come first. None would care to deny how essential such skills are to all of human culture, but at some point it becomes true that we no longer either communicate or listen effectively unless we have come to understand our culture (skill 1) and our personal strengths and weaknesses (skill 2). Empathy (skill 3) will also be of vital importance, in helping us to respect other cultures as well as to feel comfortable when interacting with people of different races and genders.

Please begin by reading through the following list, and thinking about which skills you are proficient in, which not. Think about some of the feedback you may have received in the course of your lifetime about these skills. Then decide which skills you want to work on, so as to improve your relationships and grow your business. Then keep this list handy and glance at it often; make notes on your feedback and progress; and record the successes you have had with customers, stakeholders, colleagues, and others, that grew out of your new mastery of these skills.

---

1. Know your own culture (values, beliefs, assumptions).
2. Know your own limitations (strengths and weaknesses).
3. Practice empathy with others.
4. Respect other cultures.
5. Learn by interacting.
6. Strive to be nonjudgmental.
7. Be aware of your stereotypes.
8. Learn how to communicate effectively and compassionately.
9. Listen closely, and observe carefully.
10. Strive to relate meaningfully to those you perceive as "different."
11. Be flexible; learn how to adapt.
12. Adjust yourself according to people's reactions.
13. Learn how to live with ambiguity.
14. Be as consistent as you can be, without becoming inflexible.

Now let's look more closely at each of the 14 skills in turn, and see what we can do to sharpen each. Several of the suggestions we make will be applicable to more than one skill.

1. *Know your own culture.* Culture may be defined as that which encompasses our values, beliefs, and assumptions, as well as our language, age, religious beliefs, lifestyle, gender, political orientation, geography, socioeconomic status, and so forth. Thus, it is the lens through which we view and judge the world and other cultures. Because our individual behavior is a manifestation of our culture, we must become aware of our own culture if we are to interact effectively in a setting where a wide range of cultures are represented. Here are some suggestions:

- *Reflect on your early life experiences, and on those significant emotional events that have shaped your value system and your beliefs and attitudes about those who are different from you. Put to yourself, and answer, relevant questions as to such formative influences as place of origin, family structure, socioeconomic status, religion, education, and the like.*
- *Keep a journal. Carefully note your reactions to current world events and news reports, and describe and analyze your interactions with others.*
- *Enroll in courses that examine and discuss cultures, values, and beliefs.*
- *Learn as much as you can from and about others of your own culture.*
- *Take part in values discussion groups.*
- *Identify and then participate in activities relevant to your culture.*
- *Read books and magazines that delve into your culture, especially those that outline its origins, history, and norms and that avoid one-sided discussions.*

2. *Know your own limitations.* If we are to maximize our strengths and strengthen our weaknesses, we must begin by recognizing that all of us have our strengths and weaknesses. Then we can proceed to identify what our strengths and weaknesses are, and develop an understanding of how they can help and harm us in our interactions. The following are some suggestions for heightening your awareness of your own strengths and weaknesses:

- *Broaden your perspective as to what affects your norms, values, and beliefs, by recognizing that these are influenced not only by race and ethnicity but by gender, language, age, education, and so on.*
- *Request—and really listen to—feedback from multiple sources about your strengths and weaknesses. And be sure to get such feedback only from people you are sure will "tell it like it is," not from those who will*

merely tell you what you want to hear. In particular, try to get it from those of a different race or gender.
- *Seek out those experiences that will enable you to practice your strengths and to shore up your weaknesses.*
- *Change whatever you can about yourself, and accept whatever you can't, or won't. But above all, be very aware of the consequences, for better or worse, of changing or not changing.*

3. Practice empathy with others.   To practice empathy with others means to identify with and understand the situations, feelings, and motives of others. Remember that while the ability to see the world from another's perspective is a powerful tool in life, we will fail to master skill 3 (the practice of empathy) unless and until we have worked and worked at skill 1 and skill 2. That said, here are some ways to strengthen this skill of empathy:

- *Develop friendships and relationships with as many people from as many diverse backgrounds as you can, not only at work but outside of work as well.*
- *Listen closely to the views of those friends and acquaintances, and work hard to understand them, especially if these world views differ widely from your own.*
- *Volunteer to assist friends and acquaintances of other race, ethnic, and gender groups, in efforts on which they may be embarking.*
- *Join organizations that expressly seek to advance the interests of different race and gender groups.*

4. Respect other cultures.   In our opinion, those who today do not strive to understand, appreciate, and respect other cultures, and to recognize that they are not wrong, weird, or odd but simply excitingly different, are destined to be left behind in the next century. Thus, think about taking the following steps in order to strengthen your respect for other cultures:

- *Cultivate friendships with people from as many cultures as possible.*
- *Don't "rush to judgment" when it comes to areas of cultural difference. Values are not necessarily better or worse than one another, but can simply reflect a cherishing of our differences.*
- *When judging others' cultural values and norms, refrain from using no other yardstick but your own.*
- *Continually ask yourself whether you are making a value judgment*

about others, rather than recognizing that they simply may have different ways of reaching their goals.
- *Attend cultural events, as part of your effort to develop an understanding of the history and origin of various cultures.*
- *Learn another language; travel to other countries.*

5. *Learn by interacting.* Sharing actual experiences with people of different cultural backgrounds enables us to rethink our assumptions and dispense with our stereotypes. For instance, you could:

- *Join associations that deal specifically with the concerns of a particular race or gender.*
- *Join organizations that are working toward race and gender healing.*
- *Pay close attention to the way others react to your behavior.*
- *When uncertain as to just what those reactions of others may mean, simply inquire of them, and fully absorb their responses.*
- *Delve further into others' customs, words, and actions that you find puzzling.*
- *Learn another language; travel to other countries.*

6. *Strive to be nonjudgmental.* This is a tough one, since we all have been socialized to believe that our own culture is the "right" one, and therefore superior to all others. Doing the following should help you to resist the temptation to form instant impressions of other people and their cultures:

- *Try to understand the hidden dynamics of your interactions with others, rather than merely pretend that frictions don't exist.*
- *Remember that evolution has programmed our brains to make snap judgments; learn to work with that tendency, in order to rise above it.*
- *Remember that one's own culture is only one standard, when it comes to assessing cultural norms and values.*
- *Strive to consistently maintain a positive, open attitude.*
- *Acknowledge frankly that whenever we make a snap judgment about an event or a person, it invariably does affect our next encounter with them.*

7. *Be aware of your stereotypes.* Stereotyping is normal—and dangerous. It inevitably leads to misinterpretations, unresolved conflicts, and organizational ineffectiveness. Here are some ways to become aware of your stereotypes:

- *Recognize that while stereotyping is normal, it is dangerous. And understand that while the brain and mind stereotype, we have the opportunity to frankly acknowledge that fact and then to do something about it.*
- *Develop relationships with people of other racial or ethnic groups, and of the other gender.*
- *Enter freely and openly into learning situations where stereotypes are openly identified and confronted.*
- *Ask the people you trust to gently rebuke you, if they believe you have just used a stereotype in making a judgment.*
- *Learn as much as you possibly can about people of different racial, ethnic, and gender groups.*

8. Learn how to communicate effectively and compassionately. Fragile race and gender relationships can easily be disrupted altogether, owing to poor communication skills. As we attempt to exchange ideas by means of speech, writing, or other signal, our message can become garbled, often leading to conflict and, ultimately, to charges of discrimination. Here are some ways to strengthen communication skills:

- *Carefully study Chapter 9 on communication skills.*
- *Recognize that 85 percent of our communication is nonverbal, and therefore not at all easy to be aware of and to control.*
- *Practice speaking directly and candidly, and clearly, but also tactfully and compassionately.*
- *Listen actively; paraphrase what the other person has said, and then ask him or her whether your paraphrase is an accurate version of what he or she was trying to convey.*
- *Continually check and recheck your perceptions, asking yourself whether your interpretations of behaviors and nonverbal signals have been valid.*

9. Listen closely, and observe carefully. To listen closely and observe carefully means to rise above an endless obsessing with one's own concerns and ideas, and instead to tune in carefully to the thoughts and cares of others. In order to strengthen this skill:

- *Read chapter 9 on communication skills.*
- *Ask probing questions to help you distinguish between what someone actually has said or done and your own reactions to or judgments about it.*

- *Send "I" messages, rather than insensitive words of blame: "I'm disappointed in the team for having missed its deadline," not "You guys really screwed up in missing this deadline."*
- *Ask those you trust to gently rebuke you on those occasions when you seemed to be listening, but really were not.*
- *Consider talking less and thinking and listening more.*
- *Develop your powers of observation, by taking part in workshops where trained facilitators will give you immediate feedback as to your awareness or lack thereof.*
- *Enter into no-holds-barred discussions about work situations, with people you trust of both genders, and of different racial and ethnic backgrounds.*

10. Strive to relate meaningfully to those you perceive as "different." In doing their jobs or working on a project, employees must not only produce products and services but sell them to customers. Both of these activities call for employees to work together, but to focus only on the task side of the job and neglect its relationship side is to jeopardize the final outcome. We can build up our relationship skills by:

- *Recognizing that the entire organization must continually strive to understand, value, respect, and appreciate differences, if the firm is to become more competitive.*
- *Understanding that complementary skills and strengths promote a higher level of quality in terms of tasks, products, and relationships.*

11. Be flexible; learn how to adapt. The diversity of cultures in today's global environment demands of us all that we become multicultural. That means we must upgrade our ability to adapt ourselves to the culture or environment in which we happen to be working or living, and refrain from thoughtlessly attempting to impose our own value system upon others. You might consider:

- *Spending some time with people from diverse cultures, both at and outside of work.*
- *Musing upon the role that complementary skills and strengths can play in promoting high-quality work and relationships.*
- *Consciously seeking out knowledge and experience relating to different cultures and peoples, so as to expand your own range of options and choices.*
- *Reading publications that express viewpoints differing from your own.*

- *Traveling, so as to experience other peoples and cultures in their sur-roundings rather than your own.*
- *Getting involved in groups or organizations that will not always allow you to get your own way.*

12. Adjust yourself to people's reactions. When trying to develop a team, or to influence customers and stakeholders, no ability is more vital than that of wisely "reading" other people's reactions toward us and then, when morally and practically possible, adjusting our behaviors so as to produce an outcome beneficial to all. In order to upgrade that ability, you should:

- *Solicit feedback from as many different sources as possible.*
- *Practice adjusting your behavior in response to that feedback, then requesting more feedback on your adjustments.*

13. Learn how to live with ambiguity. None of us can hope to know everything about the culture we find ourselves living or working in. There-fore, try to do the following, as ways of coping with the unavoidable stress of uncertainty and vagueness that go along with being in a multicultural world:

- *Seek out situations, both at work and outside of work, that induce discomfort; then find ways of raising your comfort level.*
- *Solicit guidance as to the appropriate behavior, when you find your-self in ambiguous circumstances.*
- *Continually push beyond the boundaries that your lifestyle and your worldview seem to have imposed upon you.*

14. Be as consistent as you can be, without becoming inflexible. Being consistent doesn't mean acting in the same way all the time. Rather, it means consistently, for us, treating people fairly, justly, and reasonably, according to their unique capacities and needs. All of us can become more consistent by adopting many of the suggestions offered in Skills 1 through 13, and especially by:

- *Soliciting feedback from a variety of people both at work and outside of work who have had a chance to observe you in widely differing sit-uations.*
- *Participating in training sessions that provide you with opportunities to deal with unfamiliar situations.*

Other Self-Assessment Tools

Like all of us, you are a complex being. Therefore, we urge you to make use of multiple approaches as you seek to understand yourself. Here are four of them:

1. *The Life Experiences and Value Inventory* As we have noted, one's first self-awareness challenge is to identify the norms, values, and beliefs that have been created largely by family, environment, and personal life-experiences. We then need to assess just how these factors influence our interactions with individuals whose beliefs, values, and norms are widely different from our own. Gaining a good knowledge of "who we are" enables us to develop clearer perceptions of ourselves and of the world around us. We then can develop better solutions and strategies for dealing with cultural interactions and issues, both at a professional and a personal level.

In order to help employees understand the diversity issues they must confront because of their socialization, we have developed two versions (short and long) of an instrument we call the Life Experiences and Values Inventory (*LEVI*). The short version covers such areas as geography, religion, language, race/ethnicity, gender, socioeconomic status, etc. Each area is explored by means of 4 or 5 such questions as the following:

Gender
1. In your family, what expectations/roles were set for boys/men? For girls/women?
2. What if any norms, values, and beliefs did you adopt as a result of your gender or of your family's expectations for boys/men and girls/women?
3. In what ways, if at all, do these norms, values, and beliefs guide your behavior in your personal and work life?
4. What changes would you like to, and/or do you think you should, make in your norms, values, and beliefs with regard to gender, so as to become better able to work and to serve and influence different race, gender, and ethnic groups?

The longer version has more in-depth questions, such as the following questions on race illustrate:

Race/Ethnicity
1. With which racial/ethnic group do you most identify?
2. What advantages, if any, have you gained because of your race/ethnicity?

3. What obstacles, if any, have you encountered because of your race/ethnicity?
4. How have these obstacles/advantages impacted your personal life?
5. How have these obstacles/advantages impacted your professional life?
6. Describe the first time that you interacted with someone of a different racial/ethnic group.
7. Was this a positive, negative, or neutral experience and how so?
8. What conclusions, if any, did you draw about this racial/ethnic group from that first experience of it?
9. What types of words/stereotypes/descriptions did you/do you hear frequently about your own racial/ethnic group?
   A. As a child?
   B. Today?
10. In general, do those words/stereotypes/descriptions carry positive, negative, or neutral connotations for you?
11. What if any impact have these words/stereotypes/descriptions had on your own view of your race/ethnicity?
12. What types of words/stereotypes/descriptions did you/do you hear frequently about racial/ethnic groups *different from your own?*
    A. As a child?
    B. Today?
13. In general, do those words/stereotypes/descriptions carry positive, negative, or neutral connotations?
14. What if any impact have those words/stereotypes/descriptions had on your view of others' race/ethnicity?
15. How, if at all, has your race/ethnicity shaped your norms, values, and beliefs?
16. How have your interactions with people of different racial/ethnic groups shaped your norms, values, and beliefs?
17. How do those norms, values, and beliefs impact your
    A. Personal life?
    B. Work life?
18. Please describe, using as much detail as you can, other ways in which your race/ethnicity has impacted you.

Completing the LEVI will help you to think about those things that are important to you, and about the influences that have shaped you. It may also be wise to further think about your answers to each item in terms of how they may influence your future interactions with other individuals, particularly those who have experiences, values, beliefs, and assumptions different from your own. Many people who have filled out this instrument have spoken to us of its use in helping them to deal with different race and/or gender groups. To further broaden your knowledge of yourself, you might wish to have others complete this instrument, using you as the subject. It might well prove to be interesting and useful to compare your own responses with the responses of others about you.

2. *Emotional Intelligence Assessment.* Although corporate executives only recently have begun to tune in to the role of emotional intelligence, psychologists and social scientists have been trying to understand and to measure emotional intelligence for a long time now. One of them, Reuben Bar-On, has developed an emotional intelligence assessment test that measures "an assortment of 15 different capabilities, competencies and skills that influence one's ability to succeed in coping with environmental demands and pressures, and directly affect one's overall psychological well-being." The questions on his test, which includes "validity scales" to ensure that the subject has given open and honest responses, are grouped into five major categories:

> Intrapersonal—*includes emotional self-awareness, assertiveness, self-regard, self-actualization, and independence*
> Interpersonal—*includes empathy, skills in interpersonal relationships, and social responsibility*
> Adaptability—*involves problem solving, flexibility, and reality testing*
> Stress Management—*covers the ability to handle stress and to control impulses*
> General Mood—*includes optimism and overall happiness.*[3]

A study was done using this instrument, with over 9000 people worldwide. And despite all we have had to say about cultural differences among the world's various populations, the researchers discovered that emotional intelligence is a consistent factor across all cultures: "The same high-score traits common to successful people in North America were also found among successful individuals in Nigeria, India, Argentina, and France. And along with culture, there were no differences between genders, either."[4]

3. *Psychoanalysis.* We recommend psychoanalysis, or some other type of professionally guided introspection, for employees. But we do caution that employees should carefully check out in advance the professional's training and experience with regard to issues of race, gender, and ethnocentrism. To work with a racist, sexist, or ethnocentric therapist, in order to gain therapeutic benefits vis-à-vis racism, sexism, or ethnocentism, would of course be counterproductive.

4. *Inside and Outside Assessment.* A third recommendation we make is to have trusted confidants, both inside and outside the organization, serve as sounding boards for your perceptions and feelings. Those inside your organization may have a better picture of the work issues you are struggling to understand and deal with; those outside the organization may have a better picture of those personal factors that tend to impact work issues, simply because they are not caught up in your own particular corporate environment. Outsiders, too, have created some excellent evaluations, exercises, and courses that can assist with self-understanding; for example, the Center for Creative Leadership in North Carolina, the Lifestyles Inventory by Human Synergistics, and the Myers-Briggs inventory.

We strongly suggest that every self-analysis method has its strengths and weaknesses; thus, adopting multiple ways of looking at ourselves will give us a clearer and more accurate picture. Then, too, we as humans are more likely to accept feedback from multiple sources than from single sources. That is all the more true, given the sensitivities that surround race and gender issues.

While we do place most of the burden of self-analysis on the employee, companies must encourage and assist in this area, while still holding employees accountable. The days of saying that an employee's psychological make-up has nothing to do with business are long gone. As long gone, as the days when it was thought that rhetoric might solve the issues of racism and sexism.

Conclusions

The first step toward the creation of our holistic model is to undercut racism and sexism by creating an environment of zero tolerance for them. The second step is to encourage each employee to conduct an accurate and honest self-assessment that will make the zero-tolerance approach work. All of us have at least some unresolved psychological issues. And because so much of our psychological makeup developed when we were babies and young children, it's hard to fully understand what makes us tick. And yet, if employees and their managers are to survive and prosper in a global arena, they have no choice but to try to find out what makes them tick. Thus not only should organizations require self-assessment, but they should provide their employees with the tools they need to do so. This chapter has presented you with some tools to foster self-awareness, awareness of others, and that tolerance which is so needed if you and your company are to flourish in a diverse, multicultural environment. Now let's proceed to some changes that organizations will have to make, to achieve that same end.

II

THE QUEST FOR EQUALITY: CREATING THE RACE- AND GENDER-FRIENDLY ORGANIZATION

7

Tearing Down the Bureaucracy

Introduction

Although their rhetoric might lead one to believe otherwise, in fact most of today's businesses are failing to see that their prospects for long-term success hinge almost entirely on the contributions, innovations, and creativity of their increasingly diverse workforces.

The reality is that instead of building organizational structures that truly value employees, customers, and stakeholders, regardless of race and gender, most businesses have opted for mere Band-Aid solutions to their problems. Under various aliases—quality circles, diversity management, sensitivity training, team empowerment, T-groups, reengineering, restructuring—many of these solutions have become quite popular over the past 25 years. Yet the results are always the same. Last year's solution soon loses its supporters' enthusiasm and is replaced by this year's fad, which in time will also lose momentum and support. And so the cycle goes on. Hopes and expectations are raised and promises are made to customers, while resources are being squandered and time wasted . . .

. . . to what end? We are not alone in asking that question. In one form or another it is on the lips of many CEOs, employees, managers, and consultants. And we believe that these stop-gap solutions inevitably wither and die because they fail to address the fundamental question of exactly *how an organizational structure and environment must change and adapt, in practical and actionable terms, if it is going to truly value all of its employees, customers, and stakeholders regardless of race or gender, and provide benefits that surpass these groups' expectations.* All we are saying is that new organizational structures are central to our constituency capitalization model, our holistic approach.

We will say it again: If businesses are to truly value their diverse employees, customers, and stakeholders, and to eliminate race and gender discrimination, they must structure themselves in a fashion conducing to those goals. The traditional bureaucratic model clearly is not in order here. Indeed, we believe it must be razed and replaced. In this chapter we will be explaining why we think that, and offering an alternative view of organizational structures.

Bureaucracy's History

Organizations hesitate to dismantle their bureaucratic structure, in part because of the very long, productive, and distinguished history that bureaucracy has had. The bureaucratic model replaced what has often been referred to as the "craft" or "feudal" structure. This prebureaucratic structure was one "riddled with arbitrary, unfair, untimely, chaotic, corrupt, unpredictable nepotism and cronyism."[1] It was characterized by unproductive conflicts and inefficiencies. Rewards and promotions were doled out on the basis of family name and social networks. Well-connected individuals, regardless of ability or accomplishments, were substantially rewarded, while unconnected workers were left frustrated and disillusioned. For most employees working under this system, the American Dream remained exactly that—a dream.

Prior to the Civil War, U.S. businesses managed to be successful in spite of the inefficiencies that were part and parcel of the feudal structure. The technology of mass production, which requires an abundance of specifically skilled workers, had yet to be developed, and U.S. consumption patterns were still local or at most regional. The Civil War changed all that. In order to meet the wartime demand for military goods, many businesses had to raise their production levels and to churn out standardized products. Technology gave them the tools to do this, but in many cases the old feudal business structure still stood in the way. Nonetheless, the bureaucratic model did make its first appearance in a limited number of specialized industries during the Civil War. By the 1920s it had become the model governing most U.S. businesses, and by the 1950s the details of bureaucracy had been worked out not just in theoretical but also in practical terms.

By the 1950s, bureaucracy's two chief elements—hierarchical structure and scientific management—had significantly altered the way work was being done in this country. Bureaucracy altered organizational communication patterns, reporting relationships, reward and recognition systems, performance planning and development, job structures, and socialization patterns. It stabilized organizational performance levels, and thus could offer "fairness" to more of the employees, especially the white male employees. In sum, bureaucracy was able to replace the old feudal business structure so completely simply because it addressed the two predominant organizational issues of the time: technology, and people—otherwise known as human capital.

Now let's take a look at each of those two factors in greater detail. Between 1860 and 1950, technology made quantum leaps. The standardization of products, working hand in hand with the astounding developments in tools and machinery, was transforming millions of production employees from hands-on craft workers to machine-based laborers. It was these two developments that were jointly responsible for the emergence of the assembly line. For the assembly line requires that work be broken up into a series of linear tasks, with many hands touching the product along the way and each set of hands performing a specialized task with regard to it. In order for such a process to work, an organization had to structure itself so as to support compartmentalization of tasks and ensure that each worker had the skills needed to do his/her one task. The feudal structure certainly had not been efficient in arranging work in this way, since it was based upon craft workers completing whole products. Admirable as that craftsmanship was in so many ways, it couldn't hope to stand up beneath the assembly-line onslaught.

Another considerable factor leading to the demise of the feudal system was the workers' belief that the path to advancement ran through the terrain of nepotism and favoritism. And as most workers had absolutely no connections, such a belief couldn't help but lower morale. The new bureaucratic structure, by contrast, held out some real hope to these workers. It promised employees at all levels a clear career path, if they would just do what the bureaucracy was asking them to do through its written policies and job descriptions. To white male workers, who had lived for so long under the shadow of favoritism and nepotism, the promise of bureaucracy was quite real; even people of color and women believed that more opportunities would open up to them than had been the case under the feudal model. Thus, it is hardly surprising that by the 1950s, the bureaucratic model had almost entirely won the day.

Now that bureaucracy had largely replaced feudalism, America stood poised to become a fully industrialized nation. For bureaucracy had taught U.S. workers the three basic ground rules of success in an industrialized society: follow the rules, put in your time, and get promoted. It had also taught society how to structure itself so as to capitalize on and cope with this new success, thereby ushering in an age of urbanization, mandatory education, new technologies, and the various communications media. In sum, and quite simply, it was to a great extent bureaucracy that had transformed the United States from an agricultural society into an industrialized one.

Bureaucracy's Key Components

The great promise held out by bureaucracy was essentially that of meritocracy. And such a promise had much to do with the concept of differentiating the person from the office. Jobs in a bureaucracy are defined by the needs of the organization rather than by the people performing them. Therefore positions must be clearly defined in terms of duties, responsibilities, methods, and authority. Each position has its own level of power and decision-making authority vis-à-vis the other positions above and below it, and this creates what is known as "the chain of command." We ourselves refer to this as the model of *positional power*, because the power resides in the office rather in the ability or credibility of the person who at a given time happens to be holding down the job. The military, of course, is the bedrock example here: "You will execute my orders not because I am a good sergeant or a likable sergeant or a believable sergeant, but because I *am* your drill sergeant! Got that, maggots?" You get the idea. . . . Since hierarchy clearly is the key component of bureaucracy, everyone in the organization quickly comes to acknowledge these gradations of power and authority and to tailor their communications and relationships to them. Such acknowledgment results in strong control systems, with clearly delineated goals and clearly defined performance levels and rewards. And that combination of elements makes it absolutely clear what has to be done and who has the power to do it. Thus, in theory at least, the bureaucratic model, by banishing all merely personal relationships and all human frailties from the workplace, made it possible for an organization to function at "peak" efficiency.

The image of a pyramid often is employed to help us envision the bureaucratic business structure. At the top of the pyramid are a few individuals whose job it is to function as a repository of organizational information. Owing to their experience and their vantage point, they can effectively assimilate and then disseminate the information that comes up to them through the chain of command. In other words, they can put that information at the service of those decision-making processes that lead to strategic objectives. These individuals at the top also control and allocate all rewards, which of course confers upon them immense power and influence. But as one moves down the pyramid, one finds that more and more people have less and less strategic information, as well as less power and influence. At the bottom of the pyramid are the frontline workers, they who have the least amount of organizational information and the fewest available rewards.

In addition to clearly demarcating roles and relationships, the pyramid structure also lays out a well-marked career path. That which represents a reward is simple: an upward promotion. An employee who is promoted upward gains more power and authority, decision-making ability, access to information—and money. Thus the hierarchical structure creates a nominal series of career goals for all employees, a stepwise progression up the organizational hierarchy to the highest level possible.

We have seen, then, how the key structural components of bureaucracy were intended to create a fair, objective organization that could rationally allocate resources, rewards, and recognition and thereby create productive, dedicated, loyal employees. The bureaucratic model was supposed to create the most efficient organizations, because organizational rather than personal needs determined its job specifications; because powers of decision making, especially at the strategic level, were clearly allocated; and because the organizational infrastructure created a chain of command that allowed decisions to be quickly implemented.

So, did bureaucracy succeed? By and large, the answer to that question is "Yes, it did." Bureaucracy created a system that did not need to rely upon individual genius. It regularized what had previously been ad hoc structures. It allowed for the efficient processing of information, thereby leading to more accurate forecasting and planning. It lowered transaction costs, by means of systemization and the greater efficiency that such systemization made possible.

Why Tear Down Bureaucracy?

Okay. So if bureaucracy was so successful, and if it has produced such significant results, then why on earth should we fix something that many people believe isn't broken? The answer to that question in many ways parallels our earlier discussion of the conflict between bureaucracy and the old feudal/craft structure. As you will remember, the bureaucratic model replaced the feudal one because it was able to simultaneously incorporate new technologies and address the pressing people-issues of its day. Today, however, we are convinced that the spiral of progress is making yet another turn. Today, it is the bureaucratic model itself that is hindering organizations from addressing the major people issues of this our own day, those of race and gender. And that, in turn, is keeping them from fully capitalizing on the technological advances of the past 25 years.

Before we take a closer look at the shortcomings of bureaucracy, we must ask our reader to note well the following features that define today's business environment:

- *Business has become highly global and therefore highly competitive.*
- *Mergers and acquisitions have become an everyday occurrence, both domestically and globally.*
- *Product life cycles have greatly shortened.*
- *Technology is allowing competitors to duplicate and enhance old products, and to turn out new ones, in a matter of months.*
- *Technology is making it possible for smaller firms to achieve economies of scale and thus to compete with the big conglomerates. Whereas a Hewlett Packard started in a garage, today's companies can practically stay in the garage—and still compete and win.*
- *Technology has facilitated new, more efficient modes of communication, at all levels and in all areas of the organization.*
- *Employees have become far more culturally and racially diverse, far better educated, and far more demanding. All of which is great, but they are also less loyal.*
- *The same goes for consumers. They, too, are more diverse, educated, and demanding, and above all, they are less brand-loyal. They expect organizations to add value to their lives on their own terms.*
- *Stakeholder groups are more diverse demographically, more vocal when it comes to expressing their dissatisfaction, and better able to extract concessions from organizations.*

Innovation

In such an environment as the one we've just been describing for you, *innovation* is key. Innovation thrives upon the fact that "different ideas, perceptions and ways of processing and judging information collide,"[2] and it emerges only out of collaboration and teamwork based upon trust and respect. In other words, good things can come out of productive, managed conflict, as a broad range of people of different racial, ethnic, and sexual orientation backgrounds go "head to head" in a creative, non-divisive manner.

Innovation requires that business organizations view and treat their employees and customers as constituting their two most important resources. It is only through their employees that organizations are able to innovate and to deliver on their innovations. That is because those employees, regardless of level, have in their heads and psyches a vast store of information and experience that is vital to organizational success. And with respect to customers, organizations can succeed only if they are able to provide benefits to those customers—sell them products and services—over the short and long term. Since customers, too, possess a great deal of information that is important to an organization (since they "know what they want"), they can provide an organization with important clues as to how to develop the products, services, and strategies that will lead to success.

In marked contrast to all of the above, bureaucracy makes procedures and rules more important than employees and customers. Specifically, bureaucracies are bedeviled by these six failings which hinder them from finding success: They waste knowledge; they're inflexible; they're too political; they foment unhealthy amounts of internal competition and the consequent discord; they're fat; and they're too homogeneous. Now let's dissect each of those failings one by one.

The Waste of Knowledge-based Resources

Fundamental to the proper functioning of a bureaucracy is the way in which it holds individuals responsible for specific job functions and duties. The attitude of the effective bureaucrat is, "That's not my job. That's Person X's job. Go talk to Person X."

This attitude has some obvious limitations. It systematically constrains the intelligence, knowledge, and experience of employees within a specific set of parameters so as to get done a specific set of tasks. Employees are encouraged and rewarded only if they *limit* their contribution. And yet research has shown that:

> Whenever employees, at whatever level, have been involved in decision making beyond their limits of usual job descriptions, they have proved capable of developing improvements that their superiors could never do alone. . . . They always produce gains unforeseen by industrial engineers whose "office" it is to maximize their effectiveness.[3]

In other words, such "unforeseen gains" come only as a result of innovation. And yet in a bureaucracy, employees are not allowed to innovate. They don't share ideas, information, experience, or knowledge. They don't challenge the proposals of their superiors. Not only is that not their job, but to do so would disrupt the hierarchical order created by the chain of command. It might well even ruin their career.

The direct result of the waste of knowledge- and experience-based resources is that organizations make decisions on a basis of less-than-complete knowledge. In a competitive global marketplace that becomes particularly perilous, especially in terms of strategic decisions, because a company's competitors will quickly capitalize on its mistakes and its customers, who are less loyal to begin with, will be slow to forgive them.

By now, we hope that the basic problem with bureaucracies has become clear to our readers. In a bureaucracy, strategic decisions are made at the top on the basis of only that information which has successfully fought its way up through the chain of command and managed to remain intact in the process. That means they are made by the executives farthest away from customers and their recommendations and complaints. Although employees at the bottom of the hierarchy are those closest to customers, they aren't thought to be in possession of any valuable information. And that's why important customer information is always getting either lost or filtered away by the chain-of-command process. Executives are left having to merely guess what customers want, and far too often they base their guesses on the values, attitudes, and norms of their own race, gender, or socioeconomic group. And when they guess wrong, as they often do, the results can be costly.

Inflexibility

Once upon a time, bureaucracies could effectively respond to changes in the marketplace and the workplace, simply because such changes came about quite slowly. Today, business conditions tend to change far more rapidly. But nonetheless, a close look at the bureaucratic response to change will reveal a certain lumbering inefficiency about the process, as a result of three factors:

1. *Change relies on, and is entwined with, the personalities of executives.* The executive first must identify a need to change, and then determine how the firm is to do so. This is no easy task, because as we have seen, the traditional executive, a white male, doesn't have at his fingertips important information about employees and customers, especially about women and people of color. Also, the system that an executive may finally genuinely see a need to change is the very one that brought him his success in the first place. Therefore it is very, very hard for him to commit to any alteration of the status quo. Finally, the average executive generally has only a limited amount of time in office in which to make changes; this artificially forces him to consider only a very narrow range of alternatives.[4]

2. *In order to change behaviors, bureaucracies generally must restructure.* The point here is that bureaucracy is based upon a formal set of relationships; for change to occur, these must be replaced by a new set of formal relationships. But restructuring is painful; it's slow; it's disruptive, to both individuals and the bureaucracy itself; and employees have had little experience of it. Thus a built-in resistance to change is inherent to bureaucracies, especially when the contemplated changes are far-reaching and fundamental (rather than incremental), and the costs of identifying and implementing them are high.

3. *The segmented, structured nature of bureaucracy promotes inertia.* Employees at all levels become comfortable with the status quo, and take structural criticisms of it personally. Also, the rules that guide behavior in a bureaucracy tend to proliferate. Every time a mistake is made, a new rule is added in an effort to preclude that mistake from ever happening again. Over time, the rules become so cumbersome that the focus shifts to following the rules rather than doing the job. The rules become an end in themselves, and therefore change begins to be perceived as nothing more than "having to learn a whole new set of rules."

When one considers the cumulative impact of all three of the above factors upon the issues of race and gender, it isn't at all hard to see why 34 years of equal employment opportunity and affirmative action have had so little effect upon the bureaucratic workplace.

Politics

Although bureaucracies are indeed supposed to be based upon formal, structured relationships, anyone who has ever worked in one knows that there are other forces at work as well. In other words, bureaucracies contain a whole set of *informal* rules and relationships. Most of these are hidden; sometimes they even directly contradict the formal protocol. Quite simply, bureaucracies are intensely *political* organizations.

Now, make no mistake, the kind of informal and expected rule-breaking that makes up so much of the "politics" of a bureaucracy is necessary. For in the absence of such politics, everyone would follow every rule every time—and nothing would get done. In many ways the art of leadership in a bureaucracy is simply a matter of understanding these subterranean processes—how things *really* "work around here"—and turning that understanding toward the support of collective goals.

But although politics can indeed benefit an organization, they can hurt it as well, in several ways and for several reasons:

- *They emerge out of chance personal contacts that are difficult to manage.*
- *They bring people into the decision-making process strictly on the basis of personal criteria, notably including race and gender.*
- *They emerge and function best within homogeneous groups, where trust and respect are easier to develop and harder to subvert.*
- *Disagreements among political groups are hard to manage and resolve, since they are unofficial and informal. Thus, each and every misunderstanding or difference can result in turf battles and power struggles.*
- *They are directly at cross-purposes with that chief tenet of bureaucracies, objectivity. Rewards are given out not on a basis of objectively defined career paths but because of the high status of one's particular political network.*

Unhealthy Internal Competition

Directly related to this issue of politics is the problem of unhealthy internal competition. Competition, both vertical and lateral, often is created on purpose simply because organizations have only a limited number of rewards to distribute. Therefore they create vertical (functional or business unit) competition, by assigning competing objectives to various individual business entities; each unit knows that it is competing with others for resources and recognition. While the intent is to egg everyone on to higher levels of productivity, the unintended effect often is to merely shift the focus to internal competition while forgetting all about the real competition—the other firm. In such an environment, functional teamwork and cooperation are neither expected nor encouraged, and distrust and resentment are all too likely to make them impossible.

The same scenario holds true within any one given business function, and again mainly because of the limited number of rewards. In a bureaucracy, "reward" invariably equals "promotion." But as a person moves up the hierarchy, he or she finds that there are fewer and fewer slots open. Employees thus have to compete for them and that brings on an "every person for herself/himself" mentality. In order to advance their own interests, individuals may purposely sabotage others by, for instance, withholding vital information from them. Teamwork and cooperation, so vital to innovation, are nowhere to be found. Add different races, and the two genders, to the mix, and a tense environment can suddenly turn into an explosive one.

Fat

In the 1980s and 1990s, lots of organizations went on a diet. They downsized, rightsized, and delayered, in an attempt to get rid of all those inefficiencies brought on by a common bureaucratic ailment, the need to have "supervisors . . . supervise the supervisors . . . and supervisors above them . . . and managers to watch the higher-level supervisors and higher-level managers to watch the lower-level managers."[5]

As bureaucracies grow and age, they, like all of us, tend to get more than a little paunchy around the middle. How come? Well, to a great extent because growth leads to a belief that additional managers and supervisors must be needed, to supervise all those additional production workers. That belief is itself based on the principle that a supervisor always should oversee only a limited number of people, usually fewer than eight. But the bigger problem here is that growth leads not only to *more* managers; that is to be expected, and forgiven. It also leads to *more layers* of management, in an attempt to boost the sum total of reward opportunities. Therefore, when the number of promotional opportunities inevitably begins to shrink, bureaucracies seek to remedy the problem by further segmenting responsibilities and power—in other words, by creating yet more layers of management.

Homogeneity

The homogeneity that still characterizes most bureaucracies can take one or both of two forms. The first has to do with employees, the second with customers. But both are based on the same invalid (because overly simplistic) assumption: that when you get right down to it, we're all pretty much the same.

Employees and Homogeneity. That just-stated assumption affects employees on two levels. The first is that of workplace equity and it encompasses benefits, scheduling, time off, holidays, and the like. Bureaucracy assumes that since everyone is the same, therefore rules and regulations, regardless of their specific nature, must impact everyone the same and thereby create a fair, equitable work environment. But in fact that assumption is invalid. We are all different. People have a wide range of wants, ambitions, and needs, and simply to ignore those differences does not constitute "fairness." Rather, it creates malcontents, inequity, and rampantly "political" behavior.

And this assumption that we're all the same also adversely affects employees in another way: by inducing conformity of thought. Bureaucratic rules and procedures, working in tandem with hierarchical structures, have the ill effect of virtually "laying down the law" as to the behaviors and relationships open to employees at any given level. Therefore to move up in the ranks, an employee must not merely master his or her firm's spoken and unspoken rules, but actually adopt the style and behaviors of a prototypical employee of that firm. In other words, employees must assimilate or die.

The result of all this is a group of people who value the same things and who think alike. What also inevitably results is that the commonly shared image of a successful organizational member is that of those already in leadership positions. Therefore not only does everyone think alike but they also tend to look alike, especially in terms of race, gender, socioeconomic background, education, and so forth. White, middle- to upper-class men with Ivy League educations are likely to choose other white, middle- to upper-class men with Ivy League educations to fill the decision-making positions. This creates covert, institutional racism and sexism, and thereby denies these companies access to a significant portion of that talent pool they must in fact draw upon in order to succeed in a competitive global marketplace.

Customers and Homogeneity. The homogeneity of bureaucracies also has a direct effect upon customers. Bureaucrats see their customers, like their workforces, as being homogeneous. They believe that the needs, wants, and aspirations of their customers must necessarily resemble their own. In fact, however, generational-based attitude shifts, working in tandem with shifting demographics, are causing the gap between bureaucracies and their customers to grow ever wider. It's really as simple as a five-step process as this:

1. Bureaucracies tend to lose touch with their customers.
2. They then must guess at what their customers want and need.
3. They develop products with little appeal.
4. They adopt marketing strategies on the basis of false assumptions and incomplete data.
5. The assumption that their customers are homogeneous proves to be a costly one, leading to severe financial hardship and possible bankruptcy.

If Not Bureaucracy, *What?*

Over the past several years, a growing number of business practitioners—including many leaders of highly bureaucratic organizations—have not only joined in the debate about bureaucracies but have expressed a readiness to try some new ways of doing business. Nonetheless, little real change is occurring out there. Why is that, you ask? Well, among the many obstacles standing in the way of organizational change, we believe that this one is the most significant: Few even among the self-styled "visionaries" have thus far told the business community what the new organization should *look* like. Academics and researchers are continually coming up with models—learning organizations, closed-community organizations, interactive organizations, virtual organizations, organizational communities—but they never seem to be able to specify the models' actual components or to frame the discussion in the language of actual day-to-day business.

We, on the contrary, will be so bold as to offer, on the basis of our analysis of these models and our 25 years of experience in this field, several changes that bureaucratic organizations can take that will bring about real efficiencies. We believe that once they have taken these steps, bureaucratic organizations will then have built up sufficient momentum to transform themselves into postbureaucratic organizations. The transformation will of course be slow and incremental in nature, and riddled with many setbacks. Elements of bureaucracy will necessarily remain even in the supposedly entirely postbureaucratic organization. But change really can and will come at last. Our purpose in the rest of this chapter is to show you how to make it happen.

The Structure

The postbureaucratic organization will be small in texture, or "feel," if not in actual size. Even if it has thousands of employees it will function like a small, entrepreneurial business, with employees working together closely on an ongoing basis. Here's how the future looks to us:

1. The postbureaucratic organization will consist of a network of satellite offices that are physically close to the customer and linked to each other through a corporate office. The most essential difference between this satellite structure and today's decentralized structure is that the corporate office will act as coordinator and enabler rather than as power broker. To that end, the corporate office will be staffed primarily by satellite employees who work there in short (perhaps 18-month) rotations. This will ensure that the corporate office will serve as a storehouse of knowledge that has originally been acquired at, and is systematically recirculated through, the satellite offices.

2. Each satellite office will have control over its business. It will determine human resource policies, staffing levels, type and depth of product lines, marketing strategies, alliances, and the like. Such local control will keep each office in touch with its customer base, thereby enabling it to develop more appropriate products and services.

3. Staff at each satellite office will consist of a mix of local employees and of those with experience of other satellite offices. Staff at each satellite office will experience a moderate amount of turnover, because satellite offices will shuffle staff to accommodate each other's need for specific expertise.

4. The work at each satellite office will be carried out by high-performance, diverse work teams. It will be the prime directive of these teams, which are discussed in Chapter 8, to deliver value-plus products and services to customers, as that is enabled by trust, respect, and mutual accountability.

The net result of these changes will be smaller organizational structures with few layers of management and fewer status distinctions. Each employee will be valued for his or her unique contribution and his/her ability to get along affably and creatively with other employees and customers. Communication will become far more honest, open, and timely, since employees will be able to (a) get their information "right from the horse's mouth," and (b) direct their feedback to the spot where it will be most valuable.

In such a new business universe, the chain of command will no longer be able to dictate communication norms and patterns, to determine career paths, or to define organizational success. Advancement will largely be a matter of lateral moves, job rotations, and global assignments. No longer will achieving management status be the only sign that one has "made it"; no longer will managers necessarily earn more than technical workers. But to whatever extent management status and perks remain in place as a perennial object of employee aspiration, that will simply reflect our human admiration of the ability to effectively facilitate and coordinate diverse talent.

Reflecting the smaller size, relative flatness, and team orientation of the postbureaucratic organization will be its reward-and-compensation system. Every employee's compensation package will have a fixed and a variable component, with the latter comprising 60 to 85 percent of that employee's annual compensation. Gone will be the annual guaranteed raise. Simply doing a good job won't lead to a raise, because *everyone* will be expected to do a good job. Increases in the fixed portion of an employee's pay will come through demonstrated mastery of a new job skill, the assuming of greater responsibility, or the success of the business unit as a whole.

All of this will serve to create what one writer has called an *ownership culture.*[6] In an ownership culture, every employee has a vested interest in seeing his/her organization succeed. And indeed, a few organizations already have created ownership cultures on a small scale by opening up stock options to their employees. In postbureaucratic organizations, large-scale ownership cultures will be created by compensating employees in part with actual shares of stock, either newly issued or purchased in the open market.

An ownership culture pushes decision making down to the lowest possible level, and in so doing it both increases efficiency and customer satisfaction and redistributes power and authority. Those closest to the customer—customer service representatives—will have greater decision-making authority than they currently do in bureaucracies. They will be able to treat their customers differently—i.e., in close accordance with those customers' needs—and thereby bring real value both to customer and firm.

In the cause of providing added value and better service, the traditional divisional turf boundaries will be eliminated to whatever degree that is feasible. Marketing, manufacturing, and customer service will work as teams, and share information during all phases of product development, introduction, and service. Because of the diversity of the customer base, the types and numbers of products and services will proliferate, which will require the communication channels and processes in the new organization to become highly developed and sophisticated.

Cross-training and job rotation, both in and out of the worker's specialty area, will become the norm, precisely because they will help to facilitate communication. (Also, employees possessed of broad knowledge are better able to size up the various challenges confronting the various functions.) These also help to create a common organizational language and to increase flexibility. It is always the flexible, broadly skilled workforce which most quickly and effectively makes the changes leading to competitive victory.

Guiding Principles

Exactly how a specific organization adopts and installs the structural components outlined above will vary with the business's history, sector, size, workforce makeup, and the like. Yet if they are to be successful, all postbureaucratic organizations will have to commit to do the following:

1. *Develop shared goals, values, and codes of conduct, by means of consensus-building conversations.* Since all kinds of people contribute to and benefit from every organization, its leaders cannot hope to define goals, values, and codes of conduct in isolation, and then present them at an annual meeting as the things to be accomplished in the coming year. Rather, the new leader seeks to manage the process of discovering what is important to employees, customers, and stakeholders regardless of race and gender; of seeing how that discovery can help the organization to deliver value; and of merging the goals of employees, customers, and stakeholders with those of the organization. And make no mistake, amazing things can happen when everyone's goals are intertwined within the organization. Loyalty is created. Solutions are freely offered. Obstacles are easily overcome. The level of complaints goes way down. Productivity and performance levels go way up. The excitement of being a part of an organization becomes infectious.

2. *Focus on innovation.* Since organizations gain and maintain their competitive advantage through innovation, the postbureaucratic organization must consciously strive to foster it. Remember that innovation requires constructive conflict. Different people with different ideas must rub against one another, challenging one another and suggesting alternatives to every approach.

At least four factors must be in place for such an environment to bloom. First, differences must exist at all points within the organization. They have to be broad-based, and include both observable differences in race, ethnic origin, gender, and age as well as nonobservable differences such as thinking style, sexual orientation, and religion.

Second, these differences have to be seen as constituting an asset. People who propose different and perhaps even difficult ideas must be rewarded, however much they may seem to be merely "rocking the boat." Systems and processes that lead to the creative rubbing together of ideas have to be put in place. Communication patterns need to be based upon everyone's actual need-to-know, not upon politics or status.

Third, trust and respect in both internal and external relationships have to be nurtured. They don't just happen; they have to be earned through open conversations initiated and sustained by leaders who actually live by their core organizational principles. Such leaders communicate and celebrate victories; they communicate and learn from failures. In sum, trust and respect are won when leaders draw upon a broader knowledge base and delight in practicing the art of influence-based decision making.

Fourth, organizations must prove that they cherish differences both in the workplace and marketplace by developing fair and equitable employment policies, practices, and benefits, and by providing differentiated products and services that bring value to widely differing market and stakeholder segments.

3. *Cultivate and use the entire available knowledge base.* In notable contrast with bureaucracies, postbureaucratic organizations recognize that only a limited amount of the knowledge needed for an organization's success can come straight out of its leaders' heads. Thus, even as the leader shares organizational strategy with employees at all levels, with customers, and with stakeholder groups, she or he also is listening intently to these groups' comments and complaints, and incorporating their goals into organizational strategies. Leaders consciously go about bringing employees, customers, and stakeholders into the decision-making processes by forming high-performance teams composed of diverse individuals who are seen as possessing information vital to the continued well-being of the organization. These teams are rewarded for sharing this information with leadership,

4. *Consciously acknowledge cultural differences based upon race and gender.* In the postbureaucratic organization, team members will be asked to remain aware of cultural differences, and to consciously work to understand different races, ethnicities, and sexual orientations, and the two genders. Leaders will strive to incorporate team members of different races and both genders, and to encourage these team members to share their experiences and perspectives. They will acknowledge out loud the barriers that women and people of color have faced, and work to eliminate those barriers. They will talk about how customers who are women or people of color have too often been accorded second class status, and will demand of all employees that they provide all customers with fair and equitable service. Finally, they will ask themselves how stereotypes about race and gender impact their own decision-making processes and behavior, and continually try to minimize the amount of institutional racism and sexism.

Conclusions

We have seen in this chapter how bureaucracy, as an organizational structure, has done much to make possible the success of American business in the post–Civil War era. And yet changing economic circumstances have exposed numerous flaws in the bureaucratic structure and made clear the need for some type of postbureaucratic organizational structure. Bureaucracies make power-based decisions; postbureaucratic organizations make influence-based decisions. Relationships and communications in bureaucracies are constrained largely by status considerations; in postbureaucratic organizations, they are far freer because they are based upon trust and respect. Bureaucracies function as secretive and obsessively closed-off units; postbureaucratic organizations are open enough to let in the feedback of customers and stakeholders. One succeeds in a bureaucratic organization by knowing the rules and regulations, but above all how to navigate around them to get things done; one succeeds in a postbureaucratic organization by basing all of one's knowledge, skill, and decision making on the trust and respect that one has worked hard to acquire from one's coworkers.

Changes like these will have a positive impact on the treatment and career paths of women and people of color in corporate America. Organizations will need the expertise of women and people of color to understand diverse market segments and to form high-performance, diverse teams. As a result of this expanded role, women and people of color will occupy and wield more persuasive power. Combined with the leveling of organizations and the diminishment of positional power, women and people of color will find that many of the barriers traditionally facing them in corporate America will tumble.

8

Trust, Respect, Equality: How Team-Based Organizations Can Solve the Problems of Race and Gender

Introduction

In Chapter 7, we tried to show why the bureaucratic, over-hierarchical organizational structure is a source of competitive disadvantage in today's dynamic, global economy. We also gave an idea of what the postbureaucratic organization will look like, as it delivers value to ever-more-diverse groups of employees, customers, and stakeholders. In this chapter we will be proposing that cross-functional, high-performance teams are the best way to deliver this value. The key to going beyond rhetoric so as to actually solve the problems of race and gender is to develop and work on those essential ingredients which jointly make high-performance teams possible.

We should note, however, that while teams are indeed becoming a more important feature of U.S. firms, they also are becoming more difficult to form. The following list gives you some of the major present barriers to developing effective teams:

- *Products and services are becoming more complex, therefore, business is becoming more complex.*
- *Teams are becoming more complex. In order to solve complex problems and/or create complex services and products, teams are having to become increasingly multifunctional, multidisciplinary, and interorganizational.*
- *The customer base is becoming more diverse, and customer tastes and needs are becoming more sophisticated and demanding. Both of those factors necessitate more diverse teams that can better understand the new customer.*
- *Employees are becoming more diverse not only in terms of race, gender, and age but also of culture, language, religion, lifestyle, ability,*

and status. And diverse work groups have more difficulty becoming effective teams.

- *Change is the norm. Change is rapidly occurring in many aspects of our societies: in their economies, globalization efforts, governments, societal norms, demographics, technologies, and relationships.*
- *People are becoming more aware of the need to subordinate at least some aspects of their individuality in order to become good team members. And yet while they are consciously aware that they must put aside their egos and work for the common good, the need to do so subconsciously conflicts with their desire to compete as individuals.*
- *The constant downsizing, rightsizing, reductions in workforces, lay-offs, takeovers, and buyouts have resulted in decreased employee job security and have created a great deal of distrust and lack of loyalty among employees.*

Cross-functional, High-performance, Diverse Teams

Definitions and Characteristics

Here are some of those essential ingredients of cross-functional, high-performance, diverse teams that we referred to a moment ago in the Introduction:

- *They are made up of a small number of diverse, interdependent people.*
- *Team members have complementary skills, and are personally committed to a common mission, vision, and purpose.*
- *Team members share performance goals for which they hold themselves and their team members accountable.*
- *Power is shared, and decisions are arrived at, through a collaborative, consensus-building process.*
- *Conflict is common and is openly expressed; and yet it also is constructive, because it is expected and is purposefully managed.*
- *The focus of the team is on both task behaviors and interpersonal behavior.*

Key to all definitions of "real" teams are words like *interdependent* and *mutual*. The top priority of the members of real teams is not competition and the needs of the individual but rather the integration of their talents, skills, and abilities through collaboration in order to meet team and personal goals. Table 8.1 lists in more detail the characteristics of real teams as these are made up of people from different racial, ethnic, and gender backgrounds who have different life experiences, perspectives, values, and skills. The list not only gives you a step-by-step progression toward team formation, but can serve as a diagnostic tool as well. For instance, your firm could make specific personnel choices so as to strengthen weak links in the team chain. Also, since trust and respect are essential to real teams, deficiencies in this regard might well become central to policies and practices vis-à-vis hiring efforts intended to support teams.

Table 8.1
Five Steps toward Building Effective Teams, and a List of Their Characteristics

Step One: *Define the Mission*

1. **Clear Purpose:** The vision, mission, goal, or task of the team has been defined and is accepted by everyone.
2. **Clear, Positive Values, Norms and Behaviors:** The team has developed values, norms, and behaviors that have been entirely understood and accepted by all the members, and that foster better communication among them.
3. **Specific Responsibilities and Expectations:** There are clear, fairly distributed responsibilities and expectations for each team member. Team members accept and carry out their responsibilities with enthusiasm.
4. **Action Plans:** Action plans are developed that contain specific responsibilities, action steps, and time frames.
5. **Shared Leadership:** Although the team does have a formal leader, leadership functions shift from time to time along with the circumstances, the needs of the group, and the skills of the members. The special responsibilities of the formal leader are to model the appropriate behaviors and to help establish positive norms.
6. **Diversity of Styles:** The team contains a broad spectrum of team-player types, including members who stress attention to tasks, goal setting, and the overall process; it contains promoters, analyzers, and those who question how the team is functioning.

Step Two: *Establish and Instill Team Values*

7. **Trust:** There is a high degree of trust and confidence among all team members.
8. **Respect:** As a result of the aforementioned trust and confidence, team members have a great deal of respect for one another.
9. **Employee Value:** Members recognize that each has her/his own strengths and weaknesses; but everyone is valued nonetheless, as long as he/she is doing her/his job well and giving 100 percent to the team effort.

10. **Acceptance of Diversity:** Team members are understood, valued, respected, and appreciated, regardless of race, gender, age, religion, sexual orientation, language, family structure, disability, etc.
11. **External Relations:** The team spends time developing key outside relationships, mobilizing resources, and building credibility with important players in other parts of the organization.

Step Three: *Stipulate the Proper Operational Behaviors*

12. **Listening:** The members use effective listening techniques such as questioning, paraphrasing, and summarizing in order to best elicit and to fully comprehend their fellow team members' meanings.
13. **Open, Proactive Communication:** Team members feel free to express their feelings about both the task and the group's ongoing attempt to fulfill it. They recognize and accept the concept of proactive communication; i.e., if you need the information and are not getting it, go after it rather than just complain about it.
14. **Participation:** There is a lot of discussion, and everyone is encouraged to participate.
15. **Cooperation:** Team members cooperate when it comes to generating excitement and achieving goals, and protect each other throughout the process.
16. **Intergroup/Intragroup Cooperation:** Team members consciously acknowledge the need not to be turf-oriented.
17. **Productive Conflict:** Conflicts and disagreements inevitably arise, but the team is comfortable with these. It understands how important it is not to attempt to avoid, smooth over, or suppress conflicts or disagreements. There are few, if any, hidden agendas.
18. **Consensual Decisions:** When it comes to the important decisions, the goal is to arrive at substantial—but not necessarily unanimous—agreement, by means of open and thorough discussion of everyone's ideas.
19. **Compromises:** Compromises are important, as long as they do not adversely affect the quality of the products or the services provided.
20. **Climate:** The work climate fosters risk taking. Failures are looked upon as opportunities to learn rather than to criticize or to punish.

Step Four: *Continually Assess Progress*

21. **Personal Self-Assessment:** Each team member periodically conducts a self-assessment, to ensure that she/he understands her/his strengths and weaknesses.
22. **Team Self-Assessment:** Periodically, the team stops its work in order to examine how well it is functioning and what may be interfering with its effectiveness.
23. **Rewards:** While the individual still is rewarded and recognized, the team receives the greatest amount of recognition and reward. In short, rewards and recognition should reinforce the idea of *team* effort.

Step Five: *Continually Compare the Team's Realities with Its Principles of Quality*

24. **Effective Processes:** Team members are committed to the quality processes, and understand the intimate linkage among diversity, team building, and quality.
25. **Process Improvements:** Team members are committed to improving processes in order to eliminate waste and remedy defects.
26. **Client/Customer Relationships:** Team members are committed to satisfying clients/customers.

Based upon work done by Glenn Parker, and adapted by Advanced Research Management Consultant, Inc.

What Table 8.1 reveals is a clear progression. In order to be effective, team members must first be entirely clear as to their mission, what they are expected to accomplish. Then, in order to fulfill that mission, they must create an environment of shared values and interdependence which, in turn, leads to the stipulation of specific operational behaviors designed to ensure a high level of communication based upon trust and respect. Finally, teams need to assess their progress, both on the personal and the team levels, and to issue the commensurate rewards; and in a team environment, assessment and rewards are all about revitalization, or what Steven Covey describes as "sharpening the saw."

How Team Members Rate Their Own Teams

Ever since 1991, our surveys have included questions about the 26 characteristics of teams seen listed in Table 8.1. The results of those surveys, shown in Table 8.2, clearly demonstrate that considerable work remains to be done, if corporate America is to actually make optimal use of high-performance teams of diverse employees who find ways to continually surpass the expectations of their companies' diverse, demanding customers. As you review the table's findings, please note well that trust and respect receive some of the lower marks from our survey participants. That is a real danger sign, if only because any environment not conducive to risk taking and constructive disagreement is likely to breed dysfunctional behavior, much of it racist and sexist. Two other points of significant interest are the following. First, these employee responses showed little correlation of opinion with the gender or race of the opinion-giver, but high correlation with his or her organizational level and department. Second, lower-level employees tended to be far harsher in their criticisms than did higher-level ones.

Table 8.2

Responses of Survey Participants about Teams: 1995

45%	of survey respondents strongly agree or agree that each team member is encouraged to go outside his/her "paradigm" or frame of reference; and that a free-thinking, risk-taking environment is encouraged.
48%	of survey respondents strongly agree or agree that the team members or the team recognizes the importance of not avoiding, smoothing over, or suppressing conflicts and disagreements. There are few hidden agendas.
48%	of survey respondents strongly agree or agree that risk taking is supported; and that failures are looked upon as opportunities to learn, not to find blame.
50%	of survey respondents strongly agree or agree that team members recognize and clearly understand the need not to be turf-oriented.
52%	of survey respondents strongly agree or agree that there is a high degree of trust and confidence among all team members.
53%	of survey respondents strongly agree or agree that as a result of trust and confidence, team members have a great deal of respect for one another.
54%	of survey respondents strongly agree or agree that there are conflicts and disagreements, but that the team is comfortable with them.
56%	of survey respondents strongly agree or agree that team members cooperate in generating excitement, achieving goals, and supporting team members in the process.
57%	of survey respondents strongly agree or agree that team members accept and carry out their responsibilities with enthusiasm.
61%	of survey respondents strongly agree or agree that team members understand the crucial linkage among diversity, team building, and quality.
65%	of survey respondents strongly agree or agree that employees are given the appropriate responsibilities and levels of authority and empowerment to get the job done.
65%	of survey respondents strongly agree or agree that team members recognize and accept the concept of proactive communication; i.e., if you need the information and are not finding it, go after it rather than just complain about it.
72%	of survey respondents strongly agree or agree that team members are committed to improving all processes in order to eliminate waste and remedy defects.
78%	of survey respondents strongly agree or agree that team members are committed to educating internal clients and customers.

The following are some representative comments made by our survey participants with regard to teams:

There has been a control problem in our group—manipulation and intimidation.

> *Hispanic female, lower-level manager*

My department doesn't have conflicts. It's almost too good to be true.

> *Black female, lower-level manager*

Most are two-faced, who will stab you in the back the first chance they get!

> *Black male, occupational*

My team cuts corners, does poor work, and most do not even care about their process here at work.

> *Black male, occupational*

There are a lot of people who just don't care—the rest of the people carry them.

> *Black male, occupational*

Most have their own agendas, but will work with others only if they have to.

> *Asian male, middle-level manager*

I have worked in this department for fifteen years. I have never seen such poor management, lack of trust, and fear, as I have in the last six months. Something needs to be done here.

> *White female, occupational*

There is no respect or regard for each other anymore.

> *White female, occupational*

There is no team.

> *White female, middle-level manager*

The team doesn't work as a team anymore—too much back-stabbing.

> *White female, occupational*

Maybe it's because of my own personality, but I find it difficult to be accepted as part of a team that has had a long existence and I am the newcomer.

> *Hispanic female, middle-level manager*

Employees here are afraid of their shadows. It is truly sad to see adults so unempowered. There is no trust.

> *Hispanic female, middle-level manager*

Coworkers are interested in teambuilding. Most supervisors stifle that.

Hispanic female, occupational

Our upper-level management communicates on a confrontational basis, producing an us-vs.-them atmosphere. Lower management is considerably more teambuilding in their approach.

Asian female, occupational

Team work in my office is discouraged. We are treated like robots. There is no room for creativity. There is no sense of communication in our office. There is a big power struggle going on.

Black female, occupational

We talk continuously about team/teamwork, but there is no team/teamwork here. It is highly discouraged and frowned upon.

Black female, middle-level manager

What teams? Is that a joke?

White female, middle-level manager

My department is generally poor in interpersonal and interactive skills. We're not very nice to each other in team settings.

White male, middle-level manager

The Organizational and Structural Environments

In the following two subsections, we will examine two critical success factors that underpin the formation of cross-functional, high-performance teams. The first has to do with worker behaviors as those have a direct bearing on interpersonal relationships and skills. The second has to do with an organization's responsibility to develop a bias in favor of teams, and to dedicate resources to creating and maintaining them by means of effective human resources policies, practices, and strategies.

The Organizational Environment: Building Trust and Respect from the Bottom Up

Teams function within the context of the firm's overall environment. And that means that the only way trust and respect can become the standard modus operandi of team relationships is for those same qualities to permeate all of a company's activities and communications.

Trust and respect have to be *built,* however; they can't simply be decreed from on high by the firm's CEO. And yet, ironically enough, what the CEO and other occupants of the executive suite *can* do is to take actions and implement policies which cause employees to conclude neither their organization nor their individual fellow workers can be trusted. The following are some of the common organizational patterns and behaviors that undermine trust and respect.

1. *Leaders not walking their talk.* Nothing so effectively subverts trust and respect as leaders saying out loud how much they value the 26 characteristics of teams, and then failing to epitomize them in their behaviors. In other words, they are in effect saying, "Do as I say, not as I do."

2. *Untimely, inaccurate communication.* Organizations that do not impart information directly, straightforwardly, accurately, and efficiently to all employees undermine trust and respect. Such practices teach employees to place their trust in the grapevine rather than in the official company communications.

3. *Downsizing and layoffs.* Organizations which acquire a track record of consistently implementing downsizing and layoff programs undermine trust and respect. These actions undermine employee loyalty and goodwill and such programs, especially if cyclical, teach employees to remain always on the lookout for opportunities outside the organization. Thus, their best energies are wasted in looking out for themselves rather than for the company.

4. *Special standards for executives.* Organizations that give special rewards to executives undermine teamwork and the notion of shared prosperity. What is especially hurtful is for CEOs to receive major incentives at a time when the organization is not doing well, even while workers are asked to be satisfied with a 2 percent pay raise or no raise at all. It is simply wrong to neglect to hold senior executives accountable and to release lower-level managers and occupational employees first, when a company's fortunes turn sour.

5. *Inaccurate and/or little performance feedback and career planning.* Organizations which only promise all employees upward mobility and endless opportunities are misleading their workforces with unrealistic expectations. Couple this with a tendency to overlook employee faults until after disaster has struck, and to not provide/gain objective feedback for/from all employees, and it is not to be wondered that hostile, angry employees distrust their company and its management.

In order to put these self-defeating practices behind them, organizations must formulate and carry out a new contract, one that entails rights and responsibilities for both the organization and its employees. Such a statement would articulate the following beliefs, at the very least:

- *Our individual team members should identify what trust and respect look like to them personally, and then all of us must recognize that open communication will never exist without that trust and respect. We understand that when these are missing, skepticism and fear rush in to fill the vacuum. Since a team is interdependent by definition, it will fail if it is filled with fear. After all, who would be willing to give honest feedback to someone they feared? Who would be willing to propose ideas to someone who had a history of verbally attacking them?*
- *Our team members must consciously acknowledge that building trust and respect is a behavior-driven process; it doesn't just happen. We all hereby commit ourselves to making a conscious effort to develop new paradigms on a basis of respect for process, of behavior modeling, and of continually reminding ourselves of our mission.*

Now let's begin to elaborate a bit on this contrast, beginning at the employee end of the scale.

As Steven Covey puts it in his book *The 7 Habits of Highly Effective People*, each member of a team has an emotional bank account, as it were, with her/his other team members. Each account's balance represents the level of trust that exists between the account's owner and the other team members. As the members work together and bicker in the process, deposits and withdrawals are entered in the account. Kindness, honesty, reliability, and acceptance increase the balance; politicking, racism, sexism, ethnocentrism, and disrespect decrease it. The team's norms and standards are the currency which allows team bank accounts to be measured in terms of it. One way that team members can begin to make deposits into each other's accounts is by acknowledging and indeed honoring differences, whether based on race, gender, or personal preference or style.

In order to build up his or her team relationships, each member must develop and sustain an emotional commitment to each fellow member and to the team's success as a whole. And that in turn means that he/she must find the team's goal to be important, rewarding, and attainable. Initially, such confidence can be secured through the careful selection of team members. But once the initial excitement of forming a team embarked on a new mission has been replaced by complacency or even outright disappointment, it is vital that the team reiterate its goals and restress their importance. Often this task falls to team members whose special competency it is to challenge team goals and their importance. Such open questioning can help the team to collectively redesign itself so as to heighten commitment, alter goals, modify team roles, or reconfigure the team's membership.

Team members can do at least two things to intensify their commitment to the team. First, they can strive to develop self-awareness—the topic of Chapter 6. Second, they can make themselves very aware of each team member's particular responsibilities and areas of expertise. That kind of task clarity will allow the team to deploy its resources most effectively. And by *effectively*, we don't necessarily mean *efficiently*. For if efficiency were a team's only goal, then the same team members would always perform the same tasks, thus undercutting two key characteristics of teams: cross-training, and individual development. The effective team is that which deploys its resources in such a way as to avoid unnecessary duplication of job tasks, constant checking and rechecking in the name of quality, under-utilization of resources because of poor planning, and persistent reliance on a manager, rather than on each other, to provide information and project assistance.

It is also this task clarity which makes innovation possible. Innovation happens when team members allow their different ideas, perspectives, and experiences to rub against one another and thereby to produce *creative* friction. The idea always must be not to attack or to belittle but to arrive at the best team solution. And that happens only when all team members feel free and unafraid to share their own perspectives and criticisms with a view to figuring out how to make an idea *work*. It happens when they feel empowered to say, "What the heck, let's give it a try," rather than, "But what will management say?"

The Structural Environment: The Employer's Responsibilities

There are two basic steps that an organization can take, which will foster the development of the kinds of teams we're talking about.

1. Develop a mission and vision statement. If teams are going to understand exactly how their work contributes to their organization's overall success, and thereby to really believe that their contribution is important, that organization has no choice but to clearly articulate its mission and its vision. And it had better make darn sure that those excite employees and evoke in them a feeling of pride and ownership.

2. Develop new values and behavioral norms. The vision and mission statement also must make entirely clear the kinds of behaviors the organization will rely on as it goes in pursuit of its strategic goals. We believe that the possession and articulation of such a core set of norms can do much to help an organization develop the kind of collaborative, consensus-based environment that greatly raises the likelihood that it will reach its goals. Table 8.3 provides the reader with our own core set of norms.

Table 8.3
Core Behavioral Norms Needed to Create a Collaborative, Consensus-based Environment

1. Zero-tolerance Environment	An organizational environment is created in which the threshold is very low, ideally zero, at which personal behavior is deemed to pass from acceptable to unacceptable and where the appropriate consequences ensue upon passing. In other words, people are held to a high level of personal accountability for their behavior, including language, feedback, and behaviors. The appropriate workplace behaviors are deemed to be those that create trust and respect between all employees. There is zero tolerance for discrimination, harassment, off-color jokes, and so on.
2. No Secrets	Organizational information is widely distributed and is made available to all employees. Although there is a limited set of information—e.g., personnel files and patented processes—that remains off limits to most employees, the true reasons for this are shared openly with employees.
3. Trust and Respect Are Deserved	It is assumed that employees who pass the employment screening process and are hired by the company are trustworthy. In other words, it is assumed that *all* employees are trustworthy. As a result, all rules designed to protect the firm from the wrongdoing of a minority of non-trustworthy employees—e.g., time cards—are eliminated. Managers thus become enablers, not gatekeepers, and the artificial barrier between managers and nonmanagers is broken down. Peer pressure, training, and formal intervention are the tools utilized when an employee breaks the bond of trust with her/his organization. If necessary, that employee is reassigned or released.
4. People Want to Do a Good Job	Managers' role is to help people do what they want to do and are trying to do, which is a good job. Thus, managers help employees to find the resources and develop the tools they can use in order to excel. Performance goals are mutually set and when they are met, the success is celebrated.

	When they are not met, the manager and the employee jointly look into the reason why, and together develop a strategy to ensure future success.
5. More Is Achieved Together than Apart	The organizational assumption is that people *want* to work together, and that working collaboratively in teams, and sharing knowledge, are the best ways to assess and solve problems. It also is assumed that the team is its own best judge of how to manage itself, determine roles and responsibilities, and continuously monitor the process.
6. Emotional Expression Is Normal	It is understood that people do not leave their emotions at the door when they enter the workplace. Employees will always become upset, frustrated, angry, afraid, etc. Rather than asking them to suppress their emotions, managers teach them how to express their emotions honestly and productively and how to interact with those who are equally or more emotional than they. This does *not* mean that employees can act abusively or disrespectfully toward each other, or toward the organization, just because they "feel like it." What it *does* mean is that employees who *appropriately* express their feelings need not fear retribution or reprisal.
7. Learning Is Important	On-going, job-related learning and personal enrichment activities are highly valued and fully sponsored by the organization. The organization also sponsors job training for all employees. This training is in the areas of skill development, understanding the business as a whole, and interpersonal skills. The company also encourages its employees to seek enrichment activities outside of work by offering them flex-time so that they can take courses etc., and by providing them with tuition assistance. Those employees who dedicate themselves to continuous learning and to developing new, job-relevant skills are recognized and rewarded.
8. Change Is Positive	Change is seen as being both positive and necessary. When it finds itself presented with a new approach or opportunity, the organization's reflexive response is not "Why should we bother?" but "Why not?" In other words, the organization has a predisposition to change.

Right at the heart of these norms—we'll say it once again—are trust and respect. And since both of those terms are so critical, let's take a closer look at what we mean by them.

Deal openly with race and gender issues. Diversity has a number of faces. It includes job-related factors such as skill level, background, experience, years of service, and the like. And it includes non-job-related factors, not only demographic ones such as race, gender, ethnicity, religion, socioeconomic status, sexual orientation, disability status, and so on, but "hidden" factors such as thinking styles and value systems.

But the point we really want to make here is that it isn't enough for everyone just to look different. In order for it to become a real business asset, diversity must be both valued and *used*. In a company that has fully bought into our notion of "constituent capitalization" (see page 19), having vocal disagreements with peers and supervisors, regardless of race and gender, is accepted, commended, and understood. That is because such creative tension leads to better decision-making, since more alternatives and potential outcomes are developed and reviewed beforehand. It enables an organization to become more attuned to, and thus to provide better value to, a wide variety of diverse customers, and to please and/or influence a broader spectrum of stakeholders.

A few years ago, it was widely reported that in an internal publication, AT&T made use of a cartoon map that depicted people on different continents talking to each other on the phone. Each continent showed actual people—except for Africa, where a monkey was depicted instead. You had better believe that AT&T got some free publicity from this—the kind that drives many customers and some shareholders away in droves. So, what led to this seemingly racist debacle? Well, although the team that produced the publication was diverse in terms of race, ethnicity, age, gender, experience, and point of view, when team members were questioned they made some telling observations. A few—but by no means all—African American team members thought that the cartoon was amusing. Other team members thought it was not amusing, but didn't feel comfortable saying so out loud. Others knew that to print that cartoon would be a big mistake, but they said that whenever they mentioned race, they were accused of having a chip on their shoulders or of being too liberal. So they also kept silent.

In other words, here we have a splendid example of a team that "had" diversity, but no real constituent capitalization. Since it was lacking in trust and in respect for diverse viewpoints, the team lost a valuable opportunity, afforded by its diversity, to head off this public relations disaster in the making. You say it's impossible to affix "hard" numbers to such "soft" factors as trust and respect? Don't try telling that to AT&T!

Encourage cross-functionality. A key aspect of constituent capitalization is that teams are in possession of complementary skills that enable them to plan, manage, execute, and deliver an entire work product or service either to another team or to the end-user. In order to provide their employees with both in-depth skill training and a broad grasp of the many skills needed to bring any project to fruition, organizations must learn to rotate them around the various functions and to provide them with cross-training. For the truth is that cross-trained employees are better positioned to analyze a work situation and to offer feasible alternatives. An added bonus is that when teams are dismantled and new ones formed, team members can easily transport a wide array of skills to their new teams and new objectives.

Reward and recognize teams. Team-oriented behaviors and team accomplishment must be rewarded, more than individual accomplishment. This is a tough, yet necessary, transition that a bureaucratic organization must make if it wishes to become postbureaucratic. The organization's reward system must reinforce the belief that it is the team, as a unit, which has it in its power to deliver value to the customer. There is simply no room for intrateam competition and rivalry.

In Chapter 13 we will discuss rewards and recognition and how new reward and recognition systems must be put in place so as to fill the void created when the old bureaucracy was torn down. To review:

1. The bulk of each employee's compensation package must be related to team performance and be based on his/her collaborative behaviors. The level of compensation should be determined by the team's contribution to the broader organizational mission and by its ability to deliver superior value to customers.

2. That portion of compensation which is linked to individual performance should be based on business-related knowledge and aptitudes, not upon longevity.

3. Most of the compensation, both individual and team-based, should be variable, rising (and falling) with the fortunes of the firm.

4. Demarcations between both teams and levels should be eliminated, unless they clearly lead to some competitive advantage. For instance, a company's policy might be that everyone flies coach, and yet a particular team that does a good bit of its work overseas might be allowed to fly business class in order to be well rested for its upcoming meetings. By contrast, a policy that requires lower-level employees to fly coach but allows higher-level employees to fly business class serves no competitive purpose and should be eliminated.

Have a commitment to training of all kinds. It goes without saying that organizations must devote a good deal of their resources to training their workforces in current and future job skills. But training in interpersonal skills is equally important and such training should take two forms. The first sort of training seeks to raise the employee's level of self-awareness. It embraces such topics as personal culture and values, views about race and gender, thinking styles, personality styles, learning styles, and the like. The second sort is interpersonal training, and it delves into such matters as understanding other cultures, races, and genders; mediation; communication skills; and conflict resolution, to name a few.

We stipulate all of the above aspects of training, simply to remind you that training can do so much more than merely provide employees with the skills they need to do their jobs. It also can serve to revitalize the entire organizational culture, to reinforce the firm's behavioral norms, and to encourage people to seek out learning outside of the organization and thereby to create a community of resident experts and greatly augment the organization's store of knowledge.

Let the teams do the hiring. Cross-functional, high-performance teams hire their own talent. Sure, the organization probably still reviews and screens applicants for skills and abilities, as well as for an ability to function well in an environment based upon trust and respect and to abide by organizational norms. Nonetheless, the actual hiring decisions are left to the team members, who have been trained to objectively evaluate the skills and competencies needed for their team without regard to the race or gender of the possessor of them.

Teams also play three additional roles in the hiring process. First, they identify the positions that need to be filled and the aptitudes that candidates will have to have in order to add value to the team. Second, they examine their team's makeup, and make decisions about reshuffling team responsibilities, in such a way as to, if possible, obviate the need for a new position and/or provide developmental opportunities for current and future team members. Third, as a direct result of its training in this area, the team has a very clear conception of the thinking and personality styles of its present members, and actively searches for new team members who will bring with them different yet complementary skills.

Conclusions

What many look upon as being the chief benefit of utilizing high-performance teams composed of diverse individuals, is the ability to innovate which they bring to a company, to generate better solutions to complex business problems. And yet before a team can begin to realize innovation, its members must develop a wide range of new skills and behavior patterns. In other words, a great deal of time, patience, and resources have to be invested before innovation can begin to occur. Trust and respect have to be continuously fostered. Each team member has to fully engage in the team-building process, so as to develop relationships based upon trust and respect with all of her/his teammates, regardless of their race or gender.

By helping employees to develop and to implement teams, and by holding them accountable for their work, corporate America can make some major inroads against racism and sexism. It must begin to do so by helping people to get excited about working in teams, by giving teams real decision-making authority, by rewarding teamwork and team accomplishment significantly more than individual accomplishment, and by creating an organizational bias in favor of structuring work in ways that are meaningful to teams.

9

Communication and Conflict Resolution: Tips for Minimizing Race- and Gender-Related Difficulties

Introduction

In previous chapters we have in passing touched upon the topic of how all of us need to improve our communication skills in multicultural environments, and of the difficulties we encounter in our attempt to do so. In this chapter we're going to zoom in on communication skills and conflict resolution, and offer some tips as to how organizations can improve them. Our special emphasis, of course, will be placed on putting these skills to work so as to solve the problems associated with race and gender.

Communicating effectively is a crucial part of our constituency capitalization strategy and holistic model for moving beyond the rhetoric of race and gender. And the simple reason for that is that we have noticed how, in the vast majority of cases in which people are alleging discrimination or believe themselves the targets of discrimination, it is clear that communication has broken down. More specifically, charges of discrimination often are made merely because people have not received timely, accurate, honest feedback about their job performance and/or career opportunities. Because they are then left to fill in the communication gaps as best they can with their own perceptions of past experiences, it isn't surprising that those perceptions tend to be of racism and of sexism, regardless of the reality of the situation.

We all pay lip service to the importance of communication. And yet in the whirl of our daily lives and the heat of our business interactions, we rarely give much thought to the overwhelming complexities of communicating. Take a moment to do so now, by recalling that game in which one person makes a simple statement to another, who in turn passes it on to yet another, and so on. We all have seen how, by the time the message reaches the last person in the chain (and it doesn't even have to be a very long chain), it bears little resemblance to the original message. Or just recollect the trouble you probably have had in staying in close communicative touch even with the loved one closest to you. Add to these examples the ways in which we are socialized in this country, and is it any wonder that the task of communicating with people in a racially and sexually diverse environment is fraught with difficulties?

One of the factors that makes communication especially difficult is our natural shyness. We generally withhold much of what we really have to say. We avoid airing issues of personal importance for as long as possible. And when we do finally bring them up, we feel awkward about doing so in a straightforward and honest manner. Especially when the issues have a race or gender component, we have become very skilled at avoiding those topics; we tend to discuss them only indirectly, while using plenty of qualifiers and euphemisms. And it is that subtlety and indirection which, however politely intended, can easily lead to incorrect assumptions and miscommunications, which in turn can directly lead to charges of unfair treatment on a basis of race and/or gender.

Thus, it no longer comes as a surprise to us, in the work that we do to help other organizations and even our own, when we find the roadside littered with communication breakdowns. Leading up to that sorry sight have been such scenarios as the following. Personal grievances and misunderstandings have been allowed to fester beneath the surface. Employees have been denied access to the information they need, and so have spent too much time on an assignment or have provided ineffective customer service, or done something else incompatible with organizational or team goals. Internal resentments have filtered under the doorways to infect customer and stakeholder relationships as well. Managers have been at odds with employees, employees at odds with customers, and everyone at odds with every other stakeholder who has a race or gender background different than their own.

Let's take a closer look at the dynamics of that last one. A manager, let's say, is not all that good at giving employees feedback as to their job performance. He/she would rather do anything than confront an employee who he/she believes isn't working up to par; far better just to avoid making a scene, and hope the problem will go away on its own. Let's say that in this particular case the employee believes that she/he is doing a great job, whereas the manager considers her/his performance to be barely adequate. Formal appraisal time comes along at last, and finally the manager's real opinion has to come out. The employee is deeply disappointed by her/his quasi-negative appraisal; the manager is upset, because the employee is alleging unfair treatment. In the now-poisoned atmosphere, with its lack of trust and respect, it is all too likely that the employee will begin to believe that she/he received her/his low evaluation because of her/his race or gender (or her/his age, sexual orientation, or some other subjective factor). It won't be long until she's/he's on the phone to an attorney, ready and indeed eager to file a discrimination suit.

The same type of thing is always happening with customers. Let's say that a white customer-service representative, with a very indirect manner of communicating, is interacting with a very straightforward, self-assured black customer who never shrinks from conflict. The employee "reads" that self-assurance as arrogance, feels uncomfortable, and communicates that discomfort through his or her demeanor and body language; the customer in turn reads those signals as a clear sign of racially based disrespect. How easy it can be, in other words, for a firm to lose a valued customer, not on account of a poor product but merely owing to a garden-variety communication misfire.[1]

It Isn't Just Words

Five barriers to communication can be found in place in any company, but especially in the most highly diverse organizations:

1. Language differences.
2. Numerous forms of nonverbal communication.
3. Cultural stereotypes that distort meaning.
4. The bad habit of making snap judgments, i.e., of not really listening to what others say.
5. High levels of anxiety, especially in the most highly diverse environments.

We hope that in thinking about these five barriers you also have been pondering the need to be aware of the signals we routinely send to others—and the signals they send to us—as we speak or listen. A good rule of thumb is that 15 percent of communication is verbal, 85 percent nonverbal. Thus, the effective communicator pays close heed to such nonverbal factors as eye contact, body language, amount of interpersonal distance, tone of voice, and pace and volume of speech. A particular problem here, of course, is that race, culture, and gender all bring wide variations to these nonverbal norms. People from the Middle East, for example, are accustomed to having only small amounts of personal "space" in their face-to-face conversations; people whose roots are northern European tend to want more space, which means that they easily can feel their space being "invaded" if someone walks up and starts to talk to them from only six inches away. Mix in gender so that we have, let's say, a Middle Eastern male manager and a northern European female direct report and you've got the perfect ingredients for a perception of sexual harassment springing out of purely cultural norms and expectations.

So, yes, body language, etc., is important, and we neglect it at our peril. But words still count, plenty. Therefore, if we are going to communicate effectively, the words we use had better have roughly the same meaning for the sender and the receiver. Alas, "linguists have estimated that the 500 most often used words in the English language can produce over 14,000 meanings."[2] And as if to make matters worse, those word meanings generally have a direct relation to personal and cultural experiences; the more dissimilar those experiences, the less likely it is that sender and receiver are attaching the same meanings to their words. A good current example might be "babe," a word often used by both men and women in a way that has no gender implications; a synonym, in the right context, for "pal" or "buddy." But a man who is trying to be chummy with a female direct report, and who therefore exclaims "Hey, babe!" will be lucky indeed if the woman hears the word in the same sense as he intended it!

Our natural insecurity and defensiveness can also do much to foul up the communication process. Some common reasons for defensiveness include the following:

1. All of us tend to cherish our own opinions, so any disagreement with others leaves us feeling attacked and vulnerable and causes us to be overly zealous in defending our own position.
2. We don't hear what the other person is actually saying, but rather merely note the fact that she/he seems to be disagreeing with us. This naturally disappoints and frustrates the speaker; we interpret that frustration as hostility, and respond in kind.
3. We are deeply bothered by our seeming inability to clearly articulate our own views. We project that frustration onto our hearer, interpreting his or her merely befuddled reactions as hostile, and the result, yet again, is hard feelings all around.

The problem of defensiveness can become especially acute when one is attempting to communicate with a person of a different race or gender. Let's say an older, female chief of surgery disagrees with a younger, male direct report as to the best way to treat a patient. The younger surgeon becomes defensive, insisting that his course of treatment is best. He begins to wonder whether his supervisor really is disagreeing with him merely because he is a man. His tone and body language reflect this uneasiness, a fact which in turn makes the chief of surgery defensive . . . and on it goes. In such situations *no one's* message is getting through, because widely differing interpretations of motives, values, and affects are distorting all content. And meanwhile the poor patient—or in our case, the customer—becomes the *real* victim of this communication breakdown.

Having Healthy Communications: Minimizing Race and Gender Issues

Yes, defensiveness is widespread, but it doesn't have to be that way. The corporate environment can just as easily nourish open, honest communication as it can harbor defensiveness and bruised feelings. And it clearly is the former kind of atmosphere that increasing numbers of women and people of color are telling us they need, if they are to be effective on the job. The accompanying box will show you some of the differences between defensive climates, which hurt everyone including women and people of color, and supportive climates, which lessen the perception of race and gender discrimination and of unfair and cruel treatment in general.

Defensive Climates	Supportive Climates
Partial listening	Holistic listening
Indirect communication	Direct communication
Overhasty evaluation	Patient and fair evaluation
Control	Collaboration
Strategy	Spontaneity
Neutrality	Empathy
Superiority	Equality
Arrogant certainty	Mellow provisionalism

Now let's examine each of these pairs of environments.

Partial versus Holistic Listening

To listen holistically means not only to hear the words but also to "listen" to all of the nonverbal factors discussed above. All of these send messages with regard to enthusiasm, confidence, agreement or disagreement, friendliness or skepticism. Remember, too, that nonverbal cues can actually contradict the message of the spoken words. The words may be "Yes,"

"I understand," or "Go ahead," while the body language or tone of voice is screaming "No!," "I don't get it!," or "Stop!"

Indirect versus Direct Communications

In many cultures, including our own, people only very rarely verbalize what they truly mean. Thus communication becomes indirect and cryptic, and results in messages that are vague, distorted, or misinterpreted, or that just plain get lost in the shuffle. We can vastly improve our communications if we will simply say exactly what we mean, but do so in such a way that is highly respectful and sensitive of the needs of others.

Overhasty versus Fair Evaluation

Verbal and nonverbal communication that is evaluative in the sense of overly judgmental is often lost on the receiver. And to make matters worse, competing cultural groups too often blame, label, and question what the members of other groups do, on the basis of an overly dogmatic belief in their own version of reality. By contrast, communication can be open, straightforward, and honest without arousing defensiveness, provided that it is more descriptive than judgmental. It should simply and soberly state the facts of a case—for instance, "It's important for us to meet these deadlines because . . ." rather than be over-emotive and accusatory: "Damn it, Harry, you're always making us miss our deadlines! For God's sake, shape up, Harry, or ship out!"

Control versus Collaboration

Far too many of our human interactions are devoted to doing something *to* someone else—influencing behavior, changing attitudes, curtailing activities, and the like. And this, despite our common awareness that we succeed best when we approach our communications with the intent of collaborating with others, in order to define or solve a problem, rather than of controlling them. There is all the difference in the world between "Damn it, Harry, you're always making us miss our deadlines!" and "Harry, what can we do to help you with next month's report?" And make no mistake, racism and sexism are the ultimate forms of control in the corporate environment.

Strategy versus Spontaneity

When others see us as having a hidden agenda or as playing a role, they resent us and grow defensive. And yet when we simply freely share our information and the sources of that information, we not only create an atmosphere of trust, respect, and spontaneity, but make team members feel that they are first-stringers rather than subs.

Neutrality versus Empathy

We reassure others when we let them know that we can identify with their problems, understand their feelings, and accept their emotional reactions even when we perceive them as being excessive or even hostile to us. On the other hand whenever we deny the legitimacy of others' emotions, what we really do, even if we intend to be supportive, is to create a closed, hostile environment, a breeding ground for bruised feelings and the consequent charges of racism and sexism.

Superiority versus Equality

We inevitably set off others' defense mechanisms whenever we convey a sense of superiority springing from race, gender, ethnicity, wealth, intellectual ability, physical characteristics, and so on. The resultant feelings of inadequacy on the part of listeners cause them to hear only what their emotions are screaming at them to hear, and the subsequent resentment and hostility can quickly lead to charges of discrimination.

Arrogant Certainty versus Mellow Provisionalism

We all know the type—the man or woman who knows all the answers, needs no additional information, regards himself or herself as the ultimate authority. And anyone who is always dead-bang certain is sure to put others on their guard. Compare such a person with our thirty-fifth president, John F. Kennedy. Those once close to JFK believed that one of his finest leadership qualities was well reflected in his penchant for saying, when changing an earlier position, "I don't think that way anymore." In other words, this great leader was wise enough to look upon his ideas and solutions as merely provisional, not written in stone.

Some Tips for Effective Communication

In previous chapters we have suggested that if we are to have good communications with people of different racial or gender groups than our own, we must begin by closely examining our own values, beliefs, and assumptions, our strengths and weaknesses, our all-too-human tendency to stereotype. Table 9.1 provides you with some specific tips for communicating with members of different races and genders. The idea behind all of them is to help you make your communications direct, clear, specific, and concise, so as to minimize those misinterpretations and bridge those gaps that can lead to conflict and to charges of discrimination. Remember, it is easy for us to point a finger of blame for our communication problems. But if we are trying to influence others we have no choice but to communicate effectively, which means causing our message to be accurately heard by its receiver.

Table 9.1
Tips Furthering Effective Communication with Different Races and the Other Gender Groups

---

- Address communicational and other problems head-on, but also in an empathetic fashion, rather than merely pretend they don't exist.
- Avoid using qualifiers that reinforce stereotypes. "We would hire people of color if they had the skills."
- Avoid using identification references that highlight race, gender, physical disabilities, etc.
- Do not use words that offend racial and gender groups.
- Refrain from speaking more loudly when communicating with individuals whose English is limited. Instead, try to speak more slowly and to pronounce each syllable. But don't do so unduly, or you will inadvertently give offense.
- Do not tell offensive jokes that stereotype or demean people.
- Use words that are gender neutral and recognize both genders—e.g., salesperson vs. salesman; supervisor vs. foreman; etc.
- Avoid the use of jargon, but nonetheless keep it simple. Use specific, concise phrases.
- Use a wide variety of analogies, metaphors, and references, rather than just sporting or military expressions, for instance.
- Be patient. It may well take longer for individuals whose native language is not English to process information.
- Use pictures, signs, or diagrams, when appropriate, to assist you in getting your message across. Demonstrating what you are explaining will often do the trick faster than words will.
- Use "I" messages as an assertive, culturally neutral way of saying that certain behaviors are causing you difficulty but that nonetheless you respect the rights of others.
- Be aware of nonverbal cues; e.g., your body language.
- Say it again. When you are finding it hard to make yourself understood, repeat yourself while using different words, and/or rephrase. Frequently ask questions, to see whether you are getting through.

- Yes, you want your questions to be direct, concise, and clear, but make sure they also are open-ended rather than close-ended.
- Make sure that all of the responses are indeed answering your questions; if they aren't, ask the questions of your hearer yet again.
- When listening, be sure to find ways to acknowledge and affirm the speaker's emotional state. Strive to pick up on any and every cue the speaker is providing you with.
- Summarize your conversation before concluding, so as to ensure that mutual understanding has been reached.
- Always remember to follow up in writing, so as to confirm discussions and agreements and avoid rework and nonconformance.

The Importance of Feedback in Eliminating Racism and Sexism

Employees simply must get feedback, if they are to know where they stand as performers, to receive career counseling, and to develop in every way possible. Feedback helps employees to change their behavior when it needs changing, to keep on doing what they're doing right, and to continuously upgrade their knowledge and their skills. It also gives them information about whether their behaviors are having the effects they sought, whether they are reaching their hearers in the manner they wish. And best of all, feedback is a two-way street. It allows companies and their managers to gain an appreciation of the needs and desires of employees, customers, and stakeholders, and to assess whether they are effectively meeting those needs.

Table 9.2 provides you with some of the characteristics of good feedback.

Table 9.2
Characteristics of Effective Feedback

1. Most essential of all is that feedback be timely and be shared at the right place. Therefore, relaxed surroundings and sufficient time for complete discussion are vital to any good feedback session.
2. The specific focus should be on the task and the behavior, not the person. Feedback provided by a manager should be about specific shortcomings that the employee can take steps to rectify in the future, or about specific things he/she is now doing well. In other words, good feedback confines itself to an employee's actual behaviors, and doesn't attempt to assess or critique them in depth.

3. Feedback must take into account the needs of the employee, his/her concerns and desires.
4. If it is to be effective, feedback must be two-way. The person giving feedback must make himself/herself an active listener, by continuously seeking and getting clarifications.
5. Feedback should be given not just when improvement is needed, but also when the employee seems to be doing just fine.
6. Feedback should not be given when you are too busy, angry, or tired—i.e., in any of those states of emotionally induced mental instability that we all go through.
7. Feedback should always be checked up on, to see if it has been received accurately.
8. If your goal is to build trust and respect, never, never rely upon feedback from anonymous sources.

Conflict Resolution

In many previous contexts we have trumpeted the value of diversity for every business trying to compete in a rapidly changing, global market— the creative sparks that can fly whenever diverse ideas and perspectives "rub against one another." But now is the time for us to expressly acknowledge the fact that diversity can and does create conflict—that sometimes those perspectives *collide* rather than merely rub.

The sad truth, however, is that many U.S. corporations still are unable to deal directly, openly, and honestly with conflicts among employees, customers, and stakeholders. From an early age most of us have been trained to avoid the unpleasantness of conflict, at all costs; we fear nothing more than the accusation of being a "boat-rocker." These conformist tendencies in us are aided and abetted as we enter corporate America by the structure of the old bureaucracy. For as our look at bureaucracy's history has shown us, it loves hierarchy to a great extent simply because the hierarchical structure serves to minimize conflict. But since conflicts do inevitably arise even within bureaucracies, both our own and our organizations' unwillingness to face up to them leads to a situation in which many conflicts are interpreted as being race- and/or gender-related when in fact they aren't. Of course they sometimes *are*, but corporate America is unwilling to admit it.

The effects of such conflict avoidance on an organization can be devastating, both internally and externally. One obvious effect is litigation and the resulting judgments against organizations. Prime examples include Texaco ($175 million), Denny's ($100 million), State Farm ($300 million), Home Depot ($85 million) and Mitsubishi (hundreds of millions). Other more hidden costs are incurred as well: negative publicity, lost business, reduced productivity, poor customer service, low morale, wasted energy, missed opportunities, towering legal fees, and squandered management time. Dina Lynch has done some calculations on the costs of conflict to organizations, and her conclusions certainly are revealing:

> Industry statistics reveal that managers spend up to 20 percent of their time resolving disputes. For each manager earning $60,000 per year, the company is spending $12,000 on conflict resolution. And for managers with higher salaries, the figure can climb to as much as $50,000 annually.[3]

The other factor here, in terms of why we err in so resolutely avoiding all conflict, is that some people *thrive* on productive conflict, as do some cultural groups. At one end of the scale are the Japanese, who some might assert have a certain genius for downplaying conflict; their tight and racially quite homogeneous island culture places a high value on consensus and agreement, on ensuring that everyone "saves face." At the other end of the scale, perhaps, are African Americans, who strike some as being quite comfortable with direct conflict. Of course, the reason for that may well be that throughout their lives they have had to fight to get their share of the American Dream, in a dominantly white culture.

At any rate, this much is clear: If companies wish to resolve their race- and gender-related problems—and to avoid the hassle and cost of all the accompanying lawsuits—they simply must develop their skills in the area of conflict resolution. One of the keys to forming diverse, high-performance teams is to teach both managers and team members how to view conflict in a positive light—to use it constructively, rather than just focus obsessively on "how to win." Some of the potential benefits of productive conflict include the following:

1. A heightened awareness of the problems that exist, and of approaches to their solution.
2. Getting people to consciously consider problems and novel solutions, rather than to just allow those problems to percolate away beneath the surface.
3. A greater awareness of injustices such as sexism and racism, and a determination to eliminate them.
4. Heightened sensitivity toward the needs, styles, values, frustrations, and resentments of others.

5. The open expression of opposing views, so as to critique old reasoning processes and develop new decisions-making tools.
6. Energizing people to dig down to the roots of conflict, and to
openly assess what they find there.
7. The fostering of an exhilarating atmosphere of creative risk taking.
8. Motivating people and improving morale, by granting them
express permission to come up with, and articulate, new solutions to old problems.
9. Greatly raising workers' skill levels.
10. Decreasing costs, by increasing efficiencies, by dealing with
problems in a direct and timely fashion.
11. Improved customer relations, springing out of a new awareness
of their real needs and concerns.
12. A reduction in the level of the organization's legal exposure.

Make no mistake: Avoiding conflict doesn't make it go away. Instead, it
starts seeping into other areas of work and eroding the cohesion of teams.
When employees feel that they are in a war zone they expend most of
their creative energy in "hunkering down," particularly during times of
actual crisis: reengineering, downsizing, mergers, implementation of new
technology, and—not least of all—changes wrought by the struggle to
achieve constituent capitalization and to implement affirmative action.
Conflict avoidance also is a big mistake in relations with customers and
other stakeholders, as it creates dissatisfied customers and disgruntled
stakeholders who gradually stop doing business with the firm.

Dealing with Conflict Effectively

The problem vis-à-vis conflict is not that it exists, but how it is managed.
Thus, it is important to acknowledge that there are two types of conflict:
interpersonal and operational. *Interpersonal conflict* arises out of disputes
between persons as a result of individual differences in the areas of personality, style, race, gender, and the like. It can easily be a manifestation
of new, more subtle forms of racism and sexism, but regardless, it is counterproductive because it causes employees to get obsessed with personality and character rather than get the job done. In contrast, *operational
conflict* is all about nonpersonal issues. It arises out of debates about marketing strategy, the best way to resolve customer service problems, and
the like. Operational conflict should be viewed as a positive thing,

because it focuses not on personalities but on products, services, and procedures—on creative differences about how work should be done and what products and services should be delivered, and how to exceed customer expectations. It is to a great extent operational conflict, which, when hammered out by diverse people bringing their varied skills and perceptions to the table, helps organizations produce optimal results.

So, in general terms interpersonal conflict is "bad" and operational conflict is "good." And yet interpersonal conflict *can* be constructive, if it is managed properly. The two keys here are to approach all differences in a collaborative manner and to trace each conflict to its proper cause. We noted in Chapter 1 that conflict can indeed arise because of racism and sexism, but that it can also be the product of poor management practices, ill-conceived human resource policies, or clumsy implementation of those policies. At any rate, what is certain is that corporations which fail to embrace conflict are less likely to locate its root causes and to take steps to "root them out."

Let's zero in for a moment on interpersonal conflict that has its roots in racism and sexism. The fact is that corporations have a hard time dealing with these problems, largely owing to simple denial. Sad to say, but over the years we have met very few corporate managers who tried to directly address the issues of race and gender. Rather, the vast majority of them have responded by vociferously denying that the conflict had anything to do with racism and sexism. What we have become very used to hearing are such things as these: "We don't have any racists or sexists in our company." "The employee [or customer or stakeholder] is overacting." "He's being too sensitive." "She has a chip on her shoulder." And so these managers run away from their company's problem, suppress it, or cover it up—until it explodes right in their faces.

Compounding the problem of confronting racism and sexism in the workplace is the fact that widespread managerial denial creates an atmosphere in which women and people of color are reluctant to do their share of the confronting. Given the current mood of society with regard to affirmative action and so on, many women and people of color simply don't dare to express their true feelings about disparate race or gender treatment. To do so would only cause them to be labeled "troublemaker," "whiner," "complainer," "not a team player," "militant feminist," and on and on. And any employee who has been thus labeled feels, probably rightly, that he/she is at the head of the line to be "reengineered" or "rightsized" or "delayered" right out of the company. Customers, too, are less likely to bring up the issues of racism and sexism these days, either because too many of their past complaints have fallen on deaf ears or because they feel that the company in question sees them as being the problem rather than the source of an exciting new solution.

Ten Steps toward Conflict Resolution

The first conflict-management practice that organizations need to implement is the viewing of conflict as being entirely healthy in today's workplace. The second is the creation of an atmosphere in which the topics of racism and sexism can be discussed and explored rationally and productively, in hopes of changing many minds on the subject. Easier said than done, you say?

To the contrary, much of what we have had to say in previous chapters comes in very handy here: creating a zero-tolerance environment; creating a learning organization where mistakes related to race and gender are accepted as one of the risks associated with constituent capitalization; encouraging team members to coach one another when it comes to the issues of race and gender; acknowledging the powerfully deleterious effect that stereotyping always has upon trust and respect. As for the specific steps we provide for you in Table 9.3, please note that these steps simply can't be taken in a traditional bureaucratic organization. They can be, however, in the postbureaucratic organization that we believe will be the new model in the 21st century and beyond.

Table 9.3
Ten Steps toward Conflict Resolution

1. Whenever a conflict arises, immediately acknowledge that fact and bring it out into the open. Describe and clarify the conflict, but don't yet try to dissect it.
2. Find a suitable time and place in which to begin the conflict-resolution process. Acknowledge and allow ventilation. This is extremely important, because it helps people not to get side tracked when the real give-and-take occurs.
3. At the second meeting, set up the ground rules for the process and for team behaviors. Focus on solving the conflict, not on attributing blame. All conversations must be marked by trust and respect. Everyone will be open and honest; everyone will have a say and be heard. Everyone will listen to each other without interruption, argument, or negative reaction. All will refrain from rushing to judgment, and will have a positive, caring attitude. Questions will be open-ended, and opinions and feelings supported by facts and specific behaviors. *Everyone must be empathetic.*
4. The conflict should be clearly defined and dissected, in terms of what the conflict is and what caused it.

5. Each person involved in the discussion should feel that she/he is responsible for solving the conflict, should recognize the continuing cost of conflict, and should feel responsible for coming up with a mutually beneficial solution. Again, everyone must practice empathy and refuse to assign blame.
6. Everyone should employ those communication skills we discussed in the section on "Some Tips for Effective Communication" in this chapter.
7. Generate a number of possible solutions. Evaluate the pluses and minuses of all solutions.
8. Once the most appropriate solution has been agreed upon and an action plan developed, assign responsibilities for implementing the action plan.
9. At every step in the process, time-outs should be called in which to share feelings about how the process is going.
10. Hold people to their commitments to successfully resolve the conflict.

Conclusions

If our past 25-plus years of actively consulting and working with and in corporate America have led us to any one belief, it is that many of the race- and/or gender-related problems in corporate America arise out of poor, ineffective, or nonexistent communications. This has become a virtual truism for us, which is why we feel so certain that building effective communication skills is one of the greatest challenges facing corporate America. An especially high hurdle will be effective communication between different racial and gender groups.

We have seen that one factor hindering the development of effective communication skills is that only 15 percent of communication is verbal, while 85 percent is nonverbal. And even within the verbal component, different words have different meanings for different people. The situation gets even more complicated when people who have different first languages try to communicate effectively, regardless of the cultural background of the person. All of which brings us back to our earlier position, which is that we must struggle to gain self-awareness, so as to understand both our personal and our cultural strengths and weaknesses. For without such self-knowledge and cultural knowledge, our own "issues" will always be interfering with even our sincerest attempts to be empathetic. And he or she in whom a lack of knowledge of self and of culture is hindering the ability to be empathetic and to communicate effectively, is all too likely to be part of the race and gender problem rather than of its solution.

Another related reality that corporations always will face is conflict among employees, customers, and stakeholders. If companies are inept and cannot effectively resolve conflicts among their employee body, their ability to solve conflicts between the company and its customers and stakeholders will also be ineffective. When these conflicts are based on the emotional issue of race and gender, conflicts can become explosive and hostile. Thus, corporations must develop strategies to teach their employees the skills and behaviors needed to resolve conflicts productively. Most of the preceding and following chapters provide knowledge in that regard. Corporations must encourage the resolution of conflict. Corporations must clearly assist their employees in understanding the pluses and minuses associated with their not dealing objectively, openly, directly, and in a timely manner, with conflict not only among employees in the organization but also among customers and stakeholders.

Finally, companies should hold everyone accountable for productive resolutions of conflict. Those who are the positive role models should be rewarded and celebrated. Those who are not should be educated, counseled, and given the opportunity to alter their behavior. If their behavior does not change, they should be asked to leave the organization.

The costs of avoiding conflict are considerable, as are the costs of destructive conflict. The benefits of productive conflict justify an investment in the learning of conflict-management skills, especially vis-à-vis the issues of race and gender. How many more legal suits will have to occur, before we all get the message that race and gender conflicts cannot be ignored, they must be constructively and quickly dealt with?

10

Recruiting and Retaining a Diverse Workforce

Introduction

"Gee, if only we could find some truly qualified women and people of color, we would be so glad to hire them all!" "Those folks just don't have much interest in our industry. But we sure would love to hire them if they were."

Those words sound familiar? They should. In all the years we've been assessing the problems of race and gender in corporate America, you had better believe we've heard plenty of remarks such as those, purporting to explain the paucity of women and people of color either throughout organizations or in the middle- to senior-level positions.

When we ask women and people of color to give us their own take on such remarks, only a handful ever grant them any validity at all. Many are especially skeptical about all of those employment opportunities that are supposedly just rolling into their laps, as a result of their race or gender. For instance, one educated, experienced Hispanic female, who holds a senior-level executive position, had this to say: "If women and people of color are receiving such tremendous offers, why am I one of the lowest-paid senior executives in my company? Why am I not being sought after by headhunters, like my less experienced, less educated white male colleagues are?" Or listen to these blunt words, from a black, female midlevel manager: "I have heard comments for 30 years, about how I have it made just like other women of color—we are a double count, women and minority status. Yet if we have had it made, if we are getting all of those fantastic offers, why do we make less than white men, black men, and white women?" Clearly, then, for many women and people of color the quoted assertions with which we have opened this chapter are pure bunkum. And in our own opinion such assertions really do reflect the new more subtle, yet equally dangerous, forms of racism and sexism that women and people of color working or seeking to work in U.S. corporations now are up against.

Quite simply, we don't believe in the arguments about the dearth of qualified women and people of color. We see them as being at best unfounded assertions, at worst, the code words masking a new brand of racism and sexism. Qualified women and people of color *are* out there, if the work environments and the offers are right, and there's no secret to finding them. It's simply a matter of committing ourselves to developing systematic, objective, rational, and fair recruiting strategies, implementing those strategies aggressively, and fostering a team environment that treats people fairly, regardless of race or gender.

And there's more to be said here. Specifically, that as corporate America's labor pool of the 21st century will comprise very large numbers of educated, capable women and people of color, especially in the high-tech and service-oriented industries. As for the demand side of things, some researchers are saying that the United States currently is producing only one qualified graduate for every five technically oriented jobs there are out there. On top of that, unemployment is at a 30-year low. The joint significance of those two trends is that both old and new recruits are going to have lots of job offers to choose among. Which in turn means that any U.S. corporation that wants to stay competitive is going to have to find, recruit, and retain the best employees, regardless of race or gender.

The Traditional Recruitment Process

Too often, recruiters and their companies evaluate new recruits solely on the basis of how they "fit" our culture and other subject areas. That is one indication of how, even though today's jobs and today's business environment do indeed require new skills and the highly intelligent and well-trained employees who possess them, many companies continue to measure new recruits with antiquated tools. Another such tool is the face-to-face, one-on-one employment interview. Too often such interviews are unstructured and haphazard; the interviewers have been poorly trained in how to conduct an objective interview, with one interviewer giving primacy to an employment factor that the interviewer down the hall sees as being less important. The result is a selection process that is biased by the way in which interviewers over-rely on "impressions," and thereby leave plenty of room for subtle racism and sexism to slip into the recruitment process.

Clifford E. Montgomery, vice president of human resources at Quaker Chemical Corporation in Pennsylvania, has shared some interesting but in our opinion dangerous observations about new skills and how his company goes about determining them. Writing about how his company conducted a "resign/rehire" exercise with its employees, he asks, "If all of our employees resigned on Friday, changed their minds over the weekend, and requested to be rehired on the following Monday, would we rehire every one of them?"[1] The company used a form that evaluated five areas: education, language skills, industry, job expertise, and interpersonal skills. The last item included such characteristics as likability, sense of humor, and ability as a team player. Montgomery writes:

> From this exercise it soon became clear that although [the five areas were rated] equally on a scale of 1 to 10, employees who rated high on objective criteria (proficiency credentials) and low on subjective qualities (personal credentials) were five times as likely not to be rehired as those who scored the opposite way. These subjective, unquantifiable personal characteristics appeared to be a major key to the success or failure of an employee, and while most hiring managers intuitively understood this, it had been virtually ignored in our staffing process. As a result, interpersonal characteristics and cultural fit have become highly regarded assessment criteria. . . . Hiring profiles—gathered in addition to technical criteria—clearly define interpersonal styles that fit well with the corporate culture and strategies.[2]

A Better Recruitment Process

While we agree that interpersonal skills are important, we have some major concerns as to Quaker's approach, which seems to be suggesting that corporations should look for people who conform to some arbitrary standards of interpersonal conduct that boil down to "act like me, talk like me, look like me, make me feel comfortable." Our view is that companies should look both at an employee's intellectual, technical and professional skills and at their desire, their understanding of their personal culture, their strengths and weaknesses, their emotional intelligence, their ability to be empathetic, and their willingness to accept and value different race, ethnic, and gender groups. In earlier chapters, we have suggested some ways in which all employees can strive to get a handle on these competencies. Additionally, however, companies must rely upon the opinions of highly trained and skilled recruiters, interviewers, and hiring managers, as these employ a wide variety of instruments and multiple inputs when they go about making their hiring decisions. Finally, we offer the steps depicted in the box, as specific ways of avoiding race and gender bias in the recruitment and hiring process.

Step 1 *Develop specific selection criteria.* It is essential to develop specific hiring criteria, and to make sure that all of the interviewers and hiring managers make use of them.

Step 2 *Develop specific instruments to measure the criteria.* And again, firms need to make sure that everyone involved in the hiring process is using these instruments.

Step 3 *Train interviewers.* Interviewers need to go through their own self-analysis, so as to assess their own culture, norms, values, emotional intelligence, racial and gender attitudes, and the like. They should go through the recruitment process, just like any other new job candidate. And they should even receive feedback from recruits about their skills.

Step 4 *Have diverse interviewers.* Because of our natural tendency to hire people like ourselves, it is crucial that women and people of color should be recruiters and interviewers.

Step 5 *Use a team-review approach.* All parties to the process should meet as a team, to review candidates and to arrive at a team decision.

Step 6 *Evaluate the recruiters.* Recruiters should be evaluated in terms of their number of hires as well as of the race and gender, types of positions, and the success or failure of their recruits.

College Relations Programs

As labor shortages continue to occur, more and more companies are acknowledging their need for a systematic, year-round college relations program that can begin to woo candidates when they are just embarking on their educational careers. The following are some key elements of an effective college relations program:

1. Evaluate and select a limited number of specific schools that have a good track record in terms of producing talent that matches the company's needs, especially vis-à-vis women and people of color.
2. Dedicate to each college a diverse team headed by a senior officer.
3. Train team members in their roles, and include race and gender training on an ongoing basis.

4. Maintain a year-round presence at the college; don't just show up at recruitment time, when most likely the best candidates already have been snapped up anyway.
5. Evaluate the teams in terms of their success or failure in attracting women and people of color.

Here are some specific actions that recruitment teams can take:

1. Have formal and informal lunches and dinners with key students, faculty members, and administrators.
2. Seek out and develop relationships with various students clubs and professional associations; and don't forget those devoted to meeting the needs of returning, part-time and evening students.
3. Volunteer to personally give lectures and conduct classes, and/or recruit some suitable employees who are not on the team to help you out in this regard.
4. Support student activities, and provide financial or in-kind help so as to bolster the image of your company.
5. Provide year-round, ongoing internships for students, and get the jump on other companies by letting them begin in their senior year of high school.
6. Provide externships for students—short periods of time (a week to a month, usually during school breaks) spent working at a company on specific projects as a way of learning the ropes of your business.

Strategies to Recruit Seasoned Employees

Given today's ever-changing markets, companies can't afford to overlook the recruitment of experienced employees to fulfill particular needs or to fill higher-level positions. Here are some ways to recruit experienced women and people of color:

1. Develop contacts with stakeholders of diverse backgrounds.
2. Develop relationships with local and national religious, professional, political, and social organizations whose focus is on women and people of color.
3. Locate, and develop relationships with, recruitment firms dedicated to women and people of color.
4. Develop a recruitment directory that contains listings for minority and female search firms, colleges and universities, sororities and

fraternities, professional and political associations, community organizations, publications to advertise in, and vocational and technical schools.

5. Never bring up the issue of quotas. Be very careful about the issue of "qualified" candidates, and how it is brought up in conversation. This also applies to college recruits, especially people of color.

Notice that most of those foregoing tactics have less to do with money and benefits and more to do with building relationships.

What Are the Concerns of Women and People of Color?

Our conversations with women and people of color have told us plenty about what is important to them as they go about selecting a company to work for. Organizations truly committed to creating a constituent capitalization environment might do well to bear these concerns in mind.

1. The level of representation of women and people of color in senior positions.
2. The company's philosophy of, and commitment to, developing women and people of color, and whether managers are held to these.
3. The content, extent, and commitment to diversity and affirmative action.
4. How the company has handled charges of discrimination in the past.
5. How sensitive, aware, and comfortable interviewers are with candidates of backgrounds different from their own.
6. How honest, straightforward, and candid interviewers and recruiters are, during the recruitment process.
7. The extent to which the company keeps to the commitments it makes throughout the recruitment process.
8. How other women and people of color view the company.
9. The company's reputation in its community.
10. The company's involvement in and with its community.
11. The company's attitude with regard to the balance of work and personal life.

Notice, again, that the list talked about environment, atmosphere, relationships, commitments—not salary or 401(k)s.

Employee Retention, Work Design, and Minimizing Racism and Sexism

New, rapidly changing technologies; restructuring; downsizing; mergers and acquisitions; flattening—all of these are providing corporate managers with significant opportunities to restructure work. Unfortunately, few corporations are making the best of their opportunities. As one pair of researchers has written:

> One of the most common complaints about reengineering is that, while processes are properly redefined, new job responsibilities are either ill-defined or not defined at all. Employees are left confused. They respond by seeking new alliances, rather than focusing on working efficiently within the new environment. Is the problem in how jobs are defined? In part, yes. More likely, the problem lies in the difficulty in aligning job definitions with the newly defined processes and ways of working.[3]

Let's face it: Poorly designed jobs lead to unhappy employees, which in turn leads to increased conflict, subjective and therefore often erroneous evaluations, poor career development and planning. The intermediate result is a loss of trust and respect, as people feel they are not valued or being rewarded properly. Add in today's higher and higher levels of diversity, and too often the end result is people's perception that they are being treated unfairly as a result of their race or gender. In such an environment it is a daunting task to retain good employees once they've been recruited.

We have noted earlier how employees increasingly are expressing a lack of satisfaction with their jobs. Several reasons account for this, and explain why effectively designed work is becoming evermore vital to the long-term success of organizations. One of these is that the workforce is becoming more educated. Educated workers demand not only a good salary and job security, but also challenging, interesting, rewarding work. Another is the lack of loyalty that employees feel on the company's side; they want compensation for that lack of loyalty not only in dollars but in a chance to use and develop their skills. A third reason here is that in many industries the number of opportunities for promotion is declining. With the gradual disappearance of the traditional career ladder, employees are demanding a healthy, challenging work atmosphere at the very least. Finally, employees are troubled by their perceptions of unfair performance appraisals and a lack of training, development, and career planning. Proper work design is a key prerequisite for correcting these ills and keeping an optimal workforce challenged and yet relatively content.

The Key Elements of Properly Designed Work

If managers are to achieve employee retention through properly designed work, they must consciously acknowledge the very human dimensions of work. After all, work means far more than a paycheck to most people. At its best, work provides them with a sense of identity, self-esteem, and order. It satisfies their social need, the need to be part of a group and to carry on social interactions in furtherance of a common task. It gives them a sense of participation, by bringing them in to those decision-making processes that can have important outcomes for all stakeholders.

And of course, the opposite is also true. Work that is boring; that doesn't allow us to have any control over our own work environment; that excludes us from the decision-making processes and having a say as to overall corporate objectives; that saddles us with red tape, paperwork, insufficient resources, and micromanagement—all of that tends to breed workers who are alienated, powerless, unproductive, unhealthy, antisocial, and at times even violent. It also leads to charges of discrimination, as unhappy employees come to feel that their performance is being evaluated on the basis not of their work but of subjectively perceived factors such as race and gender.

Now let's take a close look at some of the key components of job design, ones that can help organizations to steer clear of potentially disastrous outcomes while still retaining their best employees.

Variety on the Job

One of the great benefits of the team approach is that it gives organizations the chance to turn bad jobs into better jobs. Particularly in a climate of reengineering, it enables team members to perform a variety of tasks rather than perform the same task over and over. It also allows them to draw upon a variety of skills and to spread out the dull and routine tasks among the members of the team. Researchers have pointed out, however, that this approach won't work if employees merely are given a greater number of boring tasks, or if they are assigned additional responsibilities without a corresponding increase in the *breadth* of their functions.

Some people in your organizations doubtless believe that women and people of color received their current positions solely on the basis of their race or gender, and such individuals are unlikely to provide women and people of color with jobs that feature variety. Thus, one key to solving the problems of race and gender is to ensure that the company has in place an effective, systematic method of matching up employee skills and abilities with a variety of tasks. Employees who are working at jobs that provide them with both variety and the chance to exercise new and different skills will expend their energies constructively, rather than brood about perceived discrimination.

Whole, Identifiable Jobs

And yet, if employees or teams perform only a portion of a whole job, how is their performance to be measured accurately? How can they get usable feedback from their job? The simple answer is that they can't, because it is the nature of fragmented or narrowly designed work to vary from day to day along with subjective determinants. And that means that employees' opportunities to make valuable contributions are limited, which in turn leads to job dissatisfaction, disengagement, antisocial behavior, and heightened perceptions of discrimination. Further, managers holding stereotypes or biases will intentionally or unintentionally deny women and people of color whole, definable jobs, and thus as evaluators be unable to provide objective job assessments.

Autonomy

Employees cannot be held accountable for a meaningful end result when they are not granted any real autonomy. It is unfortunate how often they are viewed as being unable or unwilling to make decisions, when in fact they are given no opportunity to do so. For the fact of the matter is that simply by empowering employees to make decisions, organizations can vastly boost team members' sense of responsibility and of ownership of the team's work product. So too, the quality of decisions can be greatly improved simply by increasing the amount of information that is made available to team members as they prepare to make them. And another great benefit of autonomy is that it puts decision-making power closer to the point at which operational problems occur—in most cases, the place where the company and its customers and/or outside stakeholders cross paths. To sum up: The organization that masters this aspect of work design will be forestalling the persistent complaint that women and people of color are not given the same power and authority as white men holding the same or similar positions.

Feedback

Another key component of high-quality work design is the ability of the job to provide employees with feedback on their performance, in addition to any feedback that coworkers, supervisors, customers, and stakeholders can provide. This component of work design permits employees to adjust their performance *before* formal performance evaluation and *before* failure can occur. And that means that providing feedback is a crucial way of minimizing discrimination complaints, when we recall that many women and people of color believe they have to perform better than whites to get ahead and that they are not evaluated fairly owing to their race and/or gender. To structure work in such a way that all employees get ongoing feedback from multiple sources is a crucial strategy for minimizing the ill effects of corporate racism and sexism.

An Integrated Management System

Properly designed work is not the sole maker of good jobs; however, it is simply the beginning, serving as the foundation of a larger management-development system that can reduce perceptions of discrimination by bringing a more systematic, rational approach to career development for all employees. Work design affects not only an employee's performance but her/his potential for advancement and the ability of both the corporation and she/he to meet the shifting terms of their mutual contract. Hence the vital importance of the relationship between work design and the features of an integrated management system, as that relationship has been outlined for you in Fig. 10.1. An integrated management system has the following features:

A. Work functions are designed or redesigned into functionally complete units containing consistent relationships. The design process is applied team by team, at all levels of the organization.

B. The power to act is then defined for the functions contained in each job. The power to act may be phased into the job according to a plan that identifies when the employee is ready.

C. The skills and knowledge needed to perform each set of functions/decisions will emerge during this process, and should be documented as they do so.

D. All of the above information is a prerequisite for the establishment of substantive, measurable objectives.

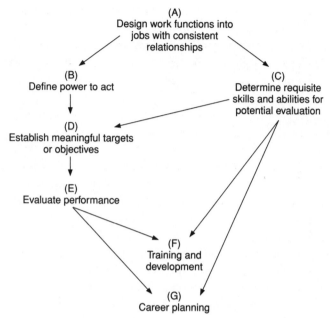

Figure 10.1 A Systematic Management-Development System

E. Said objectives are then used to evaluate performance.
F. Said objectives also are used to plan training and development programs.

The design of work at each layer of the organization (A) also is essential to determining whether the skills and abilities to be evaluated (C) reveal a potential for advancement. Unless this step is taken, the employee's gauged potential to perform at the next level will be based only upon performance at the current level or on the subjective assessments of managers at the next higher levels—many of whom landed in those jobs as a result of the Peter Principle. Training and development (F) can then be planned for those employees who have demonstrated a potential to perform at the next level (C), so that the employee's potential can be realized. Once these steps are in place, the foundation has been laid for a true career-planning process (G).

Conclusions

We believe that there are more than enough qualified women and people of color out there to fill any and all corporate positions at all levels. And we know that all managers will come to share that belief with us, if they will first rise to the challenge of developing and enacting systematic recruitment strategies that make the subjective evaluation of candidates a thing of the past. Quite simply, organizations need to face a number of realities, if they are to prosper in the global environment of the 21st century:

1. Our highly technical, service-oriented, global economy demands that corporations take a more active part in improving the educational system, so as to provide students with the skills that corporations eventually will draw upon and benefit from.
2. Regardless of how many competent women and people of color there are out there, companies will be severely limited in their ability to find them unless they employ diverse recruiters who can and indeed love to operate in a multicultural setting.
3. Companies must make use of multiple approaches to the measurement of skills and competencies, if they are to eliminate subjectivity and bias from their recruitment programs.
4. Companies must become actively involved in various groups and associations having large numbers of women and people of color as members.
5. Companies should make a point of using minority and women recruitment firms. White-male-dominated firms simply don't have the cultural skills needed to recruit large numbers of women and people of color. Indeed, most are worse than the corporations that hire them, when it comes to being race- and gender-sensitive.
6. Companies must define and utilize very specific criteria, as they go about measuring recruiters and the recruitment process.
7. Recruitment has more to do with relationship building and the corporate environment than it does with money, titles, and perks.
8. The presence within an organization of upbeat, highly valued employees will always be its best recruitment tool.

And of course, that last point reminds us that, even after competent employees have been recruited and hired, companies still must find ways of keeping them on. Job design is an important component of our holistic strategy for retaining women and people of color, particularly in a diverse, rapidly changing global economy characterized by massive changes in the structures of companies. For as we have noted, workers who are in thrall to boring, repetitive jobs that deny them any opportunity to make decisions, particularly at the point of contact with customers and other stakeholders, are more likely to be dissatisfied—and therefore to brood upon perceived acts of discrimination, and perhaps even bring charges. Therefore, if companies are going to eliminate subjectivity, enhance employee self-esteem, cut down on the number of charges of discrimination, and boost their bottom-line performance; they are going to have to give their employees at least these four things: a broader range of tasks that draw heavily on their skills and abilities; whole tasks, so that performance can be fairly evaluated; the autonomy to make many of their own decisions; and fair, systematic feedback on their performance.

11

Leadership in the Age of Racially/Sexually Charged Organizations

Introduction

One of the greatest difficulties associated with the implementation of a holistic, constituency capitalization approach to the solving of race- and gender-related problems in U.S. corporations is that it requires totally committed leaders. Although leadership on this issue has to come from all levels of the organization including frontline managers and so on, it must start at the top, with the board members and the senior officers. There is simply no hope of workplace racism and sexism ever being eradicated without the ongoing commitment of these individuals.

One of the first realities that corporations must address is the skills and abilities to be found at all levels of management. Most of us are aware that management has become the poster boy for everything that is wrong with corporate America, yet we hesitate to admit that managers—whether due to bigoted personal beliefs or to a lack of training in this area—can and do contribute greatly to creating a climate of racism and sexism in their companies. At the very least, many do not feel accountable for solving these problems; they have learned as if by rote the politically correct words to say, but few of them feel compelled to confront the issue head-on. These are not necessarily racist or sexist people. But when they say things like, "Our problems with racism and sexism are minor compared to those in other corporations," and insist that their corporations are race- and gender-blind, they are perpetuating a myth and thereby bringing discredit upon corporate America.

T. Teal, a Harvard University professor, has said that, given the way in which management has come to be equated with all that is wrong with organizations, it would be helpful to do some thinking about what management *is*. At the most basic level, a manager is someone who creates an environment that enables a group of people to get their jobs done. So at that most basic level, "people" are the critical component of effective management. And yet, when one calls to mind the typical types of qualifications and training programs for managers, people skills don't come in high on the list. In fact, when the first cost-cuts come to most organizations, it is training related to people skills that takes the hardest hit. And generally right at the top of the people-skills list is anything having to do with race and gender issues.

Thus, a big part of the problem here has to do with the way in which our managers are educated. In recent years, the MBA has become the management credential. But the focus of MBA programs is on such "core" areas as economics, finance, marketing, and strategic planning, rather than on those important people skills that managers will have to call upon if they are to create an environment that allows a group of people to get a job done. These people skills have to do with such major aspects of corporate life as hiring, promoting, mentoring, and supporting employees in a fair and equitable manner, regardless of their race or gender. And although technical expertise clearly is essential, it remains the case that many managers are unwilling or unable to develop the people expertise they need to manage a diverse group of employees. And who can blame them? Listen to Professor Teal on this subject. We feel that no one could have stated any better than he has done just what an almost impossible task we are asking "good managers" to perform:

> And still the troublesome fact is that mediocre management is the norm. This is not because some people are born without the management gene or because the wrong people get promoted or because the system can be manipulated—although all these things happen all the time. The overwhelmingly most common explanation is much simpler: capable management is so extraordinarily difficult that few people look good no matter how hard they try. Most of those lackluster managers we all complain about are doing their best to manage well.
>
> In one form or another, managing has become one of the world's most common jobs, and yet we make demands on managers that are nearly impossible to meet. For starters, we ask them to acquire a long list of more or less traditional management skills. We also demand that they master the management arts—strategy, persuasion, negotiation, writing, speaking, listening. In addition, we ask them to assume responsibility for organizational success, make a great deal of money, and share it generously. We also require them to demonstrate the qualities that define leadership, integrity and character. Finally, we insist that they should be our friends, mentors

or guardians, perpetually alert to our best interest. Practicing this common profession adequately, in other words, requires people to display on an everyday basis the combined skills of St. Peter, Peter the Great, and the Great Houdini. No wonder most managers seem to under-perform. One reason for the scarcity of managerial greatness is that in educating and training managers, we focus too much on technical and professional proficiencies and too little on character. . . . We're still in the Dark Ages when it comes to teaching people how to behave like great managers.[1]

And then recall that on top of all that, we now routinely expect our managers to free themselves and others from racism and sexism, and although racism as we know it has been around for at least 500 years and sexism for *thousands* of years. We are asking them to do this, even though most are personally ill equipped to do so, and do not have the organizational support they require in order to confront these issues effectively and efficiently. Finally, they don't really feel accountable, and in reality they usually are not *held* accountable.

Old Leaders versus New Leaders

As we have seen, the old style of leadership operates in a pyramid-shaped organization that reflects an antiquated command-and-control model. In order to effect their control, those at the top of the pyramid impose elaborate sets of protocols designed to manage the people and processes below them. The organization's success, in this model, has everything to do with its ability to design these protocols and to effectively implement them. And for employees, to get ahead under such a system means to move up the hierarchical ladder by conforming—by learning, modeling, and internalizing the behaviors of those above them. In such an environment there is little need for managers to develop their people skills, because the goal is not to build trust and respect but rather to command and control.

In a 1995 study, Christopher Lorenz showed us just how crippling are the effects of this style of leadership in today's team environment:

Top executives are forever preaching at their employees these days about the importance of better teamwork, whether in Total Quality Management, customer service, new product development, or re-engineering.

Yet most top managers, themselves, are either poor or disastrous team players. At worst, they act in a fragmented way, defending their own departmental, divisional, or personal interests like warring barons. At best, they are so like-minded that they suffer from "group think." Either way, their companies have difficulty making decisions, and are inept at executing the few which they do manage to make.[2]

We agree. But what we also have shown in this book is how the old bureaucratic model of management puts organizations at a substantial disadvantage in today's world, because its structure renders them incapable of adapting to diversity not just in the workforce but also among customers and key stakeholders. We showed in Chapter 7 how organizations have to alter their structure if they are going to effectively compete in this changing world. And in order to support that alteration, organizations are going to have to dedicate themselves not only to promoting effective leadership behaviors but also to holding their managers accountable for those behaviors.

In the postbureaucratic organization, the chief function of effective leaders and managers is to impart to employees a vision of the mutual benefits, both tangible and intangible, that are every day being attained through the combined efforts of one and all. And subservient to that chief function, they also: build relationships based upon trust and respect; explain to employees why the organizational vision is important to the individual, the team, and the larger community; motivate employees by empowering them to make this vision their own: help employees to break tasks down into actionable pieces of work, then hold them accountable for achieving the results; and behave in a manner that lets employees of all races and ethnicities and both genders know that they are the company's most valuable resource. The latter goal is reached when a manager finds that he/she is helping employees to balance work and family; to create a zero-tolerance environment; to get and give timely, ongoing feedback about performance and career development; and to fairly and equitably provide rewards and recognition suitable to a diverse workforce and a relatively "flat" organization.

The Survey Data on Leaders: Not a Pretty Picture

Over 25 years of conducting leadership/management surveys, we have found that most managers have received mixed reviews of their skills. Those reviews don't vary significantly with the race and/or gender of the critics, but they do by department, division, business unit, and level in the organization. Table 11.1 summarizes the findings of our 1995 survey; interestingly, these results do not differ appreciably from the findings in our 1978 and 1988 surveys.

Table 11.1
Survey Data on Managers and Their Skills, 1995

Opinions of Top Managers

Bad news often is passed upward. (Strongly Agree or Agree)	30%
Discipline is applied equally across the organization. (Strongly Agree or Agree)	33%
Information received from top management is straightforward and honest. (Strongly Agree or Agree)	43%
In my opinion, the organization as a whole is well managed. (Strongly Agree or Agree)	52%

Opinions of Other Managers

To what extent does your supervisor handle discipline fairly and constructively? (To a great extent or to some extent)	57%
To what extent does your supervisor enhance open communication? (To a great extent or to some extent)	63%
To what extent does your supervisor foster trust? (To a great extent or to some extent)	64%
To what extent is your supervisor usually open to suggestions or changes from employees? (To a great extent or to some extent)	65%
To what extent do you respect the supervisors in your department who are at the level above your immediate supervisor? (To a great extent or to some extent)	67%
To what extent does your supervisor encourage employees to come up with new and better ways of doing things? (To a great extent or to some extent)	67%
To what extent does your supervisor allow you to disagree without fear of retaliation? (To a great extent or to some extent)	68%
To what extent do you respect your immediate supervisor and his/her peers? (To a great extent or to some extent)	70%

Here are some typical employee comments to add flavor to the data:

> There is no effective communication and listening.
>
> *Black male, nonmanager*

Everyone is trying to cover their own butt.

White male, nonmanager

They talk down to you, like they know everything.

Black female, lower-level manager

I think they are scared of the fact that I'm a minority and coming up with good ideas.

Asian female, nonmanager

Deadbeat supervisors who have problems making decisions really damage morale and attempts at creativity.

Native American female, occupational

You don't use powerful thinking. You don't want to give anything to us—board gives everything to the top—they don't want to empower powerful people who may ask for incentives. I don't think the company cares about much except taking care of their own management people. People are left to feel expendable. Therefore, no one ever wants to stick their neck out. Don't want to be involved—just do your thing and get the hell out of here!

Hispanic male, middle-level manager

They talk down to you like they know everything. Not honest, and always trying to get in your personal life. No respect and no trust.

Black female, lower-level manager

My job performance and that of my co-workers could be greatly improved if my supervisor and my supervisor's supervisor were more receptive to employee ideas, concerns, and problem-solving strategies. Unfortunately, job performance is inhibited, not due to my inability or unwillingness, but to the supervisor's negligence—i.e. unwillingness to listen to employees, inadequate and incomplete instructions and training, and directive rather than cooperative work effort. Employees are uninformed, misinformed, and excluded from decision-making processes. This lack of communication, from the top down, leads to a lack of teamwork and a decrease in job effectiveness.

White female lower-level manager

Due to apathy in the past from supervisor and/or "the old boys' network," anger, frustration and disappointment in my positions was present.

White female, middle-level manager

> Management is not friendly since I returned from my maternity leave. Not happy with my sick leave to care for my baby.
> *White female, middle-level manager*

The data depicted in Table 11.1, and those remarks we have provided to accompany them, suggest that our leaders still have plenty of work to do. Indeed, they are sitting on a time bomb, because their lack of leadership proficiency can lead race and gender groups to perceive discrimination rather than just incompetent management. And the trend here is clear: The lower that employees are in the organization, the more likely they are to perceive management and leadership as being incompetent and ineffective. And since many of these lower-level positions are held by women and people of color, they are the ones more likely to look upon their managers as incompetent, particularly under a bureaucratic, command-and-control system. Then, looking around for some factor to help them explain this incompetence, they blame it on racism or sexism regardless of whether it is or not. Interestingly, employees at each level of the organization point to the higher level as being the source of the problem, so when we use the term *manager* we're referring to managers at *any* level, from the frontline supervisor of production workers to the board of directors that oversees the activities of corporate executives.

Competencies and Skills of Effective Leaders

Effective leaders share a core set of traits and behaviors. In this section we will take note of those we believe to be most important for firms that want to implement our holistic model for eliminating racism and sexism. While the mix of these characteristics certainly will vary from one leader to the next, any leader's effectiveness increases as he or she exhibits the most inclusive possible set of these characteristics:

1. *Leaders must understand themselves and their strengths and weaknesses.* Effective leaders and managers have a keen awareness of themselves, and above all their strengths and weaknesses. They nurture and develop their strengths and constantly work on their weaknesses.

2. *Leaders possess a good deal of emotional intelligence.* They are empathetic, and also vigilantly concerned about how their attitudes and behaviors impact others regardless of their level in the organization, their role, their race or gender. They are so highly empathetic, largely because they so clearly understand and highly value themselves.

3. *Leaders have a clearly defined set of values, based upon trust and respect.* They respect and value people's varied cultural backgrounds. They cherish honesty, openness, equity, and fairness as their key values. Since they do not have double standards, their behaviors match their values. In short, they are the models of excellence.

4. *Leaders recognize the crucial role that effective communication plays in life.* They recognize the complexities and difficulties of effectively communicating, and therefore highly esteem straight, honest, direct communication. They continuously work on their communication skills, bearing in mind the principles laid out in Chapter 9.

5. *Leaders understand the need for diversity, and continually champion it.* To effective leaders and managers, diversity is not just a business strategy but a way of life. They have a zero-tolerance policy as it relates to racism and sexism. Leaders and managers understand and recognize all forms of racism and sexism. They continuously work on their issues, and they develop strategies for their employees to work on their issues. Because of their high emotional intelligence skills, they are comfortable with diverse employees in all settings at work and at social functions not related to work. Leaders revere individual worth and achievement. Nonetheless, they place their day-to-day faith in *teams* of diverse and dedicated individuals.

6. *Leaders believe in continuous learning.* They learn from multiple sources, making certain that those sources are diverse in terms of race, gender, and ethnicity as well as other factors such as thinking style. They look upon their own and their employees' failures as constituting opportunities to learn and to grow. They look upon learning as a way of developing team strategies that will benefit all of the organization's various stakeholders.

7. *Leaders are proactive and future-oriented.* The best leaders look upon change as being a way of life. They not only meet change head-on, but in fact consciously try to foster it as a way of growing the business through the creation of better products and services for an ever-more-diverse customer base. They are risk-takers, and, by continually engendering trust and respect in those around them, they empower their employees to take risks as well. They are highly cognizant of people's inborn resistance to change, and are always seeking out new and compassionate ways of overcoming that resistance.

8. *Leaders believe in diverse teams, and know how to build them.* They believe in the efficiency of diverse teams versus individuals. They believe that building trust and respect among team members is crucial to team success. They know how to resolve conflicts.

9. *Leaders believe in two-way accountability.* It is easy for "leaders" to tell others what to do and to hold them accountable for the results. But *true* leaders also hold *themselves* accountable for results.

Some Examples of Effective Leadership

Now let's turn to some specific examples of effective leadership, primarily with regard to race and gender issues. The theme that will emerge from these brief profiles is that the battle against racism and sexism demands of its generals an ongoing commitment and a willingness to "walk and talk" through active personal involvement and full utilization of their company's resources.

Niagara Mohawk. Despite the fact their company has been confronted with some very difficult regulatory and financial issues, Bill Davis, Al Budny, and David Arrington of Niagara Mohawk have never lost sight of the importance of diversity as a business issue. Not only have they devoted much of their own time to diversity initiatives, but they have continued, despite the firm's financial condition, to fund diversity initiatives simply because they regard that as being not only the right thing to do but a business imperative. They are intimately involved in the construction of a performance accountability model that will change their organizational culture from a noncompetitive, conforming one to a competitive one that values and uses the talents of individuals of all races and both genders.

Walt Disney Attractions. Under the leadership of Judson Green, president of Walt Disney Attractions, this organization's leadership team has embarked on some diversity initiatives that have significantly increased the attendance of people of color at the company's theme parks. They have reached this goal by hiring people of color at middle- and upper-level management levels, by altering their previously homogeneous advertising, and by actively seeking out key stakeholders in communities dominated by people of color. Green has required his leadership team to attend diversity training sessions, and to be held accountable for its diversity efforts. In championing these efforts, he has spent considerable amounts of time grappling with race and gender issues as they exist not only in his organization but also he has made his own personal journey to ensure he is free of racism and sexism.

US West. Dick McCormick, chairman of US West, has been trying and succeeding for years now to solve the race and gender problems of his company and community. He also has been on a personal journey of discovery as to his own attitudes and approaches to race and gender issues, and is deeply committed to holding himself and his staff accountable for their attitudes and behaviors. He has supported and pioneered unique assessment tools, development programs, and training programs, as ways of effectively dealing with these issues. And to an ever greater extent, he has pushed his organization to develop products and services that will meet the needs of US West's diverse customer base.

American Express. As one of the highest-ranking blacks in all of corporate America, Ken Chenault, president of American Express, makes his every move under a microscope. Despite the growing disenchantment with diversity and affirmative action efforts in the United States, Ken has continued to champion them, for he sees the inarguable business reasons for eliminating sexism and racism. Thus, despite his packed schedule, Ken still finds time to serve as cochair of his company's Diversity Action Task Force, and he requires all of his senior executives to attend a two-day diversity training program. Even more remarkably, these initiatives did not commence with the upswing in Amex's fortunes in recent years; rather, they did so at that bleak time when the company's stock price had bottomed out and the company was losing market share. For Ken Chenault knew that the demographics of the United States were changing, and that global opportunities for his firm were ripening. Here is a leader who has done just what we have been advising you to do throughout this book: he decided that trust and respect among employees, customers, and stakeholders were key to his firm's being able to take advantage of the new trends.

Conclusions

Many of the problems that continue to plague corporate America today can be attributed to a sheer lack of effective leadership, especially when it comes to the divisive and emotional issues of racism and sexism. If they are going to be competitive in the 21st century, organizations have no choice but to seek out managers who are secure, healthy people, able to build up trust and respect among diverse employees and to envision win-win outcomes for all stakeholders. Such leaders, far from being afraid of change, will embrace it. They will firmly grasp the negative impact that racism and sexism are having on their companies, and will develop systematic strategies and ongoing programs to deal with them. And they will hold everyone, themselves above all, accountable.

Regardless of an organization's structure, if it does not have the proper leadership/management, it will not be as successful as it can and should be. In some cases, it will simply fail. Given all of the challenges faced by corporations in the 21st century with regard to employee, customer, and stakeholder issues, we believe that leadership/management development is a crucial component of our holistic model for solving race and gender problems. As Professor Teal has correctly noted, corporate America still has a long way to go if it is to develop and sustain effective leaders of people.

III

MANAGING RACE AND GENDER IN THE NEW MILLENNIUM

12

Minimizing Race and Gender Bias in Performance Appraisals and Career Development

I USED TO WORK at AT&T. Every two years or so, the company would institute a new performance-appraisal system. And every two years or so, employees were promised that *this* system would finally be providing us with the accurate, candid feedback we so craved.

It didn't.

My colleagues and I always were in agreement that the performance-appraisal system, whatever its retailored form, never worked because one key ingredient always was missing from it: the development of trust and respect between managers and the people who reported to them. And in the intervening years my firm's conclusions have only underpinned the belief that perceptions about performance appraisals get skewed on a race and/or gender basis simply because of the gap in communications about how employees really are doing. As we noted in an earlier chapter, one way to close this gap is to structure individual and team jobs so that the job itself provides some feedback. After all, if the cars coming off the production line all run, if the doors don't fall off and the paint doesn't peel, then the production team must be doing *something* right. If everyone has clearly defined responsibilities and objectives, and if the ways of measuring job performance have been jointly agreed to by employees, supervisors, and both internal and external customers, then performance evaluations are far more likely to be based on the job done rather than on subjective factors. Quite simply, if organizations are going to minimize racism and sexism and provide all employees with a fair and equitable appraisal of their performance, they must find and adopt performance-appraisal systems and procedures that are more objective and valid than the poor substitutes for them which they are using today.

Now, giving feedback is easy when it's positive. But when the feedback is going to be critical, many managers shy away from giving it. We don't think we're announcing anything new and startling when we maintain that providing constructive critical feedback is a crucial element in improving employee job performance. Feedback, both formal and informal, that is candid and ongoing lets employees know where they stand, and thus minimizes the damage to a firm caused by race and gender issues.

Dick Grote, author of *Discipline without Punishment,* has provided an excellent analysis of the common fact that many employees believe they are doing a good job simply because their supervisors do not tell them otherwise. Thus, when they expect a promotion because they are doing a good job, and they don't get it, they become confused and angry. In addition, Grote reminds us that a day of reckoning may come, when a company wants to dismiss an employee but can't because it lacks documentation of poor performance and because no one said anything or gave the employee a chance to improve. Can we then really blame that employee for thinking that race or gender were in play there? Who is really to be blamed when the employee sues, with all the negative publicity and dislocation that accompanies such suits?[1]

Is It Discrimination? Some Survey Data

Consistently over the past 25 years, our surveys have found that significant percentages of employees do not see their performance appraisals as being timely, objective, or providing them with useful developmental suggestions. Table 12.1 summarizes their responses to our 1995 surveys. Note that two out of five employees do not agree with *any* of these statements; only 50 percent would describe the overall quality of their supervisors' evaluation as being "excellent" or "good." We also have found that, in most cases, there are no significant differences in responses by race or gender, but that there are by level of the organization and part of the organization that the responding employee is from. At any rate, what emerges clearly here is that when employees are deprived of timely, objective, useful feedback, they inevitably will begin to feel that their poor evaluations have been a function of their race or gender, even when they are not. But sometimes they are. As we have noted earlier, a considerable body of evidence suggests that women and people of color are not evaluated fairly because of the widely held stereotyped belief that they "lack qualifications." And remember: 50 percent of whites believe that people of color hold their current positions because of their race.

Table 12.1
Perceptions of the Performance-appraisal Process

Percentage of respondents who strongly agree or agree

Question: To what extent do you agree or disagree with the following: My immediate supervisor provides me with:	
Useful development suggestions	44%
Useful feedback on my job performance	53%
Timely feedback on my job performance	58%
Objective feedback on my job performance	59%

Overall quality of supervisors' evaluations of job performance

Question: How would you rate the overall quality of your supervisor's evaluation of your job performance?	
Excellent	14%
Good	36%
Fair	31%
Poor	19%

As we have done in past chapters, we again provide some employee comments to help you put a face on the impersonal data provided in Table 12.1.

> We have lost many people due to negative attitudes about their evaluations, which have not been objective.
>
> *White male, lower-level manager*

> People don't want to tell their subordinates that they're not performing well.
>
> *Black male, lower-level manager*

> It is hard to know, since I get almost no feedback.
>
> *White female, lower-level manager*

> If you are a minority, forget it. The top ratings are saved for the white males.
>
> *Black male, lower-level manager*

> Until you have machines or computers monitoring performance, we will have what we have now: ignorant, timid supervisors rewarding favorites and discouraging the competent.
>
> *White female, lower-level manager*

Our supervisor avoids providing performance reviews. She never has time.

Hispanic female, lower-level manager

What performance review? Are you kidding?

White female, occupational

The system stinks!

White female, lower-level manager

My supervisor has a problem with my accent. She gives me low ratings based on her stereotypes.

Asian male, lower-level manager

It's awful, ridiculous. It's useless. Why do it?

Hispanic male, occupational

They would rate it as lousy, horrible, disgraceful. They only count what you do wrong, not what you do right.

Black female, lower-level manager

No matter how good you are, whites don't see minorities as competent.

Black male, middle-level manager

Clearly, some employees attribute the perceived low quality of their performance appraisals to race and gender, when it could just as easily be the result of those plain old poor management or appraisal processes that, as one survey respondent put it, "stinks."

So let's turn now to some strategies that companies can adopt to fix their performance-appraisal process.

Performance Appraisal That Forestalls Discrimination

Before we begin to talk specifics, it's important that we note that formal performance appraisals are used for two purposes: *development* and *evaluation*. Appraisals used for development give employees feedback and help them to improve their performance on their current job. Appraisals used for evaluation help to determine compensation. Most corporations believe that by linking performance evaluations to compensation, they can motivate employees to change their behaviors and become better performers.

We take a very different view. We believe that the chief use to which performance appraisals should be put is to provide feedback to employeees and teams about how well they are meeting their current objectives and how they can better meet both their current and their future objectives. Appraisal should not be a place where decisions about advancement are made; that is a more complicated and detailed task, one that should fall under the rubric of career planning, counseling, and development, the subject of a later section in this chapter. And yet far too often, the issues of *performance* and *potential* are combined in the appraiser's mind, and thereby confused.

In addition, we have a major problem with the idea of using performance appraisals as a way of measuring the contribution of individuals to their teams and thereby of determining compensation. As we will be seeing in a later chapter, we believe—and employees are telling us—that the power of money as a motivating factor has been overrated, and does in fact have its limits. What seems to outweigh money are such informal rewards as the timely word of praise, a mere "thank you," with regard to a job well done.

We also believe that companies absolutely must stay away from "forced distribution" systems—the kind of appraisal system in which 10 percent (and only 10 percent) of employees are allowed to be rated outstanding, 15 percent excellent, 65 percent average, and 10 percent below average. Such a system tells the vast majority of the workforce that they're not cutting it—hardly an inspiring motivational message! In fact, this forced-distribution system has gotten some companies into trouble, because what has emerged out of many lawsuits is that women and people of color are not proportionately represented in the top two categories. In sum, forced distribution creates a lose-lose rather than a win-win outcome.

Before we turn to our discussion of some of the key elements of a performance-appraisal process that works, we'd like to take this opportunity to quickly plug 360-degree feedback. Many companies say that they have a 360-degree performance evaluation process, but really they don't, because they're still leaving *customers* out of the loop. But customers are an absolutely crucial component of the process; it is *their* satisfaction—or dissatisfaction—with employee performance that the company should care most about. The next two most important sources of feedback should be the direct reports, followed by peer review. There are numerous methods to receive the formal feedback, such as questioning focus groups, and interviews and informals, such as daily ongoing feedback. The supervisor's primary role in the 360-degree-feedback process, is to work with the direct report in collecting and evaluating the inputs from these multiple sources, and in jointly coming to a decision as to an employee's performance. But don't get us wrong: We don't believe in anonymous input. Employees can't take steps to remedy their deficiencies when they don't know where the criticism is coming from. Anonymous feedback, we believe, is entirely inconsistent with trust and respect.

The use of 360-degree performance appraisals brings with it at least the following three benefits:

1. They can help organizations to vastly decrease the subjectivity of the evaluation process. That is important for women and people of color above all, as it is they who often are victimized by such subjectivity.

2. Employees are less likely to dismiss feedback when they are getting it from multiple sources. If a manager says to an employee, "You need to work on your interpersonal skills," the employee can blow that off as being merely the manager's own and undoubtedly flawed perception. But if everyone—from customers, to team members, to the clerk in accounting, to the cleaning crew—has a problem with this employee's interpersonal skills . . . well, the employee is more likely to conclude, "I seem to have a problem with my interpersonal skills."

3. A final benefit associated with 360-degree feedback is that it greatly reduces fear. In today's climate of more and more diversity and publicity about discrimination suits, increasing numbers of managers of all races and both genders are simply afraid to give performance appraisals. By getting the employee to actively engage with the performance-appraisal inputs and evaluations, and by getting those inputs from various sources, including customers, the manager can repose greater confidence in the validity of his or her judgments. There is, indeed, strength in numbers.

The following, then, are some of the key characteristics of any performance-appraisal system that effectively diminish the reality/perception of race and gender bias.

Timely Feedback

Performance appraisals should be ongoing, rather than a mere quarterly or annual rite. Of course, you may be wondering how you will ever get your other work done, if you're spending all that time giving performance appraisals. Two responses come to mind.

First, the mere fact that a job has been properly structured will give employees and teams clear feedback about how they are doing. For example, let's say that each member of a team is responsible for a specific, identifiable section of a market analysis report that is due on a specified date. If the report is submitted on time—and if it isn't bounced right back to the team for rework, owing to flaws—then the team can be confident it has done its task well; no formal pronouncements of any kind are needed on the matter, because responsibilities have been clearly defined. Second, much of the sort of performance appraisal we're talking about here should be informal, and come from multiple sources. No manager should be so busy that a simple "Thanks!" or "Great job!" (or if need be, "What's up with that report, Paige?") is perceived as cutting into his/her time unduly.

Too often, untimely performance feedback catches an employee off guard, and leads her/him to wonder why the issues in question weren't brought to her/his attention sooner. Think about it: You learn at a six-month review that you've been doing something wrong . . . for six months! Why, you quite naturally wonder, weren't you told about this, say, five months ago? And as that question begins to echo endlessly in your brain, paranoia sets in and you begin to wonder whether this critical piece of feedback wasn't motivated by the subjective factor of race and/or gender.

Effective Feedback

We have already suggested sharpened communication skills, and 360-degree feedback, as being two good tools to be used in providing feedback that the employee can really use and benefit from. But also remember please that feedback must be specific to the performance issue, not the person. There's a big difference between saying to a customer-service rep, "You didn't handle that customer problem effectively, Sally. How shall we approach the next similar customer problem?" and "What's wrong with you, John? I never want to hear you get hysterical like that with a customer again!" But nonetheless, effective feedback is straightforward and direct. Feedback that starts with positives, moves on to negatives, and then quickly returns to positives, however kindly intended that approach may be, tends to leave the employee feeling confused as to both *what* was really said, and *why* it was said.

Grote notes that many managers employ scare tactics, and punitive lectures. And yet, "The goals are to solve the problem and to maintain a good relationship with the individual. Traditional punitive reprimands work well in solving the problem, but certainly don't enhance relationships. We can punish people into compliance, but not into commitment."[2] By failing to foster trust and respect, such an approach can lead directly to charges of racial and/or sexual harassment.

A Few Developmental Suggestions

Our data suggest that managers are long on criticism, short on developmental suggestions. Of course, all of us are sensitive to criticism. But in diverse environments that sensitivity, when combined with an absence of developmental suggestions—"Here's what you can do to correct this deficiency, Elizabeth"—can quickly turn into perceptions of racism and sexism. That's why it is so critical that all suggestions arise out of 360-degree feedback, since feedback from multiple sources is more likely to (a) be fair and accurate and (b) provide suggestions that the direct supervisor might not have considered on his/her own. And remember that developmental suggestions should always be turned into specific action-steps within specified time frames.

Ownership and Responsibility

It is the duty of every employee, regardless of race or gender, to *seek out* objective, timely feedback. Feedback can and should be more than just a managerial responsibility at year's end.

Consistency

When the EEOC or a state civil rights commission is investigating a discrimination claim, one of the first questions it usually asks is whether there is any other employee who has similar performance deficiencies but has not received a similar evaluation. Thus it makes perfect sense that all managers should ask themselves that same question before they give a negative evaluation, and yet few do so. Taking that step on its own is unlikely to make a manager claim-proof, however. How come? Because managers who do so are likely to ensure consistency only with their own direct reports. But employees who challenge their appraisals often compare themselves not just with their immediate peers but also with employees who are performing similar tasks for other managers. And then, if she/he sees evidence of disparate treatment, the employee may have a basis for a discrimination claim. Remember managers can protect themselves from discrimination charges by building trust and respect and by having honest, open direct candid ongoing communications with their direct reports.

Minimizing Racism and Sexism through Career Planning, Counseling, and Development

Most of corporate America has yet to formalize the career-planning process, although it should be seen as a natural outgrowth of the performance-appraisal process. Managers tend to handle it instead in an informal manner, often relying on the old-boy network as a conduit that can move employees into key lateral job assignments or to higher-level positions. In a true meritocracy, such an informal system might work well enough; as things actually stand, however, such a system is haphazard at best and provides significant advantages to the white males who control that aforementioned network. The greatest boon brought by a more formal approach to career planning, counseling, and development is that it cuts back the tendency of that informal network to select for advancement those employees who entirely resemble its current members. Yet another is that such an approach helps employees to align their career expectations with reality, thereby reducing disappointment and hence the tendency to rationalize that disappointment in terms of discrimination.

Let us be clear, however, about the fact that while the aforementioned really are the two great benefits of career planning, counseling, and development, their primary *purpose* is *not* to help employees get some grip on their potential for advancement. Rather, it is to help them realistically assess their strengths and weaknesses and to develop strategies for overcoming the weaknesses while capitalizing on the strengths. A secondary purpose is to help employees contribute fully to the enterprise and to have realistic, obtainable career objectives.

We have seen in Chapter 3 how the downsizings and flattenings of the last decade have reduced the number of potential promotions, even as the number of people competing for those promotions has continued to grow. The result is that employees are likely to have to remain at their current level longer, thus creating fertile ground in which perceptions of race or gender discrimination are all too likely to grow. Our point here is that career counseling and development have to be focused not so much on advancement as on the generation of opportunities for employees to acquire the new skills and abilities associated with a variety of positions via lateral moves, temporary assignments, and/or job rotations. Quite simply, those career planning programs in downsized organizations that are not changing their focus from advancement to development, are mere exercises in futility.

Our Data: Career Planning, Counseling, and Development in Trouble

In all of our studies, the human resources area that employees consistently have rated the lowest has been career planning, counseling, and development. Few companies even have such programs in place, relying instead on the advice and discretion of their managers. And because, as we have just seen, the average manager is all too likely to extend developmental opportunities to those whom he/she perceives as being "just like me," women and people of color are all too likely to conclude that they are not being counseled and developed because of their race and/or gender. Unfortunately, even those firms that do have formal systems in place often fail to train their managers and employees in the implementation of them, and fail to hold managers accountable for the counseling and developing of all employees. The result of this mishmash is anger, frustration, and hostility, as employees see their advancement or lateral job assignment blocked, fail to take into account the part played in the situation by their own weaknesses and shortcomings, and end up blaming their lack of progress on race and/or gender discrimination.

Table 12.2 summarizes data drawn from our 1995 studies. Once again, we see few significant differences emerging out of race and gender, but many from level in the organization, and department. Overall, the data strongly suggest that far too few employees are receiving systematic career planning, counseling, and development. And even those "lucky" few don't rate their systems very highly!

Table 12.2
Career Planning and Development

To what extent does your supervisor give you useful feedback concerning your potential for advancement? (To a great extent or to some extent)	30%
Do you have a personal development plan with your company? (Yes)	35%
If yes, your personal development plan is a personal one you have developed for yourself.	69%
To what extent do you believe that your personal development plan at your company has been carried out? (To a great extent or to some extent)	58%
To what extent do you believe that you need assistance in developing a personal development plan? (To a great extent or to some extent)	49%

Do you often have personal career development planning discussions with your supervisor? (At least once a year)	38%
How useful are your personal development discussions with your supervisor? (Very useful or useful)	39%

A number of possible explanations have emerged out of our discussions with focus groups and our one-on-one interviews with managers, as to why managers and companies fail to help employees with career development:

1. The company simply has no career development strategy.
2. There is no time available, or such at least is the perception on management's part.
3. Managers have no real training or skills in the area of career planning.
4. Managers are not evaluated or rewarded, with regard to their level of competence in assisting employees with their career development plans.
5. Employees have been given no training, and therefore have little or no understanding of their roles and responsibilities when it comes to managing their careers.
6. Career development is viewed as being entirely up to the employee, not the manager or the company.

Let's look at some of the comments employees have shared with us on this important topic.

> This company does not know what career planning is, and they don't care.
>
> *Native American male, lower-level manager*

> There really isn't any clear picture of any career planning in my department.
>
> *Asian male, occupational*

> It is very frustrating to have a career plan, and no direction from management on what you need to do to develop yourself for the future.
>
> *Black male, lower-level manager*

> There [are] no career choices at this company. There is no goal direction for the current generation of workers.
>
> *White male, occupational*

Your asking questions about career counseling is not the real world!

Black male, middle-level manager

Career development and advancement at this company is a joke.

White male, middle-level manager

I have had to fight to be allowed to take a class to advance myself. Policy here is inconsistent, and changes to suit the supervisor.

White female, lower-level management

Most jobs here are filled by preselected persons.

Black male, lower-level manager

My supervisor doesn't care about career development.

White female, occupational

Career planning and development, for the majority of employees, is nothing other than nonexistent at our company.

White female, occupational

Career planning discussion? My supervisor just says, "you should feel lucky to have a job." She has made comments like that for three years.

White female, lower-level manager

Given comments like those, it's no wonder that lots of employees are just plain fed up, and that corporations are hunkering down under the barrage of an increasing number of discrimination suits related to lack of advancement.

A Career Planning Model to Minimize Racism and Sexism

The effective career planning, counseling, and development system is that which focuses on helping employees to gain a clear vision of what their realistic career development goals should be. To that end, corporations must (a) institute training programs that will provide their managers with effective and bias-free tools and approaches to guiding employees through the process, and (b) hold those managers accountable for results. Parallel counseling sessions held with each direct report should seek to enhance his/her understanding of the programs, and should stress his/her individual responsibility for making the process work.

In the accompanying box you will find the eight steps that make up our career planning and counseling model.

Eight Steps toward Effective Career Planning and Counseling

1. Train managers and direct reports both in the programs and in their roles and responsibilities with regard to them.
2. Inventory the employee's educational background, work experiences, job knowledge, and performance.
3. Conduct the sort of self-analysis discussed back in Chapter 6. In this step, employees obtain a more realistic understanding of who they are, of their norms, values, and beliefs and their strengths and weaknesses. Three-hundred-and-sixty-degree inputs, and a variety of evaluation methods, must be used.
4. Listen carefully and compassionately to the career goals and aspirations of the employee.
5. Clarify which of those personal goals are achievable and which most likely are not, given the employee's abilities and aptitudes and what is available in the company.
6. Develop a systematic overall action plan with the direct report.
7. Assess the implementation of the plan.
8. Hold managers accountable for the successful implementation of the plan.

Career Centers

Several processes and tools must be in place, before employees can be assisted with their career development. And because an increasing number of companies are recognizing that most managers are ill equipped to guide employees through the process, many are choosing to either send their employees to external career centers or to establish career centers of their own. These centers are staffed with professional career counselors, trained to help employees get a good conceptual grip on their strengths and weaknesses and to set realistic yet challenging career goals.

Such centers prove their usefulness to corporations by reinforcing the importance of having a learning and development culture; by boosting employee retention; by providing coaching support for employees and their managers; and by helping employees to apply for internal positions and, when appropriate, external ones.

3M is a good example of a company that has chosen to systematize career planning, counseling, and development. Its career resources department has three sections: career transition, career information systems, and career development. The career transition section was developed in response to constant organizational changes. Its main purpose is to help employees and managers to adapt to such changes. For example, at times of downsizing employees are counseled and helped with their job-search techniques and their networking. The career information systems section helps managers to identify internal candidates who are qualified for job openings. It also serves as a center for job postings.

At the core of 3M's career resources department, however, is the career development section. This helps employees to assess their strengths and weaknesses by means of various testing methods and assessment procedures, as well as of seminars and workshops. Before undergoing any training or utilizing any of the section's resources, employees attend a two-hour orientation session in order to familiarize them with those resources. A key component of the program is the career directions workshop, at which employees can learn more about their culture, personality type, interests, and the like. Employees are taught to look upon their current job as a stepping-stone toward their next move. Other workshops deal with such matters as interviewing skills and resumé writing, and an extensive library has innumerable resources that can be of use in career planning.

Assessment Centers

Another component of a rational career development program is the assessment center, which may or may not be part of the company's career center. As defined by Douglas W. Bray, who in fact developed the concept, an assessment center is a device "to provide an objective off-the-job evaluation of developed abilities, potential, strengths and weaknesses, and motivation." This type of evaluation is conducted

> through the observation of behavior in a variety of standardized performance situations, the rating of that behavior on a number of predetermined dimensions, the drawing of conclusions concerning potential for certain levels and types of work, and the diagnosis of development needs.[3]

Typical assessment-center techniques include interviews, in-basket and group exercises, paper-and-pencil tests of ability and personality, and projective personality tests. Assessment center staff is usually made up of managers who are one or two levels above the employee, although some companies make use of trained professionals. Upon completion of the assessment procedure, staff members meet to discuss each candidate and to evaluate his or her performance. They then prepare a report that can be used in placement or promotion, or for early identification of potential and development.

Although we do support the use of assessment centers, we want to make it clear that racial or gender bias can exist both in the assessment process criteria and in the assessors themselves. Then too, an assessment center can too easily become a kind of self-fulfilling prophet. In other words, let's say a company is looking (as it usually is) for certain characteristics in its "ideal" employee. The assessors find those characteristics in some aspirants, and label those people "promotable." Because they have been so labeled, those people are in fact promoted. Such a self-fulfilling prophecy is simply a potent form of bias, one that may or may not have a racial/gender component.

Another point we want to make here has to do with the ways in which assessment centers are used. When Bray talks about the purpose of assessment centers he tends to speak solely about benefits and aids that come to employers by maximally utilizing the managerial force as a whole. But as we see it, an equally vital role for assessment centers is to familiarize employees with their own potentials and limitations. Ideally (although this ideal is never realized in many companies) the process should not send employees back to their jobs simply feeling that their experience has been a negative one, particularly in the sense that their career with their present company has dead-ended. Rather, they should walk away glowing with a sense of learning and growth. The procedure should identify areas in which improvement is needed, offer specific techniques for achieving such improvement, and provide the employee with the option of requesting reassessment at some specified time in the future. Furthermore, employees should be reassured that other techniques are being employed in assessing their potential, besides this one-time assessment.

Also key here is for companies to have in place a succession planning system, one that ensures that all employees are being fairly and accurately evaluated. We have noticed over the years that most informal systems tend to exclude many capable employees, especially people of color and women, and we believe that mentoring must therefore be a key part of every succession planning system. By requiring managers to be mentors of a diverse group of people, and by holding them accountable for their mentees' successes and failures, companies can ensure that those who all too often have been left out of succession lists are included therein. Now let's take a closer look at the mentoring process.

Mentoring Programs

If organizations are to break the cement ceiling, and ensure that career planning, counseling, and development are not exercises in futility for women and people of color, they simply must establish mentoring programs. In her book *The New Leaders*, Ann Morrison makes a case for the idea that a lack of mentors and role models constitutes a major barrier to the advancement of women and people of color. She writes:

> Mentoring programs have proven highly beneficial in a number of diversity efforts. Senior managers are assigned to work with more junior employees, who can benefit from additional coaching and attention. These programs also encourage dialogues about diversity issues; these conversations can go a long way toward changing unconscious stereotypes and increasing comfort levels around differences.[4]

It's true that a few U.S. corporations did inaugurate mentoring programs after the landmark AT&T discrimination suit in 1973. And yet it was not until the late 1980s and the 1990s that they became a standard feature of around 40 percent of U.S. corporations.

The following two mentoring programs could easily serve as models for the one you will be instrumental in instituting at your organization.

The Bank of Montreal. The general objective of the mentoring program at the Bank of Montreal is to bring about cultural changes within the bank and to create career-enhancing opportunities that lower barriers hitherto blocking the full realization of employees' potentials. Specifically, the objectives are to

- *Increase dialogue and networking interactions.*
- *Increase the visibility of advisees in the eyes of executive officers.*
- *Provide professional development and insight into leadership styles.*
- *Boost the level, and upgrade the quality, of organizational communications.*
- *Strengthen advisor knowledge and development by means of discussion of ideas, values, concepts, and realities.*
- *Assess differing mentoring styles, specifically vis-à-vis cross-gender matches.*[5]

Managers are involved in defining the key characteristics of the program. They are thoroughly oriented to the program, and play key roles at specific stages. Employees attend day-long sessions designed to (1) help them understand the program's goals and structure; (2) help them review preprogram feedback, and prepare development plans to be worked on with their mentor and manager; and (3) prepare them for a new relationship with their mentor. An essential aspect of the process is that it allows the bank to get ongoing feedback about the program, which in turn allows it to measure it and to modify it where necessary. From the bank's perspective, the program has been a real success.

Menttium 100.   A unique mentoring program, known as Menttium 100, is the brainchild of a coalition of companies such as Charles Schwab, IBM, and Genentech. These companies have worked together in key cities to sponsor a one-year mentoring experience that matches up seasoned professional women with top-level executives from outside their organizations. It was developed as a noncompetitive forum offering participants (a) a peer network, (b) one-on-one relationships with senior-level mentors, and (c) monthly seminars on critical management and business issues. Menttium enforces a strict nonrecruiting clause, in order to protect its participating organizations from competitors.

Because the participants come from different companies, they tend to speak openly about their professional and personal challenges. "The confidentiality of a cross-company relationship is very productive," says Lisa Giarretto, managing director of Menttium's San Francisco program, "especially for the mentors, who have the opportunity to find out what high-potential women face and ask questions they couldn't ask people in their own group."[6]

Regardless of particular programs and processes, it is important that accountability be built in to any mentoring process. Over 90 percent of the employees we have surveyed over the years have agreed that managers should be evaluated, in part, with regard to how well they utilize and develop the people who work for them; 80 percent believe that managers should be rewarded, in part, on the basis of that criterion. Given that high level of support for this key component of the mentoring process, why isn't it being implemented? One answer may be that top-level management is unskilled in this area; another, a failure to recognize that this practice is essential to improving the corporate bottom line and to minimizing racism and sexism as employees are developed.

Conclusions

No feature of our holistic model for solving the problems associated with race and gender is more central than that of having in place performance-appraisal systems that provide employees with timely, objective, and effective feedback. And yet our data consistently show that nearly half of the employees we have surveyed cast a jaundiced eye on their firms' performance-appraisal systems. These systems aren't working not only because of a lack of trust and respect, but because managers and employees aren't routinely trained to implement them and managers aren't held accountable for their results. One way to improve these systems is to get rid of the old hierarchical feedback system and instead make use of 360-degree feedback from customers, peers, and subordinates. Another is to train both employees and managers in how to bring about objective, useful, timely performance appraisals. They must be taught to see that such a partnering process, built upon trust and respect, can do much to minimize racism and sexism in performance appraisals.

A crucial part of the feedback process is career planning, counseling, and development, as these have the potential to create motivated employees who care deeply about the success of themselves, their teams, and the company. And yet we have seen that still not enough firms sponsor career planning, counseling, and development, and that those which do, do so in a haphazard way. Too often they rely upon an informal good-old-boy network rather than upon formal systems that have a capacity to really eliminate bias. Such formal systems instill in managers and employees a sense of their duty to make the system work, and just as importantly, provide employees with opportunities for self-analysis and reasonable grounds for hope in their futures. An action plan is developed, and managers are held accountable for implementing that plan.

Among the tools that corporations can employ as they seek to put career planning, counseling, and development on a more rational footing are career centers, assessment centers, and formal mentoring programs. The great benefit of all of these is that they ensure that career planning, counseling, and development are extended to all employees, not just to those who have found their way into the "right" informal network or have been formally identified as having high potential. And by using these programs to build relationships based upon trust and respect rather than stereotypes and fear, companies can minimize perceptions of bias along the way. Which in turn means that, when combined with fair performance-appraisal systems, effective career planning can serve to greatly cut down on the number of charges of discrimination brought against a company.

13

Race, Gender, and Rewards: How to Reward to Elicit Maximum Performance

Introduction

Much of the race- and gender-related conflict taking place in corporate America today has some relation to the question of who is, and should be, receiving the greatest rewards for their contributions. As we have noted, no corporation in the world has on hand enough formal rewards to meet the expectations of all its employees. Especially in an era of downsizing and delayering, the traditional two-years-and-then-up, career-ladder ascent, with its attendant pay increases, is almost entirely a thing of the past.

As we will see, a large majority of the employees who have participated in our studies believe that their contributions exceed their rewards—that they are not being recognized for the work they believe they are doing. Such a gap inevitably leads many to believe that they are not being treated fairly on account of their race or gender, when in truth many companies are lacking in both effective, objective evaluation processes and in enough formal rewards in the shape of money, promotions, etc. to go around. *Informal* rewards, however, should never be a resource issue. Companies have or can create more than enough informal rewards to meet their employees' need for proper recognition. Such rewards all too often do become an issue, however, simply because many companies and their managers fail to appreciate the importance of, and are not skilled in the distribution of, informal rewards.

Now, if corporate America is serious about wanting to minimize the amount of racism and sexism it can tolerate, it must take a serious look at how it rewards and recognizes employees. For employees who do not feel that they are being rewarded and recognized do not feel valued. And they are then less likely to be creative, productive, and motivated, because they are obsessed with how they are being treated, rather than fully engaged by their jobs. They never achieve excellence in the area of customer service, because they're angry and frustrated. They don't function well in teams, because they see themselves as being locked in bitter competition with their peers for the few scraps of rewards that are thrown down to them by management. As they fight for those scraps and often fail to get them, they begin to conclude that they are the victims of race and gender discrimination.

The Power of Money to Motivate

It's important to recognize that all of us value different things. Our varying cultural backgrounds, in particular, do much to determine the value we place on rewards and recognition, and the types of these that mean something to us. Thus in order to make employees feel valued, corporations have to develop a wide variety of rewards and ways of recognizing employee achievement—all of them based upon trust and respect. Only in an environment of trust and respect can corporations avoid being charged with favoritism and discrimination, when they reward people differently but fairly.

Traditionally, money has been used as the chief motivator, the most tangible item of value that rewards employees for work: "Do this job, and I'll give you money; do this job *better,* and I'll give you *more* money." And yet far too many corporations, in our opinion, place too high a value on money as a rewarder and motivator of human beings. Up to a certain level, money is clearly a motivator, but beyond that level it is not. One outspoken critic of the inveterate habit of using money to motivate is Alfie Kohn, author of *Punished by Rewards.* Kohn suggests that the use of money as a lever to pry better performance out of employees is both exploitative and counterproductive: "The long and the short of it is, if I cut your salary in half it would piss you off. But if I double your salary, it wouldn't make you any more qualified, motivated or inclined to do a good job."[1] By the same token, corporations place too much emphasis on the power of promotions to motivate. This is especially the case in our own era, as the crush of baby boomers just now entering their peak income-earning years, combined with changes in the structural makeup of U.S. corporations over the past decade or so, is further draining promotions of their ability to motivate.

Several research studies have borne these conclusions out. In a study of 1500 employees, Gerald Graham, professor of management at Wichita State University, has confirmed that money is not a top motivator. Rather, out of the 65 potential incentives which he evaluated, Graham found that personalized, instant recognition from managers is the greatest employee incentive—and this despite the fact that 58 percent of employees reported that they seldom, if ever, receive such recognition! Coming in second on Graham's list was a letter of praise for good performance, written by a manager. In another study, the National Study of the Changing Workforce conducted by the Families and Work Institute of New York in 1994, "open communications" was ranked as the top motivator, followed by a better balance between work and family life and more effective supervisors. Money and advancement came in far down the list. And Robert Half International, a recruiting company, recently reported that the number-one reason employees give for leaving companies is a lack of praise and recognition, not a desire for more money.[2]

Survey Data about Rewards and Recognition

The data we have been compiling over the years very much confirms those above-stated findings. The most frequently cited reasons that employees gave us for why they would take a new job were "more interesting and challenging work," "better career opportunities," and "more supportive managers." And our open-ended survey questions also show that what tends to motivate the majority of workers are intangibles such as being appreciated for a job well done, thank-yous, being kept informed, having a say with regard to issues that affect them, and having an empathetic manager who takes the time to listen to their cares and beefs.

Please take a close look at our 1995 data, as it has been summarized in Table 13.1. Other analyses not shown in the table showed that there are few significant differences by race and gender, but significant differences by level in the organization and by department. These data, particularly when buttressed by the accompanying employee comments, show that three out of five employees say that their formal and informal rewards do not match the contributions they believe themselves to be making to their companies.

Table 13.1

Survey Data about Rewards and Recognition

Formal Rewards:

To what extent have the formal rewards (money, promotions, etc.) you have received been what you deserved, considering your performance and contributions?	
Rewards Greatly Exceed My Contribution	2%
Rewards Somewhat Exceed My Contribution	7%
Rewards Equal My Contribution	30%
My Contribution Somewhat Exceeds My Rewards	33%
My Contribution Greatly Exceeds My Rewards	28%

Informal Rewards:

To what extent have the informal rewards (praise, recognition) you have received in your department been what you deserved, considering your performance and contributions?	
Rewards Greatly Exceed My Contribution	1%
Rewards Somewhat Exceed My Contribution	5%
Rewards Equal My Contribution	32%
My Contribution Somewhat Exceeds My Rewards	36%
My Contribution Greatly Exceeds My Rewards	24%

Employees' Perceptions About How Their Company Values Them:

To what extent do you believe your company values you as an employee?	
To a Great Extent	13%
To Some Extent	38%
To a Small Extent	36%
Not at All	14%

The following are just a few of the employees' comments on this topic:

> It seems ridiculous to me that the company only seems to recognize its employees when they have sacrificed personal and family time for this institution.
>
> *White female, occupational*

> I've hit the glass ceiling; I have the respect, power and opportunity to do work related to higher positions, but never have the opportunity to receive pay, promotion, or recognition for it. Also,

workload does not really compromise quality of work, but it is taking a terrible physical toll on me.

White female, middle-level manager

If you are white, you are rewarded. If you are black, forget it.

African American female, lower-level manager

This year my supervisor recommended a raise. The department director approved. The level above took back a significant portion, to reward others. How is this merit?

African American male, lower-level manager

There are no rewards, just a job!

Asian male, occupational

White females get the rewards. We minority women are at the low end of the totem pole.

African American female, lower-level manager

I keep hearing, "If you don't like it, there are 10,000 people waiting for your job."

Hispanic male, occupational

My supervisor's personal traits interfere with fairness.

White female, occupational

Many at the VP and above levels are so far removed from reality that it is difficult for them to recognize who is performing to a level and who is not. Form is often recognized before substance.

White male, middle-level manager

A person does not need patches, pictures, luncheons, just thanks for a job well done.

White male, occupational

I've been told several times by my supervisor that I can be replaced.

White male, occupational

Minorities get all the opportunities.

White female, lower-level manager

Pay is not the only motivator; management needs to know what motivates their employees.

White male, middle-level manager

If my evaluation yearly is always above average, why is my salary below average?

African American male, lower-level manager

What rewards or recognition?
> *African American female, occupational*

A good "talker" gets more reward than a good "doer."
> *Hispanic female, lower-level manager*

My own manager does not even know me, and she's been in my department over eight months.
> *Hispanic male, occupational*

They talk about teams, but they reward individual performance.
> *Native American, female, lower-level manager*

If these comments are at all indicative of widespread attitudes, then corporate America still has plenty of work ahead of it.

Rewards and Recognition: What *Doesn't* Work?

In our view, two types of reward-and-recognition approaches are fraught with problems. One of the most destructive is the so-called "merit award," given each year to a select number of people for outstanding performance. Corporations that use this system create a great deal of tension and politicking during the final months of the performance period, as employees vie to be among the chosen few to receive the awards. Then the actual announcement of the awards has a very negative impact on the 90 percent of employees who have been left out, especially because even in the best of companies, people know that awards are made on a basis of subjective as well as objective criteria. In the worst of companies, evaluations are far more about who you know and who likes you, than about actual performance.

A second type of framework for rewards and recognition that we find troublesome is one that reveals companies' lack of total commitment to the team concept. Some corporations talk out of both sides of their mouths when it comes to teams: They espouse the virtues of teams and teamwork, but when it's time to disburse rewards they place more value on the contributions of individuals than teams. By emphasizing individual rather than team rewards and recognition, they create a me-versus-you climate that undercuts the benefit that teams bring in eliminating racism and sexism. In a highly competitive environment, we humans have an innate tendency to turn "the competition" into "the enemy." And such a tendency only serves to exacerbate our stereotypes about "those" people; "those" generally meaning those of a different race or gender, the ones who we believe are getting the rewards and recognition that are being denied to *us.*

So, What *Does* Work?

Many companies are coming up with some unique and effective ways of rewarding employees, as a result of their recognition that employees who do not feel valued and rewarded are unable to concentrate on their jobs and on building constructive relationships with colleagues, customers, and stakeholders. Such employees also are unable to engage in the kind of self-analysis we have been recommending, and as a result find it difficult to build up trust and respect and work toward the elimination of racism and sexism.

We are firm advocates of corporations equitably and fairly rewarding *all* employees, from the board of directors on down, based on how well the company as one big team has done. Only after corporatewide rewards have been equitably and fairly distributed should corporations reward business units, particular teams, and individual team performers. This approach is far more likely to generate a spirit of harmony, cooperation, and goodwill.

One company that is trying to implement such a system is Lyondell-CITGO, a Houston-based oil company. Craig Redding, who heads up performance management for the firm, is trying to purge the company of its multiple and redundant incentive systems and reward programs. He wants to make employees' base pay account for as much of their total compensation as possible. "I think we have created our own monster, so to speak, by all the incentive systems and money systems. We've made them hunger after money, simply because we keep throwing it in their face and calling attention to it."[4] One of the first steps Redding took to distance pay from performance was to abolish the performance management system, and instead just pay a general increase to all employees.

Of course, high performers need their recognition, too. Otherwise they will come to feel that they aren't being valued for their consistent contributions. They may appreciate a sincere thank-you, but still need some higher-order incentive as well. As for the latter, money's great, but there *are* alternatives: asking them to train others on the job that they have learned to do so well; granting them more autonomy; giving them special assignments; giving them a spot in prestigious task forces; or increasing their visibility. A good manager will make it his or her business to discover which form of recognition is of the highest value to the high-performing employee.

Other approaches to reward and recognition can work, as well. Giving out on-the-spot awards of a specific nature for specific projects, activities, or accomplishments can motivate individuals and teams. Such a reward is immediate, and directly linked to a specific accomplishment. This makes it more visible and real, in contrast to an award that materializes months later.

In addition to team awards, we urge companies to develop various career paths and incentive schemes that will meet the needs of top talents who have to stay in particular jobs for long periods of time because of some special expertise and are thereby removed from the pool of promotable candidates. In order to satisfy employees facing this kind of a barrier to promotion and higher salary, companies can develop career moves such as the following:

1. Providing employees with the autonomy, resources, and access they need, in order to resolve the business problems they face.
2. Appointing them to special assignments such as visible task forces; rotating them from line to staff jobs, and vice versa; and transferring them to other functions and departments so as to widen their range of job skills.
3. Creating a company culture that holds in high esteem not just the managerial but also the professional, technical, and staff career tracks. Let's face it, lots of people have no desire to be managers. And since they're good at doing what they do, they should be allowed and indeed encouraged to keep on doing it. By contrast, the traditional career path would insist, for example, that the gifted teacher be "promoted" out of the classroom into the principal's office, or the talented salesperson be made to stop selling and to start to manage the office. What these employees really want and need, as both they and we are saying, is different kinds of reward and recognition systems.

Of course, if one really wants to know what types of reward and recognition will work for one's employees, a good way to find out is to ask them! Here are some of their suggestions, as drawn from our surveys.

Letter of recommendation, pat on the back, "good job."
African American male, occupational

Praise and recognition from management.
Asian male, lower-level manager

To know that my contributions are meaningful to the company goals.

Hispanic male, lower-level manager

Basic respect, trust; recognition for performance.

Hispanic male, lower-level manager

Verbal confirmation that the work I am doing is good or bad; to be included in unitwide meetings as part of the whole group.

White female, occupational

"Great job," "a job well done."

Native American female, occupational

Positive feedback, for one—we are consistently criticized and reprimanded like small children.

White female, occupational

Just a friendly "good morning." Some interest in me as a person. I feel invisible.

African American female, occupational

More responsibility.

African American female, lower-level manager

Praise for a job well done, and incentive pay.

Asian male, occupational

Verbal praise for a job well done. Reassurance of competency and faith in a given task. Given a higher level of responsibility and work.

African American female, lower-level manager

What about recognizing we have personal and family lives?

White male, middle-level manager

Appreciation; just being recognized.

Hispanic female, lower-level manager

Inclusion in strategic development meetings.

White female, lower-level manager

Feedback on the positive effects of my good performance—how it ties in to the company's success.

White female, lower-level manager

And then there's the woman who was so starved for some kind of recognition that she simply wrote down, "Any reward." See, it doesn't take much!

We freely admit that that foregoing list of comments is a selective one. Yes, plenty of people did list money—and yet often only as a second or third factor. What most of these employees are saying is that besides formal rewards such as money and position, they have a deep need to feel that they are being valued for their skills and talents and for what they daily contribute to their companies. They want to hear it said loud and clear that they really *are* contributing to the company, and they would love to play a real, however small, role in determining their companies' objectives. As for women and people of color in particular, they do of course want all of these items that we have been enumerating. And yet it would seem that their biggest reward would be a company climate in which differences are accepted and women are free of sexual harassment. Overall, employees' comments tell us quite clearly that companies can reinforce a sense of human dignity in a variety of informal—and pretty inexpensive—ways.

Some of the comments we have received also indicate that companies can show that they value their employees by adopting flexible benefit programs. Employees are diverse in their needs, and companies can acknowledge that diversity at no added expense by providing a certain number of benefit dollars that employees can use in any way they want to, within the range of a wide variety of options. Thus a childless employee would have no need for a child-care reimbursement option, but might be delighted by an elder-care option for his/her aging parent. Other employees might choose more time off, educational reimbursement, a sabbatical, and so on. But regardless of how many and how innovative the forms are which such a flexible benefit plan might take, without trust and respect, it simply won't work; in a hostile, competitive environment, employees spend much of their time sitting around and grousing, "Why is so-and-so getting that, when I'm *not?*"

Some companies have found unusual ways of letting their employees know how much they value them.[4] These may seem like little things, but please believe us when we say that they send a powerful message.

1. Employees at Wilton Connor Packaging Inc., in Charlotte, North Carolina, can take their laundry to work and have it washed, dried, and folded, courtesy of the company! The company also has a handyperson on hand, who can do minor household repairs for employees while they are at work.

2. Autodesk, the software developer based in San Rafael, California, lets its workers bring their dogs to work. (Of course this raises the

delicate issue of cat discrimination, but that's the subject of a whole other book. . . .)

3. PepsiCo now offers employees working in its Purchase, New York, headquarters an on-site dry-cleaning drop-off; it also offers financial counseling services, for a fee of about $20 per month.

Conclusions

A company can raze the old bureaucracy; restructure work; offer effective performance appraisals; provide well-considered career planning, counseling, and development. But all of those innovations will go for naught, unless the company also is committed to developing effective, flexible, reward and recognition systems which encourage those behaviors that the company holds in high regard, and which demonstrate to employees that it values them and appreciates their unique needs. Companies must recognize that while they have only limited resources to draw upon as they seek to provide formal rewards, the array of informal rewards and recognition available to them is limited only by their own imagination and creativity. And they must understand that their very first step must be to create a climate in which women and people of color can feel comfortable and safe, and that affords them complete trust and respect as full-fledged members of the team.

To fail in the above, will be to have on one's hands a workforce that is upset, angry, and frustrated, focusing not on their jobs but on how they are being treated: in short, a fertile breeding ground for perceptions of racism and sexism. And remember that too many reward and recognition systems actually aggravate the problem by setting workers in competition with one another for limited rewards, thereby driving a wedge between members of the teams rather than rewarding teams as a whole for the contributions they are making to meeting corporate objectives.

Thus, a key aspect of our holistic strategy is for companies to determine the needs and desires of their employees, with regard to how they wish to be rewarded and recognized. For many, it is as simple as a pat on the back; for others, it is a need to participate in company planning and goal setting; for still others, it is a flexible benefit package that implicitly acknowledges their unique needs. And when one considers today's increasingly well-educated, highly demanding workers, confronted by dwindling chances for that traditional promotion, such a strategy begins to look all the more vital.

Diversity and Affirmative Action Are Still Crucial to Corporate Strategies for Dealing with Racism and Sexism

Introduction

The evidence suggests that racism and sexism still play a crucial role in the careers of women and people of color. Therefore if corporations are going to make the best use of high-performance teams of diverse people to deliver quality goods and services to diverse markets, they are going to have to do more than just adopt and implement the human resources practices we have outlined in previous chapters. It doesn't do any good, for example, to recruit a diverse workforce, and then fail to ensure equal opportunity for all employees once they are a part of the organization. Corporations simply must take specific steps to eliminate racism and sexism, in order to ensure that women and people of color receive their fair share of opportunities and that their talents are fully utilized.

Now, those steps definitely include affirmative action and diversity efforts. And yet one of the reasons such efforts have largely failed over the past 34 years is that corporate leaders, and thus employees, have been less than totally committed to eliminating racism and sexism from their organizations. That lack of commitment is born not of malice, but rather of the misguided notion that racism and sexism no longer exist in their companies. And whatever amount of progress has been made in carrying out diversity and affirmative action programs, has been the result of committed white male leadership combined with federal laws against discrimination, not of any specific, government-mandated, affirmative action program. The real lesson there is that affirmative action—that is, programs designed to ensure the fair and equitable representation of women and people of color throughout corporations—will never be truly successful unless and until society comes to fully acknowledge the real depths of its racism and sexism.

The research in recent years has been suggesting that affirmative action and diversity programs are in trouble. A survey cited in a 1995 issue of the trade journal *Training and Development* found that 52 percent of employees believed that federal affirmative action programs, designed to help women and people of color, had gone too far; only 29 percent said they had not gone far enough.[1] In addition, only 29 percent of employees believed that affirmative action was an effective policy. A survey done by *Fortune* in 1989 found that 68 percent of CEOs believed that affirmative action programs were good or very good; by 1995 the figure had dropped to 52 percent.[2] And yet despite these discouraging statistics—perhaps because of them—we are convinced that organizations must find a way to renew their commitment to diversity and affirmative action.

The Position of White Men

Anyone who wishes to gain a full understanding of the lack of widespread support for affirmative action programs, must first comprehend just how far-reaching have been the effects of civil rights legislation. Prior to the passage of the Civil Rights Act of 1964, white men were in essence competing with only about 33 percent of the adult population—that is, the percentage of the population represented by white males. And yet after that act and subsequent pieces of legislation were passed, white men, at least by law, also had to compete on a more equitable basis against the other 67 percent, comprising women and people of color. This meant that many white men of average or below-average ability levels began to find it considerably more difficult to advance; they now had to compete against the entire adult population, many members of which possessed credentials and abilities superior to their own.

Nonetheless, and despite these vast demographic changes, above-average white men, especially those who fit the image of a promotable manager, have had little trouble advancing in corporate America. Both before and after 1964, the most numerous and powerful decision makers have always been white men. And that means that even average and below-average white men still, in many cases, have the advantage over above-average women and people of color. Increased competition, however, has led some whites and men to cry foul, alleging unfair treatment and reverse discrimination. While it is certain that such has in fact been the case in many instances, in many more instances such allegations simply represent the natural reaction of people who resent losing their perceived "top dog" status in society.

So, how have white men as a group done, after 34 years of affirmative action and diversity efforts? Pretty well, on balance. Although they represent only 41 percent of the workforce, they own 64 percent of the nation's businesses and occupy most of the nation's highest-paying jobs. White men are still:

- *70 percent of judges*
- *70 percent of university professors*
- *71 percent of air traffic controllers*
- *73 percent of lawyers*
- *75 percent of police detectives and supervisors*
- *84 percent of construction supervisors*
- *85 percent of boards of directors*
- *89 percent of U.S. senators*
- *94 percent of fire company supervisors*
- *95 percent of senior managers[3]*

Given that overwhelming preponderance in the professional classes, some whites and men have done what anyone might well do: become fearful with regard to people and programs that challenge their perceived position of dominance, and develop, consciously or unconsciously, an array of strategies designed to shore up the status quo. They are abetted in doing this by some in the news media, which often writes and speaks as if women and people of color had it made, and by academics who write books about the negative effects wrought upon corporate efficiency and productivity by affirmative action programs. By blaming the victims, these individuals seek to maintain their own power bases and to avoid having to face up to their own deficiencies.

As Bowser and Hunt have written:

> Why have whites insisted on holding power, both historically and in the present? The answer to this question is nuanced, but its essential element is not hard to find. With a "race problem" the subordination of whole classes of people based on color is justified and competition is reduced. If the "race problem" disappeared tomorrow, however, with people of color still a significant portion of the U.S. population, approximately 3 out of 10, whites would have real competition from a minority person with whom they did not have to compete before.[4]

We want to be sure to note, however, that resistance to affirmative action and diversity can have other and more benign sources than race or gender bias. Much of it can be explained by reference to our deep-seated human resistance to change. As Robert Rosen has said in his book *The Healthy Company:*

> Employees may have a good reason for denying change, for it can be personally and professionally threatening. Underneath their denial may well be a fear, such as fear of
>
> * *Losing security—their job future is now uncertain*
> * *Losing the feeling of competence—they are asked to do new, unfamiliar tasks, and no longer know whether their skills are adequate*
> * *Losing a sense of belonging—established, comfortable groups, teams, and cadres of coworkers may be broken up*
> * *Losing a sense of direction—change may mean new priorities and goals*
> * *Losing control over psychological and physical space—work space and assignments may be altered.*[5]

Attacks on Affirmative Action and Diversity

Ever since the 1980s, the attacks on affirmative action have been intensifying. In the 1990s we have all seen numerous articles which speak about how reverse discrimination and affirmative action have been hurting whites—although interestingly, it is white women who have been by far the greatest beneficiaries of affirmative action. As late as 1996, *The Wall Street Journal* was reporting that over 50 percent of white males were opposed to affirmative action, although that figure was down from the 67 percent, reported the year before. And in an article entitled "White Men Shake Off That Losing Feeling on Affirmative Action," Jonathan Kaufmann wrote that many white men have become convinced that the high-water mark of affirmative action has come and gone, seeing as the employment of women and people of color in their companies has slowed or halted.[6]

Opposition to affirmative action is continuing to spread. For instance, in 1997 fifty-four percent of Californians supported the California Civil Rights Initiative (CCRI) Proposition 209, which ended state affirmative action programs, and more than 20 other states have drafted similar initiatives. We should note that the chief proponent of Proposition 209 was Ward Connelly, a black businessman who opposes affirmative action because he believes he has gotten to where he is today strictly on a basis of merit—a position we're inclined to question. Even if affirmative action did not help Connelly, he has achieved his successes in part because key people "liked his fit" and allowed him into the club. As we see it, Connelly's support of Proposition 209 is simply another indication of how women and people of color can be their own worst enemies, just as many white men can be their valuable allies. Let it also be noted here that Congress currently is debating the possible introduction of bills similar to California's, on the federal level.

What rightly troubles the opponents of initiatives such as Proposition 209, is the lack of hard evidence in support of those allegations of preferential treatment and reverse discrimination that gave rise to it in the first place. As Dave Barclay, chair of the National Black Business Roundtable, has noted:

> What is missing from this debate from the supporters of CCRI is evidence of preferential treatment and reverse discrimination. Instead they have misled the public to believe every time a person of color or woman has been selected for a job, a contract, or admission to a university, that person is less qualified or has been given a preference over a more highly qualified white male to meet some fictitious quota imposed by the government.[7]

And listen to these words penned by Mori J. Matsuda and Charles R. Laurence, in their response to a *New York Times* article about the U.S. Court of Appeals' ruling that the affirmative action program at the University of Texas Law School was unconstitutional:

> The . . . most damaging myth is in the court's phrase: "to the detriment of whites and other minorities." The belief is that affirmative action takes from one and gives to an unqualified other and that no white people benefit from diversity. Yet the talents and abilities that it takes to negotiate an increasingly complex world are not one-dimensional. Interaction with different cultures, belief systems and presumptions help make us smarter. Creative intelligence challenges existing premises. This kind of critical thought is what we teach in universities. We teach it best when the classroom is rich with diversity, not impoverished by it as the Fifth Circuit presumes.[8]

These efforts to do away with affirmative action are the product of the false belief that the United States, after 400 years of racism and sexism, has become color- and gender-blind. They also are based on the false belief that prior to the coming of affirmative action, the United States was a meritocracy, now supposedly in the process of being dismantled by giving women and people of color preferential treatment. A survey taken in California, right after the passage of Proposition 209, found that 67 percent of the state's residents agreed with what we believe to be a patently false assertion: "If we end affirmative action programs, people will be hired on the basis of merit and qualifications, not race and gender."

Our position should be clear: Racism and sexism exist. And they will continue to exist unless those white men who hold down the overwhelming preponderance of the positions of power in our society lead the initiative to eradicate them. Listen once more to Bowser and Hunt on this issue:

> The race problem and the power to change it—enlightened or otherwise—belongs primarily to whites, and not simply because they are the numerical majority of the nation's population and voters. It is a matter of whites having the status and associated power to maintain and advance their perceived interests.[9]

In brief, despite the widespread claims of reverse discrimination by white males, the numbers say that they still have significant advantages over women and people of color. Let us turn now to an examination of the present state of affairs as it exists in most U.S. corporations, with regard to these issues.

Employee Support for Diversity and Affirmative Action

Before we try to discover the extent to which employees support diversity and affirmative action, it's important that we get some sense of the extent to which they do or don't understand their own companies' affirmative action efforts. Over the years, our surveys have revealed that companies have done a poor job of fostering such understanding. In 1995, for example, 60 percent of our respondents said that they had an adequate understanding of their companies' overall goals—not bad, perhaps, but that still means that 40 percent *don't*. And yet only 43 percent of employees, regardless of race and gender, believed themselves to be well informed about their companies' diversity efforts. It is worth noting that people at lower levels tend to be far less likely to say they understand these efforts and are well informed about them. Table 14.1 summarizes our survey data regarding the level of employee support for diversity and affirmative action efforts.

The following employee comments drawn from our surveys, are revealing.

> I don't know much about affirmative action and diversity, except the company believes we have to do it.
>
> *White male, lower-level manager*

> Who knows what diversity is?
>
> *Asian male, occupational*

> I understand the efforts, but I totally disagree with them.
>
> *White female, lower-level manager*

> The company doesn't do a good job informing people about diversity. Everyone thinks it's affirmative action, which equals reverse discrimination in their minds.
>
> *Black female, occupational*

> Diversity is a key to our future successes. Our employees need a better understanding. We are working on it.
>
> *White male, upper-level manager*

> Who knows what this company is doing about diversity, affirmative action, or anything else. They never tell us.
>
> *White female, lower-level manager*

> I think affirmative action was necessary in the beginning, to show society the importance of equality. However, in today's society, there is a much greater mix of various cultural backgrounds. I think the words "affirmative action" should be thrown out. It has served its purpose and is now being overused. It's time to show our children that all people should be treated as equals—with no preference to race.
>
> *White female, lower-level manager*

> People are either prejudiced or not. No amount of workshops, forums, surveys, etc. are going to change their minds one way or another.
>
> *White female, occupational*

> Keeping track of how many minorities we have, in itself, is being prejudiced! It shouldn't matter.
>
> *White male, lower-level manager*

Table 14.1
Level of Employee Support for Diversity and Affirmative Action Programs in Their Companies

To what extent do you agree or disagree with the following statements regarding workplace diversity?

For your company to be successful in the 1990s, it is important to have an employee makeup that reflects diversity similar to the general population? (Strongly Agree or Agree)

	1972	1978	1984	1986	1988	1995
Black	—	—	90	92	90	90
White	—	—	82	86	83	72
Hispanic	—	—	86*	89*	89	86
Asians	—	—	86	89	84	86
Native Americans	—	—	86	89	89	91

To what degree are you supportive of hiring goals and timetables? (Strongly Agree or Agree)

	1972	1978	1984	1986	1988	1995
Black	—	—	89	94	88	88
White	—	—	70	71	65	62
Hispanic	—	—	88*	84*	89	86
Asians	—	—	88	84	83	71
Native Americans	—	—	88	84	78	65

*Because of the small number of Hispanics, Asians, and Native Americans, and because of similarities in their responses, this information was collapsed into one category, "other people of color."

To what degree do you believe that diversity/affirmative action workshops should be made mandatory? (Strongly Agree or Agree)

	1972	1978	1984	1986	1988	1995
Black	—	—	—	—	72	70
White	—	—	—	—	44	36
Hispanic	—	—	—	—	62	64
Asians	—	—	—	—	52	60
Native Americans	—	—	—	—	50	57

To what degree do you believe that your supervisor should be compensated on the basis of his or her successful efforts to foster respect for diversity/affirmative action efforts? (Strongly Agree or Agree)

	1972	1978	1984	1986	1988	1995
Black	—	—	—	—	48	75
White	—	—	—	—	36	45
Hispanic	—	—	—	—	45	73
Asians	—	—	—	—	55	71
Native Americans	—	—	—	—	33	64

Our survey data have led us to make the following observations:

1. Thirty-nine percent of white men, and 51 percent of white women, believe that diversity will assist their department in attaining better results. The figure for blacks is 79 percent; for other racial groups, it ranges from 61 to 70 percent. Lower-level employees, which means more women and people of color, are more likely to believe that diversity will lead to better results.

2. Regardless of race and gender, only about 1 in 10 employees believes that diversity and affirmative action efforts will not meet with any resistance from within their companies; 50 percent believe that resistance will be equal at all levels of their companies—that is, that even senior executives will resist affirmative action and diversity efforts.

3. White employees' support for diversity and affirmative action programs is more substantial in "soft" areas, less so when it comes to efforts that would put teeth into those programs. Since 1986, for example, our surveys have been indicating that 80 percent of employees do hold the belief that their companies' workforces should reflect the diversity of their customers and stakeholders. However, only about 45 percent of whites (and 64 percent of people of color) believe that supervisors should be compensated for in part on the basis of the success of their diversity efforts over the 1988 figures, which suggests to us that employees put some teeth into their diversity and affirmative action.

4. When employees were asked if their companies should establish hiring and promotion goals and timetables as part of their diversity efforts, there were significant differences by race and gender. Fifty-six percent of white men, and 68 percent of white women,

compared with 88 percent of blacks, responded affirmatively in 1995. This is an important issue for us, since to oppose hiring and promotion goals and timetables is to oppose a key strategy that has provided people of color and women with better opportunities over the past 34 years. All our research shows that little progress has been made toward greater diversity without such goals and timetables, as those are supported by government pressures.

Mandatory Training and Support Groups

Another indication of the softness of support for diversity and affirmative action programs is the lack of commitment to mandatory diversity training. While it is entirely clear to us that women and people of color will never get their fair share of opportunities in the absence of ongoing employee training about racism and sexism, a mere 36 percent of white employees (24 percent of men and 43 percent of women), compared to 70 percent of black employees, believe that attendance at company-sponsored diversity workshops should be mandatory. The figures for other racial groups range from 57 to 64 percent. And in the years between 1988 and 1995 the support among whites for mandatory diversity training went down sharply.

What that fact suggests to us is that many whites don't want to face up to their own racism and sexism, or believe that they and their colleagues have no racist and sexist attitudes and behaviors and/or that their companies have already done "enough of that training stuff, so now let's get on with the job of running this business." Remember, however, how large is the percentage of white women who believe themselves to be daily confronted by gender discrimination.

Another divisive issue that has emerged out of our seminars, focus groups, interviews, and surveys, is that of the value (or lack of it) of employee support groups. During the 1970s, 1980s, and 1990s, many companies found themselves unsure and uneasy how to respond to employee support groups, as those had been formed largely out of race and gender subgroups within the company that were seeking to pressure it into addressing their concerns. Members of such support groups also engage in self-help activities so as to ensure that they will be ready to seize opportunities, and some try to assist their companies by recruiting diverse employees, exploring new and diverse markets, and resolving internal conflicts.

What many white males especially object to, is the way in which such support groups often ultimately become company-financed. Responses to our survey questions on this issue reveal clearly just how divisive it is: Eighty-one percent of people of color are in favor of the use of support groups, whereas only 28 percent of white male employees are. Many white males indicated to us that in their view these kinds of groups increase segregation within the company, and they complain that they would be sure to be called "racist" or "sexist" if they started such a group in support of their *own* interests and concerns.

Employees' Perception of Their Companies' Support for Diversity

We have been seeing just how considerable is the opposition that companies face, as they seek to alter their racial and gender makeups, at all levels, so as to become truly reflective of society at large. They must contend with many employees in their current workforces whose attitudes toward diversity and affirmative action range from skepticism to blatant opposition. If a company is to make a successful transition to post-bureaucracy, however, there must be a total commitment from the corporation. And that means not merely the image the company projects, but also the actual leadership of its top executives as that is demonstrated by their behaviors and views, not their rhetoric. Over the years we have found in most surveys that about 2 out of 3 employees, regardless of race and/or gender, believe that their supervisors do show support for diversity and affirmative action efforts as that is revealed through their behaviors. And yet in terms of the company as a whole, our results in 1995 showed that slightly more than 1 out of 2 believe their companies to be involved with diversity only in order to be politically correct, and that only about 1 out of 2 believes that his/her company actually lives by the principles of diversity. (Note once again that on these questions, there were no significant differences in response by race and/or gender.) Thus what this data is really telling us is that fully half of employees don't believe their companies are truly committed to diversity and affirmative action, as many of the following responses will show.

> Mandated diversity causes more division, not less. It is very threatening to many individuals. This company is doing the "politically correct" thing to do, but I fear it does not go beyond that.
> *White female, middle-level manager*

I don't know if they work hard enough to diversify and promote women, African Americans, and Hispanics. The company talks it, but doesn't address it. Here comes another one—the token!
White female, lower-level manager

I heard them at a meeting wondering why people didn't think that they were diverse, and sitting around the table was all white males.
White female, upper-level manager

To avoid lawsuits and bad publicity.
Black male, middle-level manager

It's a fad, like "politically correct." It means nothing.
White male, lower-level manager

It's "politically correct."
White male, occupational

I don't see any commitment to diversity from the upper levels of management, other than diversity means "differences in thinking."
Hispanic male, middle-level manager

This issue being handled like this, and forced down our throats, will spell big trouble. It is already evident by the company's employee behavior. All departments sink to the lowest common denominator, i.e. an unqualified worker being placed to make the office diverse. Diversity programs are totally unfair.
White male, middle-level manager

The "white" male population has been blamed for nearly all problems here. This is just another example. It is politically correct to do so.
White male, upper-level manager

Some white males perceive reverse discrimination when a woman or a minority is promoted, because ability is controversial and supposedly unqualified promotion incites much communication along the grapevine. I don't argue, but that is the case.
White male, lower-level manager

I'm a 44-year-old white male, and to say that the company's efforts at diversity are not threatening to me would be a lie. My career goals were almost greatly affected once, and will be again because of the company's goals.
White male, upper-level manager

It is clear that the softness of employee support for diversity and affirmative action programs is based, in part, on the fact that almost 50 percent do not believe their companies to be serious about, and committed to, the principles of diversity and/or affirmative action. We should remember that although half of the employees believe that their company does support diversity, over the years only about 1 out of 10 employees has expected there to be no resistance to her or his company's diversity and affirmative action efforts. And about 1 out of 2 employees believes that the resistance will come with equal force from all levels of his/her company. Although it is no easy matter to put a single "spin" on all of that data, what we do think we are seeing here is a reluctance to acknowledge the fact that many employees are going to have a tough time accepting diversity and affirmative action, even when their company as an entity supports it. Thus it is vital to make employees understand that a company is nothing more than a collection of individuals, and that if all of those individuals, from the Board of Directors right down to the occupation workers, don't support a strategy, then "the company" will never be able to do so either.

A Holistic Approach to Diversity and Affirmative Action

Let's be real: No one method that we have suggested in earlier chapters is going to solve all of any company's race- and gender-related problems. These are so deeply inbred, and reinforced from so many sources, that only an all-out, multifaceted implementation has any hope of negating their ill effects. And without *leadership,* such implementation will never get off the ground.

If a company is going to make a successful transition to post-bureaucracy, there must be a total commitment from the corporation as that is reflected in the leadership of boards of directors, top managers, and chief executive officers. All of these individuals must demonstrate their commitment to recruiting women and people of color, and to understanding the needs and desires of diverse customers and stakeholders. While maintaining their proper reverence for individual merit regardless of gender or skin color, they also must make every effort to ensure that women and people of color are represented in all positions, including senior ones. They must listen to their customers, and surpass their expectations by having on board an appropriately diverse workforce that can fully satisfy their needs. And they must ensure that diverse customers and stakeholders are wisely and compassionately dealt with by aware and knowledgeable employees.

Such commitments on the part of top managers must be modeled through their behaviors. Too often top-level, white-male executives require their white managers at lower levels to work with women and people of color, but conspicuously fail to include women and people of color among their own peers and direct reports. Such behavior, far from fostering an organizationwide commitment to the utilization of high-performance teams of diverse people, in fact causes employees to resent and distrust managers whom they perceive to be talking out of both sides of their mouths. By contrast, when top managers actively mentor, coach, develop, and place people of color and women within their own ranks, they send a powerful message to one and all about the organization's deeply held commitment to employees, customers, and their stakeholders.

So too, it is only a company's leaders who are in a position to spearhead efforts to implement the proposals we here share with you in the accompanying box. Implementation of these recommendations will make affirmative action and diversity an integral part of the corporate culture, and create a climate in which the skills and talents of all employees are fully utilized and developed and in which diverse customers and stakeholders are valued and respected. The end result will be a more efficient and productive corporation, one that is well equipped to compete effectively in the challenging economic environment of the 21st century.

An Affirmative Action/Diversity Strategy

Establish goals and timetables for all departments and levels of the corporation; with respect to hiring and promotion of people of color, women, and white males where underrepresented, establish similar goals and timetables.

Require higher-level managers to become mentors and sponsors of high-potential people of color and women. Measure and reward their success at this task.

Develop concrete performance measurement criteria to evaluate all managers' efforts in managing diverse individuals. Set up rewards for those who do well in these areas, and penalties for those who do poorly.

Demonstrate the company's commitment to solving affirmative action and diversity difficulties, by promoting to other areas people who directly work in these areas and do an outstanding job.

Take concrete, well-publicized actions to demonstrate the company's commitment to affirmative action—such as on-the-spot awards for individuals who have contributed in a significant manner to the company's efforts.

Develop and implement diversity awareness and skills-building workshops as an ongoing part of the company's training and development programs; expand these programs, as the company continues to strive to eliminate racism and sexism from its culture.

Develop diversity awareness and skills-building workshops, using trained company facilitators drawn from high-potential, middle-level and above managers, whose participation should be mandatory.

Make certain that all training programs and systems relating to managerial/supervisory skills development have modules that deal with some aspect of diversity; the same should apply to all other relevant training, such as employee orientation education and development.

Conduct on-site and off-site educational courses that teach about different cultures. Make the taking of such courses a requirement for promotion.

Develop a systematic college relationship and intern program, one that focuses on the hiring of women and people of color.

Conduct and support, in the company and in the community, multicultural events; strongly encourage employees to attend.

Require all high-potential managers, and those being considered for promotion to middle management and above, to belong to and be active participants in community organizations concerned with the elimination of discrimination; support their involvement by channeling corporate community service contributions, financial and in-kind, to the organizations' activities and programs.

Sponsor company tours to various sites of interest within people-of-color communities, with the express purpose of helping employees to better understand, respect, value, and appreciate the lifestyles and difficulties experienced by people of color.

Make a conscientious effort to locate plant and facilities in a wide variety of communities, especially people-of-color communities. Make certain the company maintains a diverse workforce at these facilities.

Make diversity- and affirmative-action-related jobs required work assignments for high-potential persons, and especially for any such person being considered for promotion to middle management and above. These tours of duty should be for a minimum of two years.

Actively seek out people-of-color and female contractors, and take steps to ensure that they are provided with equal, fair access to company contracts.

Finally, companies must be prepared to punish—to the extent of firing, if it comes to that—any employee who shows consistent and flagrant disrespect for his/her fellow employees and/or customers and stakeholders.

Conclusions

Racism and sexism are alive and well in American society and therefore in corporate America, despite anyone's protestation to the contrary. If it is going to do its part in combating these evils, corporate America must take a number of steps, first and foremost among which is to consciously acknowledge that women and people of color have been and continue to be formally and informally denied an equal opportunity to compete and succeed in the American workplace. Although some progress has indeed been made over the past 34 years, and although numerous federal laws have been passed that are designed to banish discrimination from our midst, the lion's share of the positions of power, authority, and influence in corporate America continues to belong to white men. And they are understandably reluctant to give up those positions by having to compete for them with a broader workforce, one that extends equal opportunities to women and to people of color. Therefore many of them argue that discrimination and sexism do not really exist. In recent years all of us have seen the result: widening efforts to roll back affirmative action and other programs designed to level the playing field for all who compete there, including women and people of color.

Unfortunately, concrete and doable proposals to correct these ills are being met with less than enthusiastic support and total commitment in our nation's corporations. Almost half of employees believe that their organizations are not truly committed to diversity and affirmative action efforts, and only 1 in 10 believes that such efforts will be met with no resistance from within the organizations, at all levels equally. Such comments suggest to us that these employees do not really understand what affirmative action is all about and how it can promote, rather than detract from, fairness in the workplace. And that in turn causes us to conclude that their companies are doing a poor job of informing them about its nature and its value.

Only leadership, coming right from the top levels of organizations, can set this sorry state of affairs right. Corporate leaders not only must insist that other employees extend opportunities to women and to people of color—through recruitment, coaching, mentoring, and the like—but they must open *their own ranks* to women and people of color. Additionally, they must find new and innovative ways of putting teeth into diversity and affirmative action efforts; for example, by making diversity efforts a crucial component of the set of performance-review expectations for supervisors and managers. Finally, they must find ways, and take steps, to increase contact between all segments of the workforce. It is only in ways such as these that there can be built up the requisite level of trust and respect to make diversity and affirmative action efforts more than mere hollow exercises in political correctness. Rather, these efforts and programs will be among an organization's most valuable tools, helping it to serve diverse customer bases and stakeholder groups well into the new millennium.

15

Targeting Diverse Market Segments

Introduction

Throughout the first 14 chapters of this book, we have repeatedly mentioned customers. We haven't had much to say about them, however, since our chief emphasis has been placed on employees and their organizations. We would now like to turn our attention to customers and markets, and to apply our notion of a holistic strategy for the elimination of racism and sexism to the efforts of firms to build up their business.

We have noted earlier that racism and sexism have a decidedly negative impact upon an organization's ability to expand and to succeed in the increasingly diverse U.S. and global marketplace. Our present task is to look more closely into those current market and customer conditions that make it all the more vital for organizations to develop new structures to combat discrimination. In other words, no corporation will truly become motivated to seriously tackle the issues of racism and sexism, until it has come to appreciate the significance of women and people of color in the marketplace.

Now, at the most basic level, organizations exist because customers have needs and wants, which they fulfill by buying firms' products and services. Without its customers, any business organization would cease to exist. And since markets are comprised of customers, and since customers are human beings, it follows that in order to understand markets, an organization must understand the complex nature of human beings. Traditionally, that has not been business's strong suit. All that organizations have to do, however, to make it stronger, is to focus on the human dimension as constituting an essential part of their effort to define key market characteristics. Which brings us directly to our goal in this chapter: to provide you with a framework within which you can build up effective relationships with race- and gender-defined markets.

Race and Gender Markets: A Quick Overview

The marketplace is of course made up of many different segments. We are always hearing these days about the "mature market," the "women's market," the "ethnic market," the "gay market," and the like. But what do those labels really mean? In the past, market segmentation meant that differentiation on a basis of price, quality, and product features was *the* factor that defined market segments, and therefore organizations responded eagerly to market needs by creating products that fit each one of those segments like a glove—economy, mid-price, and luxury cars come immediately to mind. Today's sort of market segmentation is marked, however, by a recognition that certain demographic and lifestyle variables are perhaps even more important than the traditional segments.

Make no mistake, many of the new nontraditional segments have substantial influence and buying power. For instance, women-owned small businesses are the fastest-growing segment of the small business market; indeed, collectively such firms employ more people than all of the *Fortune* 500 companies put together! As for minority-owned firms, between 1987 and 1992 their receipts mushroomed from $77 to $202 billion. Hispanic buying power is currently pegged at a staggering $363 billion, and by 2010 Hispanics will be the second largest ethnic group in the United States. African American buying power is even more impressive, having reached $427 billion in 1996. As any fool can see, those are numbers that a business firm ignores at only its own peril.

Now, organizations that wish to target one or more of these nontraditional segments must both adjust their traditional marketing strategies and develop new ones precisely to target the segment in question. The first adjustment that must be made, is to get rid of the old one-size-fits-all definition of excellence, replacing it with an acknowledgment that what constitutes excellence will be decided by the norms, values, and beliefs of each particular market segment. Thus the inevitable result will be many different standards of excellence. Once again: In order to succeed, organizations are going to have to first identify how a particular market segment defines excellence, then tailor their products, services, and relationships to that market definition accordingly. And none of that is going to happen, unless each organization makes itself intimately acquainted with its current and potential customers.

One excellent way of gaining acquaintance with the demographically diverse marketplace is to be an organization comprised of many diverse members at all levels and in all functions. For it is the creativity and innovation that a diverse team generates, through its ability to consider and evaluate a broader set of viewpoints, which helps organizations to develop the appropriate products, services, and marketing strategies for targeted market segments. The results of a study conducted by the loan company, Beneficial Corporations have confirmed us in this view. As part of its effort to penetrate the African American market, the company held a series of focus groups. There it learned the simple facts that African Americans are more likely to do business with a company when they feel trust and respect, and that they look upon the employment of African Americans as a sure sign that the company in question does indeed respect and trust them not merely as a market segment but as individuals.

Another company that experienced a similar success was a Miami-based Toyota dealership that was seeking to increase its share of the Hispanic market. Indeed, over a six-year-period and through targeted marketing, this dealership was able to boost its market share by more than 50 percent, and to increase its sales by 400 percent. More specifically, it employed a multipoint approach aimed at developing a relationship with the Hispanic community. It hired bilingual salespeople, and held special events that would appeal to Hispanics. Thus it was able to build up its customer base not only through trust and respect, but more especially by showing respect for its customers' culture.

Value-Plus Products and Services

Yet even with all of the insights and benefits that having a diverse workforce does assuredly bring to an organization, such a workforce is only one prerequisite for success. Organizations must then develop their ability to develop, deliver, and market value-plus products and services. These are products and services that meet a target market segment's wants in such a way as to simultaneously fulfill other needs or preferences. For example, Hispanics of course want phone service, just as we all do. A value-plus phone service, however, might well be one that could provide Hispanic consumers with the option of conducting their transactions with the phone company in either English or Spanish. Similarly, financial institutions have become keenly aware that many Asians are highly reluctant to discuss financial matters with those they perceive as being mere strangers. Thus a bank, in developing programs designed to educate Asian customers about financial vehicles, might not set out merely to fill a basic need—banking—but also to provide a value-plus service: that of raising the awareness of shy and wary customers who, deep down, are interested in exploring a wide variety of financial options.

Framework for Targeting Diverse Market Segments

The standard procedure for the average organization, before it makes a decision to target a market segment, is to study demographic projections, its relative market share, and how that market share stacks up against that of its competitors. Once it has identified gaps and failings in its attempts to meet the needs of its market, it feels it is at last ready to launch the new product or service.

A very different approach must be taken, however, in the targeting of diverse markets. For in this case, the firm also must identify the obstacles that stand in the way of building cross-cultural relationships. And it is both the organization and the target market's unique characteristics that determine both the specific obstacles that have to be overcome and the appropriate strategies for doing so. Table 15.1 will show you the disastrous consequences of failing to take the time or devote the resources to understanding a target market before you try to win its business. In Table 15.2, you will find listed seven of the most common barriers separating you and your firm from the building of effective cross-cultural marketing relationships.

Table 15.1
Marketing Mishaps Caused by a Failure to Get Acquainted with the Target Audience

- In Hong Kong, a car-rental company unsuccessfully attempted to promote itself by giving away green hats. The company was unaware of the Chinese superstition that if a man wears a green hat, his wife is cheating on him!
- A manufacturer of golf balls failed in a marketing effort in Japan. They were unaware that in Japan, there are negative connotations associated with the number four and with items grouped in four. The manufacturer here failed to get acquainted with its market, and by doing so failed to respect a cultural difference.
- The thesaurus that was contained in a Spanish-language version of Microsoft's Word 6.0 provided a series of offensive synonyms for ethnic groups. A spokesperson for Microsoft said that it had purchased the thesaurus code from a U.S. supplier, who had failed to catch the outdated terms and the misinterpretations of Spanish idioms. Microsoft failed to educate itself and to get acquainted with its market. Rather, it made the mistake of merely hoping that its supplier had taken care of these essential tasks.

Table 15.2

Seven Obstacles to Cross-cultural Marketing Relationships

1. Assuming that the entire target market segment is homogeneous; that is, assuming that all members of that market have identical values, beliefs, assumptions, preferences, wants, and needs.
2. Conducting little or no research into the wants, needs, and culture of the targeted segment, but instead merely falling back on gut feelings or stereotypes.
3. Erroneously believing that one can reach a targeted market segment through only one marketing method; e.g., assuming that all Hispanics can be reached through television, when in fact Spanish-language radio may be the more effective method.
4. Erroneously believing that a mass-marketing strategy such as advertising can be quickly and painlessly adapted to a target market merely by translating it into that target market's preferred language.
5. Creating advertisements that are out of synch with the mood, values, and/or culture of the target market.
6. Placing advertisements only in mass-market publications rather than also utilizing publications geared directly toward the target market.
7. Blindly and expensively developing new products and services, on the basis of an unexamined assumption that the current product and service mix does not meet the targeted segment's needs and wants.

If those obstacles are to be overcome, a combination of internally and externally focused initiatives will have to be undertaken. In combination, these will support the development of a target-market strategy able to deliver value-plus products and services over both the short and the long runs. Table 15.3 gives you an outline of the components of such a strategy. While it is useful in all marketing efforts, it is absolutely vital to success in markets that are segmented by such factors as race, ethnicity, gender, age, and the like.

The following list provides you with seven basic steps toward such a strategy.

Table 15.3

Seven Steps toward an Effective Target Market Strategy

1. Understand your own and your organization's culture.
2. Understand the target market's culture.
3. Identify key stakeholder groups.
4. Develop relationships based upon trust and respect; become a proactive community citizen.

5. Identify the market segment's needs, preferences, and expectations through a variety of methods, such as interviews and focus groups.
6. Develop products, services, and delivery mechanisms that will deliver value-plus products to customers.
7. Continually check up on your progress, and ask members of the target market to provide you with ongoing feedback.

Now let's examine each of those seven steps in turn. Along with each step we will include a "best practices" box that describes some particular company's success.

1. Understand Your Own and Your Organization's Culture

In previous chapters we have had a lot to say about how a person's norms, attitudes, and beliefs drive her or his behavior. By now we're sure you understand just how vital it is for individuals to understand their own culture. And yet when it comes to dealing with market segments, an additional knowledge-component is just as important: being intimately acquainted with your organizational culture. We're talking here about an organization's preferred, traditional ways of conducting business; the written and unwritten rules of the trade; and those behavioral characteristics—for example, aggressiveness—that are formally and informally rewarded and promoted within the organization. Only marketers who are well aware of those sorts of organizational norms are going to be able to identify and surmount the barriers that stand between them and their desire to meet the needs of nontraditional markets.

Best Practices

GPU (General Public Utilities) lays great stress on the need for its employees to understand their own culture and to be held accountable for their actions and behaviors. It actively promotes such understanding by means of ongoing diversity training. At the same time the company has undertaken a major culture-change initiative, as part of its effort to understand its current organizational culture and to see how that would help or hinder the company as it competes in a deregulated utility industry. It has been on the basis of its own self-analysis that GPU has reconstructed its organizational culture and explicitly set forth the values on which its new culture is based.

---

2. Understand the Target Market's Culture

This step is so important because the values and norms of any market segment are inevitably translated into behaviors, with the latter greatly influencing how the segment views the behaviors of the organization and vice versa. When speaking to others, for example, members of a targeted market segment may stand closer than do members of the organization's traditional customer base; or they may casually arrive 15 minutes after the scheduled start of a meeting. Whereas the unaware marketer might react with surprise or annoyance to these behaviors, the savvy marketer would recognize them as simply being cultural-specific, and adjust his or her own behavior accordingly. And yet note well that the savvy marketer develops her or his in-depth understanding of the market without any resort to stereotyping. What we mean is that this recognizes, for example, that the "Asian" market actually consists of distinctive Japanese, Chinese, Korean, and other ethnic groups, and that a marketing campaign targeted toward first-generation Filipino immigrants to the United States would be very different from one targeted to fifth-generation immigrants.

Best Practice

Southern New England Telephone took the time to understand why its Hispanic accounts had a much higher delinquency rate than its other accounts. What it discovered was that many aspects of Hispanic culture were directly clashing with its customer service system. For example, the average Hispanic customer feels a need to develop rapport with a customer service representative before he or she is comfortable getting down to business; the abrupt style that SNET had taught its reps caused many Hispanics to feel alienated, and hesitant to call the company to work out a problem. SNET also found that their policy of not accepting third-party checks or cash payments made it difficult for Hispanic customers to pay their bills, and that using only English on their bills made it difficult for many Hispanic customers to understand them. Thus we see how, by simply making an effort to get to know the culture and needs of its Hispanic customers, SNET was able to significantly lower its delinquency rates.

---

3. Identify Key Stakeholder Groups

Organizations are increasingly coming to understand that their target-market strategies must be geared toward, and appeal to, the target market's key stakeholder groups. In other words, government officials, local religious leaders, community activists, and others are often in one way or another impacted by or have influence upon both the organization and the target market. By simply identifying these key stakeholders and determining precisely how they influence the target market, an organization can begin to strike up mutually beneficial relationships with them, and/or get a feeling as to possible future opposition before they are actually confronted by it. Texaco, for instance, worked with Jesse Jackson to rectify discrimination against African Americans in its organization, but only after its name had been smeared all over the media with accusations of racism.

Best Practice

In 1996, General Motors won a $1 billion automotive deal with China, in large part because back in 1986 it had hired a very prominent, American-born Chinese woman who was well connected in China. In addition they had a company support group for Asians. Thus the company's knowledge of China and its culture, and some key contacts, gave GM a leg up over the other major car manufacturers who were pursuing the same contract.

---

4. Develop Relationships Based Upon Trust and Respect; Become a Proactive Community Citizen

Let's face it, it takes time to develop relationships based upon trust and respect. An organization must invest lots of time in researching what constitutes value-plus products and services for a market segment, largely by simply asking target market members and then listening and responding to what they have to say.

Also, however, it is vital that the organization foster an image of being a community partner. To a certain degree this may mean sponsoring community events, but money can buy only so much goodwill. If it is to truly become a community partner, an organization must get truly involved with its community. Easy and natural ways of doing this include hiring as employees people who are longstanding members of the community and supporting employees who volunteer their time to the community.

Best Practice

American Express actively participates in and supports the markets it targets. So as to develop a relationship with the gay and lesbian community, for instance, the company sponsored The Names Project in 1996. That year, too, it included partner benefits as part of its overall benefits structure.

---

5. Identify the Market Segment's Needs, Preferences, and Expectations

As an organization builds up a true partnership with a target market, it inevitably learns much about its customers' needs, preferences, and expectations. Sometimes, this knowledge will be gleaned directly from the target market by means of image surveys, focus groups, and the like. At other times it will be generated through competitive product analysis. Regardless, what always remains key is not just to get information but to keep it current, so as to be sure it is continually reflecting that market segment's true needs.

Best Practice

Because 51 percent of tires are sold, perhaps surprisingly, to women, Goodyear found an excellent way of targeting this market when it discovered through interviews, focus groups, and surveys that safety features are a big plus with women. Hence they developed the Aquatred tire, with its focus on safety.

---

6. Develop Products, Services, and Delivery Mechanisms That Will Deliver Value-Plus Products to Customers

If they are going to bring real value to their customers, organizations have to focus on developing products that are perceived by the target-market members as being both beneficial and attractive. Sometimes, a product that is a part of the firm's existing mix does add value for the target market. More often, however, a firm has to either redesign products or develop new ones in order to satisfy its target market.

And don't forget distribution systems. Your firm may well have a great product, but if you don't have any way of getting it into the hands of the user, so what? The particular problem here is that firms often assume, erroneously, that the distribution channels they use for the general market will work for the targeted market as well. What they fail to see is that nontraditional markets often purchase products in nontraditional ways. Recent immigrants, for example, often shop at specialty shops or at small, local grocers rather than in big supermarkets.

Best Practice

Coors Brewing has redesigned a portion of its distribution channels so as to reflect the tendency of new immigrants to shop at small, local community stores. Coors has dedicated a diverse-markets manager to each of its regions, whose job it is to place the company's beers with smaller, non-key accounts. Coors supports this effort by providing diversity training and ongoing support to their distributors.

An essential part of "delivery" is communication with the target market, including advertising and customer service. Advertising in particular has to be tailored to the target market's culture, and merely translating mass-market advertising isn't tailoring. Tailoring means developing the advertisement's message through a creative medium that is familiar and appropriate to members of the target market.

When it comes to customer service, nontraditional customers ask three questions as they seek to assess its quality: (1) Was my question or problem resolved? (2) Was dealing with the company's customer service representative comfortable and easy? (3) Was I treated with trust and respect? Organizations always must remember that the standards for measuring customer service are those of the target market, not the organization. Thus to respond defensively to a target market's critique of customer service is only to defeat the marketing strategy. For example, many recent Hispanic immigrants to the United States do not have personal checking accounts, so they'd rather pay their bills with cash or a third-party check. Any organization that sees those as being "inappropriate" ways of paying bills is unlikely to win the business of that target market.

Best Practice

Cadillac developed a new luxury model called the Catera, designed specifically for women. Female engineering, finance, and marketing managers were key members of the design team. Cadillac conducted focus groups to identify women's preferences, and modified the vehicle's design accordingly. To test how the car's controls function when the driver has longer fingernails, Cadillac engineers put paper clips on the ends of their fingers and attempted to use the controls. Here is another good example of a company which recognizes that the market was changing, and instead of imposing a new design on the market, employed a diverse team in order to create a product that the market truly wanted.

---

7. Continually Check Up on Your Progress, and Ask Members of the Target Market to Provide You with Ongoing Feedback

An essential part of every good marketing strategy is to check up on progress, and to ask members of the target market for their feedback. The organization must then react to this feedback, and alter its marketing strategies on that basis. This stage of the marketing strategy assists organizations in returning to the first step and recycling through the entire process.

Best Practice

Ann Taylor engaged in a strategy in order to find out how its store personnel were treating nontraditional customers. They assessed performance by having a diverse group of secret shoppers make purchases and then report back to the company on their shopping experience. The company shared the secret-shopping results at their annual sales meeting, so that all stores and associates would be able to monitor their progress in this area.

Making Use of Our Framework to Target Diverse Market Segments

Understanding Markets Segmented by Race, Ethnicity, and Language

As of 1998, American people of color numbered 79.5 million, representing 30 percent of the U.S. population. Their current buying power of $1 trillion is expected to grow significantly over the next 10 years. And in addition to that increase in buying power, the number of minority-owned firms is growing significantly as well. Indeed, between 1987 and 1992 it almost doubled, going from 1.2 to 2.1 million, the latter figure representing 12 percent of all firms. Minority business owners are exerting more autonomous control over a variety of decision-making processes, such as determining with whom they will and will not do business. And you had better believe that they will be more inclined to do business with organizations whose structure and values reflect the racial and ethnic diversity of the country at large, and which treat them and their communities with trust and respect. Savvy marketers will make a point of getting intimately acquainted with this large and growing segment of the marketplace, in order to win its business.

Now, let's take a closer look at some of the segments of this market.

The "Of Hispanic Origin" Segment. In 1996, Hispanic buying power in the United States stood at $363 billion. The U.S. Hispanic population reached 26.8 billion in 1995, and is expected to pass 31.1 million in the year 2000. This group is projected to add the largest number of people to the U.S. population every year until 2050, and by 2010 it will have become the second largest ethnic group in the country. Between 1987 and 1992, the number of Hispanic-owned firms increased 83 percent to 771,708, taking in $72.8 billion in receipts—a 195 percent increase. Hispanic men own the largest share (42 percent) of firms owned by minority men. Forty-eight percent of Hispanics live in five major cities: Los Angeles, New York, Miami, San Francisco, and Chicago.

There is great variation among the subgroups that make up the Hispanic population, but some factors held in common include the great importance placed on family and children, the desire to preserve ethnicity and language, devotion to religion and to tradition, a strong interest in physical appearance, and an emphasis on quality of life and enjoyment. Families tend to be larger and more extended, and traditional gender roles are more adhered to in these cultures than in the United States overall. Communities tend to be tightly knit, providing marketers with a ready-made network for word-of-mouth promotion.

The vast majority of Hispanics, 86 percent, speak Spanish at home, but there are significant differences among the various Spanish-language dialects. Thus, translations of English into Spanish must take into consideration the fact that a word-for-word rendering could not only produce a different meaning in Spanish but also different meanings to Mexicans, Puerto Ricans, and Cubans, and other Spanish-speaking groups. Each marketer must decide whether it is wisest to try to reach this market in Spanish or in English. Forty-eight percent of Hispanic respondents to a recent study reported that Spanish-language ads are "most persuasive," but there were notable differences among the groups included, ranging from 43 percent of Puerto Ricans to 68 percent of Dominicans.

In general, Hispanics tend to be somewhat brand-loyal; however, they are less likely than the general market to pay more for quality products. Also, they are more likely than the general market to gather a lot of information about a product before buying it. Markets are accessed through various media. According to *Packaged Facts,* advertisers spent more than $1 billion in the Hispanic media in 1995. In Los Angeles alone there are more than 30 Hispanic media sources, including television, radio, and newspapers.

Best Practices

- Bank of America has attracted new depositors by targeting Mexican and Central American immigrants. These potential customers were not responding to mainstream advertising because most had had no experience with banks and had no idea what an "interest-bearing account" was. By educating these groups through advertising and seminars, Bank of America made banking less intimidating for them.
- Goya Foods, a New Jersey-based food producer, was founded in 1963 to "feed" a growing demand for familiar foods on the part of swelling numbers of immigrants from Spain, Puerto Rico, Cuba, and Central America. Goya manufactures, packages, and sells nearly a thousand products and ingredients, with annual sales of $528 million.
- Sears reached out to Hispanic customers with its "Todo Para Ti" campaign, and sponsored the tour of singer Gloria Estafan.

The Asian American Segment. Between 1970 and 1990 the number of Asians in the United States increased 385 percent to 7.3 million, and they constitute the nation's fastest-growing market segment. Buying power in 1996 stood at $325 billion. In contrast to other immigrant groups, Asian women outnumber men in most Asian American communities. The largest Asian groups in the United States are Chinese, Filipino, Japanese, Asian Indian, Korean, Vietnamese, Hawaiian, Somoan, and Guamanian. The Asian American market is the most diverse in terms of ethnicity, language, and religion; for instance most Filipinos are Catholic whereas most Japanese are Buddhists, and Indians are largely a mix of Sikhs, Muslims, and Hindus.

Two-thirds of adult Asian immigrants have attended college and are proficient in English; compared to U.S.-born white males, a much higher percentage of them earn $50,000 or more. Many Asian American households are made up of two-income families, with many generations living under the same roof. Asians have enjoyed much success in the business community, and they are responsible for 89 percent of the new small businesses that have been started up by immigrants between 1979 and 1987. In 1987, 376,711 Asian-owned firms had total receipts of $33 billion; by 1992, 606,438 Asian-owned firms had total receipts of $108 billion. So while the number of firms increased 61 percent, receipts increased 227 percent!

In general, Asians tend to assimilate into U.S. culture faster than do the members of other groups. They tend to place a high priority on education, hard work, close family ties, and financial caution. Once they have established a relationship—and the relationship counts for everything—the most important things to Asian Americans are quality, a long-standing reputation, and respect for customers. Polls indicate that the most important factors in choosing a product are quality, price vis-à-vis value received, service, and convenience. In addition, Asians appreciate any effort that is made to bridge cultural differences.

Marketers need to be on the lookout for certain basic cultural "red flags" here. In Japan, for example, there are negative connotations attached to the number four, while in Canton, China, the numbers two and four add up to bad luck. In Hong Kong, as we also noted earlier, one company unsuccessfully tried to give away green hats, unaware of the superstition that if a man wears a green hat his wife is cheating on him. In many Asian cultures, silence is viewed as a sign of deep appreciation. In Japan, there are 16 ways to say the word *yes*. These can then mean anything from "Yes, I will try" to "Yes, I'm not sure but I want you to feel good," to "Yes, I made a mistake but I don't want to bring shame on my family," to "Yes, it is unlikely that we will be able to do business but I do not want to bring shame on you." Clearly, given all of the above, organizations intent upon tapping into the Asian market must strive to be attentive to innumerable nuances of language and culture.

Best Practices

- Acknowledging that its products weren't selling well in Asia, Bausch & Lomb turned to its Asian employees for guidance. Where their inquiries led them was to the discovery that their glasses weren't fitting Asian people properly. Sales rose, once the company had modified its glasses for its Asian markets.
- The Discovery Channel's cooking show features a pork-free menu for Islamic Malaysia, and a beef-free one for Hindu Indians.
- Oxford Health Plans has one fully Chinese staff, a walk-in center in New York City's Chinatown, and an 800 number which provides the caller with Chinese-language service.

The African American Segment. There are 31 million African Americans, representing 14 percent of the U.S. population. Buying power totaled $427 billion in 1996. Between 1993 and 1994, African American households represented the only racial or ethnic group that experienced real income gains. In 1995, 1.6 million African American households had incomes of $50,000 or more. The number of black-owned businesses has grown significantly. Between 1987 and 1992 the number increased by 46 percent to 620,912; receipts for these firms increased 63 percent, to $32.2 billion.

As with most other market segments, African Americans vary by country of origin, language, family type, age, religion, education, income, and other factors. Organizations must take account of these differences if they are to market effectively to this segment. For example inner-city youths, suburbanites, the middle-aged, professionals, and blacks from sub-Saharan Africa will all tend to respond to very different marketing messages. It is a major mistake to assume that every member of the black community has had personal experience with urban ghettos, drug dealers, welfare, and crime.

The keys to marketing success in the black segment are relevance, recognition, and respect. It is vital that a company build up a long-term, honest relationship with the black market segment. Research has shown that blacks tend to be willing to pay more in return for perceived higher quality, better service, and greater respect. According to *Packaged Facts,* since the "silent demand" of the African American consumer is for respect, these customers are sensitive to all "hustle, condescension, choice of words, and body language that would connote lack of respect." In general, this market appreciates labels and brand names, and spends more on image-enhancing products than does the general U.S. population.

Organizations draw upon a variety of media as they seek to penetrate new markets. And yet according to a Burrell/Yankelovich survey, 58 percent of African Americans agree that "Most advertising was designed only for white people." The same survey found that African Americans rely on advertising for product information and brand identity, respond to advertisements that purvey a positive sense of black lifestyles, and respond best to ads that speak directly to them and to their experiences.

Thus, as they strive to get their message through to this market segment, advertisers must carefully consider their media choices. African Americans, for example, watch notably different television programs than do most other members of the general population. They also listen to the radio 50 percent more than the general population, with the urban format being their top choice. And it is true that urban radio tends to have a loyal listener base, and is heavily involved in the African American community.

African American churches, political organizations, and fraternal and social organizations, and the military, are also critical to the development of effective marketing strategies. Also, organizations must be aware that African Americans expect that a reasonable amount of the profits taken out of the black community will be recirculated within that community. *Packaged Facts* has reported that African American shoppers notice whether their neighborhood chain stores employ African Americans at the managerial and sales levels, do business with African American suppliers, and employ black models in their ads. Thus organizations that want to tap into this market must take special care to develop distribution channels, workforces, and advertising messages that include African Americans.

Best Practices

- Boston Bank of Commerce offers a Unity Visa card, targeted to African American customers. One percent of all spending is donated to one of seven African American community organizations.
- Chrysler sponsored the national television premier of the acclaimed documentary *Hoop Dreams,* in an attempt to appeal to black consumers; this was part of an overall marketing and educational initiative designed to show Chrysler's commitment to the African American community. And in 1995, Chrysler was able to report a 14 percent increase in market share among African Americans.
- J C Penney, the only national department store chain to specifically target African Americans, sells Afrocentric merchandise through a special catalog.

Understanding Markets by Gender

Markets have of course been segmented on the basis of gender for many years now. It has been assumed that "women's" products involve nurturing roles—the home, the children, the husband—whereas "men's" products involve masculine roles—big-ticket items, insurance, finances, tools. Typically marketers have targeted these segments through their advertising choices: sports events versus soap operas, *Sports Illustrated* versus *Good Housekeeping.* And yet the current gender-related demographics contain some wake-up implications for organizations that are already used to segment markets by gender.

For example as women gain ground in the areas of education, career advancement, and representation in the workforce, their buying power is steadily increasing. And that means that they now have the clout to demand not only that all goods, services, and marketing strategies meet their needs, but that organizations treat them with trust and respect. Of course men's roles are changing as well, as many men find themselves in such nontraditional roles as single parent, or guy with more responsibility for more household chores. Men also are being given broader license to express themselves and their emotions. All of which means that the image created by marketers of the rugged, manly man, wedded as much to his power tools as to his stay-at-home wife, rings true with only a small and ever-shrinking portion of our society.

All of these gender-related changes are both challenging and full of opportunity. What marketers now need to do is to segment both the male and female markets into smaller groups, targeting a broader spectrum of products and services at these market subgroups. The bottom line: it simply will no longer cut it, to base marketing and product-mix strategies on the old assumptions about men and women. Both sexes have become too diverse in age, race, income level, family structure, norms, values, and beliefs. Organizations that base their marketing strategies on any one "typical" man or woman are doomed to fail.

The Women's Segment. In the United States there are 51.9 million women at the age of 16 and over, representing 52 percent of the entire 16-and-over population. In 1950, women represented a mere 30 percent of the workforce; by 1996 that figure had risen to 46 percent. Women currently earn $1 trillion annually. And don't think for a moment that that money is just "pin money" or "rainy-day money." According to a survey conducted by the Families and Work Institute and Whirlpool, 55 percent of all employed women account for 50 or more percent of their household's income.

Another statistic graphically revealing the economic clout of women is the number of women-owned businesses. In 1996, women owned 7.9 million businesses—33 percent of all domestic firms, 40 percent of all retail/service firms. They employed 15.5 million people, and generated $1.4 trillion in sales. Women-owned firms also have staying power: Of women-owned firms that were in existence back in 1991, 72.7 percent are still in existence today, as compared to 66 percent of U.S. businesses overall. Thus, given their growing success, women business owners are increasingly in a position to make their own decisions regarding the types of companies they will consent to do business with.

In the home, it is women who make most of the important financial decisions. According to Paul Sheldon of Prudential Securities, women make 70 percent of all family financial decisions; 61 percent of family bills are paid by women; 53 percent of individual shareholders are women; 80 percent of checks are written by women; 86 percent of the personal wealth in the United States is controlled by women; and over seven of the last nine years, the all-female investment clubs have outperformed the all-male clubs.

When they are marketing to women, firms must recognize that women of various ages have different frames of reference. For older women, references to the 1950s might, for example, evoke images of the "good old days" when families were valued and the country was growing economically. For younger ones, however, the term "the fifties" might evoke images of a time when women were discouraged from entering the workforce and were unable to get credit and loans. We're sure you can see how vital it is for marketers to be keenly aware of these differing frames of reference.

In addition, firms must design products and services with women in mind, recognizing as they do so that women are interested in more than color and going out of their way to ask them what particular features they are eager to see in certain products. When Jockey made the decision to market a line of women's underwear, the company had the good sense to avoid rushing right to the design phase. Rather, it sought out women's counsel, and thereby boosted its chance of having a successful product launch. Some marketers seem to have a fear that taking such an approach will alienate the male market, but that fear appears to be unfounded. For instance when auto manufacturers redesigned seat belts on the basis of comments they had acquired from women, they found that men liked the new designs as well; as it turned out, the original seat belts, designed for six-foot-tall men, were awkward not only for women but for most men as well!

It is vital that any organization developing marketing strategies for women understand the realities of this segment, and get beyond all generalizations and stereotypes about who women are and what they want. Women are entering and succeeding in the workforce at higher and higher rates. They are in many cases balancing work and family—though some are choosing to forgo motherhood. But at any rate, this much is crystal-clear: any attempt to appeal to the women of the next millennium by means of images of women decked out in dresses, pearls, and pantyhose, while happily running the vacuum cleaner, are sure to miss the mark.

Best Practices

- Through a women's marketing committee, Ford did extensive research into the women's market before it designed the Ford Explorer. And now, with its four doors, no hump, and easy-to-handle dashboard design, the Explorer has replaced the station wagon of old to become one of the most popular cars on the road today.
- MacGreggor Gold created a set of gold clubs that features an unusual mix of clubs designed to meet the needs of women golfers. They have also introduced a Lady Petite line, for smaller women golfers.
- Ryka athletic shoes are manufactured specially for women by primarily female designers, marketers, and project managers. A portion of the sales proceeds goes to the Ryka Rose Foundation, which assists the victims of rape and domestic abuse.

Conclusions

Tremendous changes have occurred in the marketplace over the last 20 years, causing organizations to radically rethink their marketing strategies. Many have found that a one-size-fits-all approach simply no longer cuts it. Instead, they are choosing to target specific segments of the population and to develop the marketing strategies appropriate for that segment. Numerous variables segment these markets: race, language, gender, family structure, and the like.

If they are going to capitalize on today's changes, organizations will have to develop new ways to interact with customers and with diverse market segments. This chapter has laid out a seven-step plan that organizations can follow, as they seek to develop the appropriate marketing strategies for their many diverse target markets. At the foundation of this plan, like all of them, is the need to patiently build up relationships that are with the target market based upon trust and respect. For let's face it, today's consumers are nothing if not sophisticated; they can tell the difference between an organization that wants to be a true community partner and one that is just out for a quick buck. The bottom line: Any corporation that takes the time and trouble to get intimately acquainted with its target markets will be poised to succeed in the coming century, and along the way will make some major inroads against the racism and sexism that continue to corrode our society.

IV

MANAGING YOUR CAREER

16

Managing Relationships to Enhance Career Opportunities

Introduction

Throughout our book until now, we have placed most of the onus for change on organizations, tasking them with the job of implementing holistic strategies so as to minimize racism and sexism and thereby ensure the fair, equitable treatment of all employees. We have made organizations responsible, for example, for the designing of fair performance-appraisal processes and the establishment of formal mentoring programs, and as well as for their own restructuring to better become a postbureaucratic structure.

In this chapter, we propose to shift the burden onto the shoulders of employees. For although organizations do have clear responsibilities, the fact remains that it is individual women and people of color, as well as "out-group" white males, who must bear most of the responsibility for making their own careers a success. Rather than merely sitting around whining about how bad things are, members of these and other groups must constantly seek not only to raise their level of emotional intelligence but to sharpen all of their technical and professional skills as well. And as they do so, they must be fully aware that what is key to overcoming the barriers that confront them in their careers is relationship building. Therefore our goal in this chapter is to show how any employee, but particularly women and people of color, can more effectively develop relationships and thus enhance their career opportunities.

But make no mistake: It isn't easy. All business organizations have their hierarchies, their own breeds of politics, their corporate cultures, identities, organizational charts, rules, regulations, formal and informal networks, symbols, rituals, customs, and vocabularies. They all have many people eager to grab up only a limited number of resources and rewards. The environment one must navigate through is almost certain to be highly competitive, and any corporation is likely to have its share of unhealthy people who behave in unhealthy ways, particularly in the area of race and gender interactions. Given these realities, the watchword for every employee should be that ancient one, "Know thyself," i.e., continually become more aware of the image one is conveying, and not just with regard to its "what" but also to its "how" and "why." When a person understands the self, he or she is in a far better position to analyze success or the lack of it in building (a) effective relationships with members of different races or the opposite sex, and (b) successful careers. The remainder of this chapter will provide you with some paths to such self-understanding, vis-à-vis managing one's career and one's relationships.

Social Interaction: The Need to Be Part of a Whole

One study of a hunter-gatherer society in New Guinea showed that no person living in that society suffered from depression. Researchers have speculatively attributed this high degree of mental health to the fact that this society is marked by a high degree of social interaction, trust, and cooperation.

In today's corporations this deep-seated human need for social interaction has become just as pronounced—perhaps more so, given the radical changes taking place in families and other social structures and given the fact that for many of us, most of our social interactions now take place at work. As we have seen, earlier, however, a key problem that especially impacts women and people of color is their exclusion from informal work groups, and thus from the kind of social interactions we all so crave. Such exclusion inevitably affects not only their working relationships, but their mental health as well. Psychologists insist that it is critical for people to work and interact closely with others; in other words, developing trust and respect—in the home, the workplace, the marketplace, or elsewhere—is essential to our daily functioning and to our mental health as well.

Building Relationships

In order to be an effective employee in corporate America, one must have not only a clear understanding of oneself, but also some piercing insights into the natures of the persons with whom one works. In short, one needs to know, as closely as one can, the other person's *real* self. Since business situations ultimately come down to people-situations, the more we know about the person(s) we are dealing with, the better we enhance our chance of doing an outstanding job. And the only way of really learning about that person is by developing a personal, not just a professional, relationship with him or her.

Thus, we should strive to learn as much as we possibly can about the personal lives of the people we are trying to influence—where they live, how they live, what they do outside of work, who their friends are. It might of course be objected that it is inappropriate to probe into other people's personal lives; but the fact is that other people, and indeed the corporation itself, are doing so all the time, whether one likes it or not, or thinks it is ethical or not. For one thing, to do so is one good way to gain the confidence of key people. When we get to know such persons' family members and explore areas of common interest—children, good wine, reading, sports, the theater, travel—we are provided with an invaluable window into their minds—how they think; what their attitudes toward money or power or risk are; what they value; what their aspirations are for the future. In other words, a gentle but respectful "probing" can do much to build up positive, healthy, and long lasting relationships.

Nonetheless, building relationships across the boundaries of gender and race can be difficult, for at least two reasons. First, many people look upon the hiding of their true selves as being an essential survival tactic in today's ever-changing bureaucratic environment. Being politically correct, and thereby hiding many of one's true feelings, has become the norm for many white men and white women, and for some people of color. For while it has often been deemed inappropriate to discuss one's personal feelings in general, lately it has become particularly inappropriate to discuss one's feelings about race and gender. Second, it can be difficult to broaden one's relationship base through non-work-related functions. This is particularly a problem for blacks, given the fact that only 50 percent of whites, compared to 80 percent of blacks, have frequent contact with blacks or other people of color at social functions not related to work. All of which simply means that blacks—and the same holds true for women—have to make more of an effort when it comes to "reaching out and touching someone."

Networking

We have been suggesting that a great deal of the power to be found within the corporate structure resides in informal networks. Systematic exclusion from powerful and well-connected informal groups—a problem which many of our survey participants believe afflicts women and people of color much more than it does most white males—seriously blocks us from gaining access to that power and authority we so need in order to do our best work and thereby enhance our careers. Thus, it is essential that women and people of color actively seek out those informal work groups that have been formally or informally sanctioned by their companies. And yet we must not waste our energy in trying to become members of groups that are more purely social than "political." The goal is to make contacts at both work and nonwork functions with group members who are in possession of information, power, and experience. Hard and unfair as it may at first sound, women and people of color simply must try to find something they have in common with the leaders of a network, and then build on that commonality. And remember that the more diverse your contacts are, the easier it will be for you to gain access to information and to receive more targeted coaching. Such diversity also will allow you to more efficiently identify new opportunities as they arise.

True as all of that is, it also is true that women and people of color must begin to come together in their own informal work groups. Alas, women and people of color tend to have trouble forming such networks, largely because whites and men criticize them for being racist, sexist, or "not-team-approved." Still, women, people of color, and nonconforming white males shouldn't let such misguided criticisms keep them from "looking out for their own." For to be scared away from forming such informal networks because of such perceptions would be to allow others to deny them access to a crucial strategy for success.

Most networks have overlapping memberships. That is important to remember, simply because all too many groups have their snitches and "plants." Therefore informal work groups must be entered into and utilized "only" very cautiously and strategically. Note also that many "out-group" members tend to be more open, honest, and straightforward than the "in-group" members. Thus it can be a fatal error, when the in-group has let one in, to believe that their acceptance is total. Never entirely let your guard down until you have developed trusting and respectful relations. A young, high-potential black male once told us of how accepted he had felt when he became the first black member of a high-powered operating team. He began to share with the group his true feelings both personal and professional, but later found to his dismay that his supervisor and several of his colleagues were using these informal discussions to derogate him. In fact, his career soon came to a halt, and not owing to performance—his division was number one in results—but because it had been decided that he didn't have the right stuff politically. He was seen as having a bad attitude, and rough edges that needed to be smoothed away. Think of how much better things might have turned out, if this unfortunate fellow had taken the time to understand his colleagues, and to ascertain the extent to which his relationships with them were based upon genuine trust and respect.

Before we leave this topic, we ask you to heed these words well: Along with internal intelligence networks, effective employees build external networks of personal contacts. External contacts help you stay informed about what's going on "out there"—changing customer preferences, a competitors's plans and actions, social and economic trends, pending regulations, emergent technologies, and so forth. Their networks reach into different nooks and crannies; they have different perspectives; they're steps closer to vital news as it breaks.[1] We would add that such external contacts also can be invaluable sources of feedback about your interpersonal skills, strengths, and weaknesses. They can become crucial allies as you seek not only to carry out your job at the highest level but also to enhance your career prospects.

Just Corporate Politics, or Managing Relationships?

Let's face it, politics are of the essence of corporate life. As Allison and Allison have argued, "Wherever there are people, there is influence, power and competition. Add to this brewing personality clashes, differing leadership styles, conflicting goals, limited budgets, and rapid change, and you have politics, corporate politics." Of course, we would add to that list the problems of racism and sexism. But the real point here is that the political process need not be as harmful and as hurtful as it so often is. It can just as easily become a way of constructively persuading people that your way is the right way or at least the best way. But we're sure not going to deny that as of now, corporate politics still have their sinister side: exploitation, apple polishing, backstabbing, lying, sabotaging, cheating, racism, sexism, you name it.

Thus, what it is most important to remember about politics is that you can't ignore them. The question is not *whether* to play the game, but *what kind* of game to play. And once again, we stress that "playing politics" doesn't have to mean stabbing others in the back. It can become synonymous with the constructive process of finding out how an organization really works; who its powerful and interesting and helpful people are; who really makes the decisions; what the true relationships on and off the organizational chart are; where and what the rivalries and factions are; and the like. Unfortunately, racism and sexism often serve to deny women and people of color with the coaching and experience they need in order to fully learn "the rules of the game"—rules that generally are second nature to in-group white males.

Manage Your Manager, Your Peers, and Your Direct Reports

To begin with, remember that you and your manager need one another. Your fates and fortunes are intertwined. You are a team. Helping and cooperating with each other is vitally important to both of you. More particularly, each of you plays a critical role as a provider of information for the other. You only close yourself off from a vital source of information when you view your manager as an adversary.

That said, here is the single best piece of advice we can give you about managers: No matter how weak and ineffective they may seem to you to be, you should challenge them aggressively only with regard to business issues directly related to you or your team's job performance and objectives. If you challenge your managers too often, or on tangential issues, you will lose not only their support but the support of top management as well. Manage your manager; keep the manager out of trouble; make the manager look good, even if the manager *isn't* very good.

Of course, far too many of us complain about how we are managed, then turn around and do the very same things once we have become managers. But if you are going to develop trust and respect among direct reports, remember that the bad old days of command and control are over. Remember that effective managers get things done *through* others. You depend upon your direct reports, just as your manager depends upon you; therefore empower them to do their jobs better, and they will help you to do yours better. Try to think of them less as subordinates and more as partners and allies in your quest for personal and organizational integrity and success—often a damn hard thing to do, in a control-oriented, patriarchal environment.

Sometimes it's hard to understand your direct reports, and you're right that it's not just level and status that are standing in the way. When direct reports come from diverse backgrounds, then differences in language (e.g., slang), customs, and styles of interaction can make it tough to truly understand them, even for managers with high emotional intelligence. But if you simply recognize that this is a problem for which no one is to blame, then you are less likely to direct your anger at your direct report for any difficulties of mutual understanding, and more likely to seek out constructive approaches to maximizing communication.

And remember that no matter what you do or don't do, you are always going to have some employees who are disgruntled. One way to keep them from devoting all of their energies to useless carping is to get them directly involved in finding the solutions to their problems through committees and task forces. And when they do come up with reasonable solutions to the problems they've identified, be sure to support them. Make your direct reports personally responsible for implementing the solutions, and then for evaluating and refining them. Thus, this approach to carping employees has a dual benefit: it focuses on the problem and its true source, rather than on mere griping, and it gives employees a sense of ownership in solutions.

Peer relationships are yet another matter that needs to be carefully managed. Never allow yourself to forget that peers control all sorts of necessary resources: technical expertise, information, advice, political backing, and moral support. Peers make powerful friends, and very dangerous enemies. You need their support, and they need yours. Unless you are fortunate enough to already be working in a true postbureaucratic organization, recognize that you can genuinely trust very few of your peers, regardless of race or gender, simply because they are competing with you for the same organizational rewards. But be heartened by the fact that as firms move more toward teams and flexible organizational structures, your success will more and more be linked to your ability to knowingly and compassionately manage peer relationships. In the meantime, seek out those places where the interests of peers align with your own and be on the alert for competing interests.

The bottom line here is that managers, peers, and direct reports clearly are enmeshed in interdependent relationships. Therefore it is foolhardy for employees, and especially for people of color, women, and out-group white males, to believe that they can succeed without first gaining the support of all three groups. If you are going to survive and prosper, you have no choice but to actively manage these groups, rather than let them manage you.

Mentors

No one gets to the top, or into key positions, without the help of mentors. As our data in Chapter 12 reveal, lack of mentoring is a key problem for women, people of color, and white males who do not fit the corporate image. Yet only about 40 percent of U.S. corporations have formal mentoring programs; and even more disturbingly, only about 20 percent of employees believe that their corporations do.

Let's take a moment here to remind ourselves just exactly who a mentor is. Effective mentors are experienced, knowledgeable managers who are widely seen as being strong leaders. The psychosocial role they play is to coach and protect those whom they mentor. They assist them in obtaining challenging assignments, they educate them in the company's culture and informal political processes, and so on.

In most companies, mentors select those whom they wish to mentor, as opposed to vice versa. And that means, since most people naturally want to mentor those with whom they feel personally and professionally comfortable, and since the mentoring relationship necessarily entails a degree of risk to the mentor, that mentors are most likely to select those who look like themselves (in the broadest sense of the word *look*). Which in turn, as we have seen, makes it hard for women and people of color to find mentors. After all, mentors are nothing if not fond of saying that the person they are mentoring is "like a son to me," words that right away throw up a roadblock to women and people of a different color.

So, what can you do if you are one of those who simply don't "fit"? Stand out by being creative, and by taking risks. Do your work at a level of excellence that will help your potential mentor to get over any hesitancy he or she may be feeling about you and about the amount of risk he or she may be taking on in choosing to mentor you. And be gracious enough to remain consistently aware of how quickly you can become a liability to your mentor, and of how, in sticking out his/her neck for you, your mentor could suffer a "power loss" or even leave the company feet first. Thus, it is both politically wise for you, and compassionate toward mentors, to spread out the risk by developing relationships with as many mentors as you can.

Some employees who discover that they're having trouble finding mentors, try to fix the situation by creating for themselves an image of one who is promotable—that is, they emulate the dominant race and gender group in thought and spirit. That's a big mistake, in our opinion. Women, people of color, and nonconforming white males must bear in mind that in most cases a mentor selects a protégé not only because the two share some common reference point, but also on the basis of some unique characteristic that distinguishes that protégé from other employees. For a person to try to be someone else only serves to negate that advantage—not only with mentors who might themselves be women or people of color, but with those more emotionally intelligent white males who might very well serve that person as powerful mentors.

Although there aren't many people of color in real positions of power, and only somewhat more women are available to be mentors, people of color and women still can sponsor other people of color and women. Therefore, members of those groups, especially at the lower levels, should not entertain the false notion that their mentors have to be white and/or male. On the other hand, however, people of color and women also should not believe, as some have suggested, that only a person of color or a woman can effectively mentor people of color of the same race, or that women can only effectively mentor women. Nothing is more certain than that a sensitive, aware, white-male mentor of high emotional intelligence will do a far better job as a mentor than will an inconsistent, unaware woman or person of color.

One final note here: As you women and people of color ascend the corporate ladder, please be a hero or heroine and make a special effort to bring other women and people of color up with you. We say that because we have found that many people of color who make it into the middle and upper ranks are reluctant to assist other people of color, perhaps out of a fear that they will be appearing to favor their own group. This is somewhat less of a problem with women, perhaps owing to the somewhat larger number of women who have found their way into the middle and upper ranks. But the real point here, however tough it may be to swallow, is that if women and people of color don't assist others "of their kind," no one else can be counted upon to do so. And only when the middle and upper levels of management contain far more women and people of color committed to helping the corporation change its structure, policies, and practices, and to eliminating racism and sexism, will everybody have an equal chance of moving up and helping their company to compete and win in the new millennium.

To Conform or Not to Conform?

A difficult issue for women and people of color—and, as always, for a surprisingly substantial number of white males—is that of conformity, of the degree to which one should or should not alter one's behavior and/or mindset in order to fit in with a corporation's culture. We begin here by saying that we believe few people can be happy and healthy, if they are trying to be only what others want them to be. And yet we also believe that *some* degree of conformity is essential, if one is to become an active and happy member of a corporation. Indeed, conformity was an issue long before diversity was, as suggested by the widespread influence of the 1950s classic, *The Man in the Gray Flannel Suit*. Depending upon the situation, we all may well have to hold our tongues, be nice to people we despise, occasionally put aside a value we hold dear, and even don clothes we hate to wear. But the point here is that however tempted we might be to resist something like accepted business attire, some battles as Schoonmaker has noted, simply aren't worth fighting:

> You may feel that doing these things is a cop-out, a sacrifice of part of your identity. Perhaps you are right, but there is another viewpoint. Your identity is not just what you wear or the language you use; it is what you believe in and the strength of your character and self-confidence. If your sense of identity depends only on your clothes, you are really in bad shape, and letting your hair grow will not solve your identity problems.[2]

Now, no employee should conform slavishly, in a misguided attempt to meet other people's wrongheaded expectations.

And in the long run, a company's refusal to straitjacket its talents (whether those be innate or culturally conditioned) will prove itself a beneficial policy both for the corporation and for society as a whole. By allowing employees to be themselves as long as they remain within the basic norms, values, and behaviors which the corporation has established, corporations will be developing precisely the right skills as it seeks to provide products and services to diverse customers who are not about to conform to any corporate norm of looks, behaviors, and mannerisms. We have seen plenty of employees trying to become clones, and in fact making a darned nice job of it; but to what end, and at what cost? Most of them will not be rewarded for behaving as clones, because people of color will never be white and women will never be men. Some decision makers will continue to delight in continually changing the criteria for becoming a "true clone," and/or openly ridicule those who are trying. In short, what we have here is a double-bind. The "boys" will always be able to change the overt conformity criteria, whenever they want to keep employees from focusing on their problems.

We want to close this section by making two final points. First, and as we have said previously, healthy employees are those who have a keen sense of their strengths and weaknesses. Because of that they basically like themselves and feel secure, and will conform only because they want to and while recognizing and admitting to themselves that they are conforming. Second, please be seriously cautioned that those people and companies that demand of one a great deal of unnecessary conformity, even in such an area as dress, are also the ones mostly likely to find it very difficult to appreciate and value differences of race, ethnicity, and culture.

Your Attitude toward Work

Too many people fail to recognize that their attitude toward their work is another big key to building effective relationships. For the fact is that no one wants to have a relationship with someone who is not carrying his or her weight. And yet at the same time, our data show that many people who feel they are not being treated fairly by their company (presumably because they have been denied access to the networks and mentoring that we have been speaking of throughout this chapter) then begin to perform below their abilities, so they're damned if they do and damned if they don't. Such a double-bind is especially deadly for women and people of color, since it reinforces stereotypes about their lack of qualifications and inability to get the job done. For instance, let's say that a woman works hard and conforms, then is not rewarded for her efforts, which causes her future performance to slacken. Those watching her will then say "Ah-hah, see? I told you she wasn't up to that job!"

Our best counsel here is that no matter how unfairly you may be treated, always perform right up to the top of your ability—or leave the company. One manner of doing the former is to approach your job in a way diametrically opposed to that which the company culture dictates. Rather than doing what so many employees do—making your job seem difficult, and creating a lot of froth to show how busy you are—try taking complex problems and making them simple. Such a "can-do" attitude can solve problems, get the job done, and make money for stockholders—and get you noticed for the part that you and your good attitude played in all that. Also, don't fall into the trap of first complaining about overly directing managers and then complaining, when things feel directionless, that managers aren't taking sufficient interest in you and your career. Take the initiative, direct yourself. And if your manager does seem to be chary of directing you, take that as a sign of trust and respect.

Rarely, if ever, turn down a work assignment, especially if you have people working for you. After all, a big part of your job should be to figure out how to get a full plate cleaned. It's all part of the excitement and challenge of work. But also remember that to never turn down an assignment doesn't mean to never ask for help when you need it. Thus, the proper approach we're recommending here is to, on the one hand, never say that a task or a problem isn't your job or your responsibility. If it has come your way, it's your job. But on the other hand, always ask for help when you really need it.

Conclusions

All employees face many obstacles, as they seek to do their jobs effectively and to enhance their careers. And none of them can hope to successfully navigate around those obstacles without first building up a network of effective interpersonal relationships. We have seen how this problem can be particularly acute for women, people of color, and nonconforming white males, so many of whom lack both the models and the informal networks to truly "relate."

Precisely because of all the obstacles they face, members of these groups must make a special commitment to take some of the steps we have outlined in this chapter:

- *Networking, in the sense of building informal contacts within the organization; not just social contacts, but those that provide access to crucial information and a degree of power*
- *Recognizing when it is necessary to play within the rules of corporate politics; not in the negative sense of manipulating others, but in the positive sense of adapting oneself to the way things really work*
- *Managing relationships with managers, direct reports, and peers, with a recognition that all are part of a team that can make or break the fortunes of its individual members*
- *Building relationships through mentors, and then themselves becoming mentors when they have the opportunity*
- *Conforming (within reason) to the corporate culture, so as not to waste time and energy by taking fruitless stands on minor issues*
- *Maintaining a consistently positive and upbeat attitude toward work.*

If they can just summon up the courage and determination to take these sorts of steps, women, people of color, and nonconforming white males can significantly boost their chances of surviving and flourishing within the company culture. And that in turn will leave them in a far better, more entrenched position from which to work tirelessly to banish racism and sexism from their organizations.

Notes

2
The Search for Solutions

1. Wooldridge, E., "Time to Stand Maslow's Hierarchy on Its Head?" *People Management*, December 21, 1995, p. 17.

3
The United States Is Not a Meritocracy

1. Dalton, H. L., *Racial Healing* (New York, Doubleday, 1995), pp. 127–129.
2. Levinson, H., *Psychological Man* (Cambridge, MA: Levison Institute, 1976), p. 31.
3. Kanter, R. M., "How the Top Is Different," in *Life in Organizations: Workplaces as People Experience Them*, ed. R. M. Kanter and B. A. Stein (New York: Basic Books, 1979), pp. 25–26.
4. Wynter, L., "Discrimination Follows an Internal Script," *The Wall Street Journal* (10/19/94), p. B1.
5. Ruderman, M. N., Ohlott, P., and Kram, K. E., *Managerial Promotion: The Dynamics for Men and Women* (Greensboro, NC: Center for Creative Leadership), pp. 25–26.
6. Merton, R., "Bureaucratic Structure and Personality," *Social Forces*, 17 (1940), p. 562.
7. Gannon, M. J., *Organizational Behavior* (Boston: Little Brown, 1979), pp. 107–109.

4
To Stereotype Is Human—But Dangerous

1. Levinson, p. 140.
2. Goleman, D., *Emotional Intelligence* (New York, Bantam, 1995), p. 28.

3. Cole, K. D., "Brain's Use of Shortcuts Can Be a Route to Bias," *Los Angeles Times,* May 1, 1995, p. B1.
4. Zaden, J. W. V., *American Minority Relations: The Sociology of Race and Ethnic Groups* (New York: John Wiley and Sons, 1963), p. 52.
5. Cose, E., *The Rage of the Privileged Classes* (New York: Harper Perennial, 1993), p. 83.

5

Stereotyping and Discrimination in Corporate America: A 25-Year Perspective

1. Harris, L., New York, 1993.
2. Jones, R. L., "The Concept of Racism and Its Changing Reality," in *Impacts of Racism on White Americans,* eds. B. P. Bower and R. G. Hunt (Newbury Park, CA: Sage Publications, 1981), p. 43.

6

Beyond the Rhetoric of Race and Gender: Two Immodest Proposals

1. Hofstede, G., *Cultures and Organizations: Software of the Mind* (New York: McGraw, 1991), p. 5.
2. Goleman, D., *Emotional Intelligence* (New York: Bantam, 1995), p. 149.
3. Stuller, J., "E. I.: Edging Toward Respectability," *Training,* June, 1997, pp. 46–48.
4. Ibid.

7

Tearing Down the Bureaucracy

1. Nirenberg, J., *The Living Organization: Transforming Teams Into Workplace Communities* (New York: Irwin, 1993), pp. 22–23.
2. Leonard, D., and Straus, S., "Putting Your Company's Whole Brain to Work," *Harvard Business Review* (July–August 1997), p. 111.
3. Heckscher, C., and Donnellon, A., eds. *The Post Bureaucratic Organization* (London: Sage, 1994), p. 20.
4. Ibid, p. 23.
5. Gordon, D. M., *Fat and Mean* (New York: The Free Press, 1996), pp. 40–41.
6. Chambers, N., "Ownership Gets Big," *Management Review,* July/August, 1997, pp. 13–19.

9

Communication and Conflict Resolution: Tips for Minimizing Race- and Gender-Related Difficulties

1. Henderson, G., *Cultural Diversity in the Workplace* (Westport, Connecticut: Praeger, 1994), p. 152.
2. Kikoski, J. F., and Kikoski, C. K., *Reflexive Communication in the Culturally Diverse Workplace* (Westport, Connecticut: Quorum, 1996), p. 155.
3. Lynch, D., "Unresolved Conflicts Affect the Bottom Line," *HR* magazine (May 1997), p. 49.

10

Recruiting and Retaining a Diverse Workforce

1. Montgomery, C. E., "Organizational Fit Is Key to Job Success," *HR* magazine (January 1996), p. 95.
2. Ibid., p. 96.
3. Langdon, D. G. and Whiteside, K. S., "Redefining Jobs and Working in Changing Organizations," *HR* magazine (May 1996), p. 97.

11

Leadership in the Age of Racially Charged Organizations

1. Teal, T., "The Human Side of Management," *Harvard Business Review* (November–December 1996), pp. 35–36.
2. Lorenz, C., "Disarray in the Executive Suite," *Financial Times* (July 28, 1995), p. 6.

12

Minimizing Race and Gender Bias in Performance Appraisals and Career Development

1. Grote, D., *Complete Guide to Performance Appraisal* (New York, AMACOM, 1996), p. 23.
2. Ibid.
3. Bray, D. W., Lecture given at Yale University, October 2, 1974.
4. Morrison, A., *The New Leaders* (San Francisco, CA: Jossey Bass, 1992), p. 128.
5. Gray, J. D., Lee, M. J., and Totta, J. M., "Mentoring at the Bank of Montreal," *Human Resource Planning*, pp. 45–48.
6. Walker, A., "Program Matches Promising Women to Top Mentors," *Human Resource Executive* (April 1997), p. 15.

13
Race, Gender, and Rewards: How to Reward to Elicit Maximum Performance

1. Kohn, A., *Punishment by Rewards* (New York: Houghton Mifflin Company, 1994), pp. 131–132.
2. Nelson, B., "Secrets of Successful Employee Recognition," *Quality Digest,* August 1996, p. 26.
3. Filipczak, B., "Can't Buy Love," *Training,* January, 1996, pp. 29–34.
4. Dolan, K., "When Money Isn't Enough," *Forbes,* November 18, 1996, pp. 165–170.

14
Diversity and Affirmative Action are Still Crucial to Corporate Strategies for Dealing with Racism and Sexism

1. "Is Affirmative Action Obsolete?" *Training and Development,* October 1995, p. 5.
2. Pinderton, J. P., "Why Affirmative Action Won't Die," *Fortune,* November 13, 1995, pp. 191–195.
3. U. S. Census Bureau. *The Congressional Record and the U.S. Labor Department Glass Ceiling Commission.*
4. Bowser, B. P., and Hunt, R. G., *Impact of Racism on White America* (Thousand Oaks, CA: Sage, 1996), p. 15.
5. Rosen, R. H., *The Healthy Company* (New York: Perigee, 1991), p. 108.
6. Kaufmann, J., "White Men Shake Off That Feeling of Affirmative Action," *Wall Street Journal,* September 5, 1996, pp. A1, A6.
7. Barclay, D., "The Myth behind the California Civil Rights Initiative," *Minority Employment Journal,* Fall 1996, pp. 31–35.
8. Matsuda, M. J., and Laurence, C. R., *New York Times,* April 2, 1996, p. A-13.
9. Bowser and Hunt, op. cit.

16
Managing Relationships to Enhance Career Opportunities

1. Allison, M. A., and Allison, E., *Managing Up, Managing Down* (New York: Simon and Schuster, 1984), p. 64.
2. Schoonmaker, A. N., *Executive Career Strategies* (New York: American Management Association, 1971), p. 131.

Index